MARKET-NEUTRAL TRADING

Other Books by Dr. Thomas K. Carr

Trend Trading for a Living
Micro-Trend Trading for Daily Income

MARKET-NEUTRAL TRADING

Combining Technical and
Fundamental Analysis into
7 Long-Short Trading Systems

DR. THOMAS K. CARR
("DR. STOXX")

New York   Chicago   San Francisco   Athens   London   Madrid
Mexico City   Milan   New Delhi   Singapore   Sydney   Toronto

1 2 3 4 5 6 7 8 9 0   DOC/DOC   1 9 8 7 6 5 4 3

ISBN 978-0-07-181310-5
MHID   0-07-181310-1

e-ISBN 978-0-07-181311-2
e-MHID   0-07-181311-X

This publication is designed to provide accurate and authoritative information in regard to the subject matter covered. It is sold with the understanding that neither the author nor the publisher is engaged in rendering legal, accounting, securities trading, or other professional services. If legal advice or other expert assistance is required, the services of a competent professional person should be sought.
—*From a Declaration of Principles Jointly Adopted by a Committee of the American Bar Association and a Committee of Publishers and Associations*

Library of Congress Cataloging-in-Publication Data

Carr, Thomas K.
  Market-neutral trading : combining technical and fundamental analysis into 7 long-short trading systems / by Thomas K. Carr.
    pages cm
  ISBN 978-0-07-181310-5 (alk. paper) — ISBN 0-07-181310-1 (alk. paper)
  1. Investment analysis. 2. Portfolio management. 3. Investments. I. Title.
  HG4529.C3727 2014
  332.64—dc23

                                                                                    2013033965

Product or brand names used in this book may be trade names or trademarks. Where we believe that there may be proprietary claims to such trade names or trademarks, the name has been used with an initial capital or it has been capitalized in the style used by the name claimant. Regardless of the capitalization used, all such names have been used in an editorial manner without any intent to convey endorsement of or other affiliation with the name claimant. Neither the author nor the publisher intends to express any judgment as to the validity or legal status of any such proprietary claims.

Micro-Trend Trading is trademarked by Befriend the Trend Trading, LLC.
Overnight Trading is trademarked by Befriend the Trend Trading, LLC.

McGraw-Hill Education books are available at special quantity discounts to use as premiums and sales promotions or for use in corporate training programs. To contact a representative, please visit the Contact Us pages at www.mhprofessional.com.

CONTENTS

ACKNOWLEDGMENTS

It has been my distinct pleasure to work again with McGraw-Hill and its associates on this third of a three-part series on trading strategies. Everyone involved in these projects has been fantastic. I wish especially to thank Mary Glenn, associate publisher, along with Cheryl Ringer, Charu Khanna, Lisa McCoy, and everyone else involved in the editing, production, and marketing processes. You have been consummately professional, kind, and appropriately thorough.

I wish also to thank the many readers from around the world who took the time to e-mail me comments on the first two books. What a joy it has been to connect with new and experienced traders in China, Korea, Japan, Malaysia, Thailand, New Zealand, and so many other places around the world. Trading has truly become a global phenomenon! Thank you, new friends. Your words of encouragement are singly responsible for this present volume, and your helpful comments have made it a better read.

My wife, Ina, deserves an enormous "thumbs up" for the many evening hours she spent watching the kids while

I was chained to the keyboard. Thanks, sweetie, you're awesome and I am truly blessed! To my beautiful daughters, Natasha and Nadia, and my handsome son, Nathan, I need to say sorry for being so preoccupied during these months of research and writing. Thank you for patiently waiting to play! You are all my true treasure. I am so proud to be your dad!

WHAT THIS BOOK
IS ABOUT

I hated every minute of training, but I said, "Don't quit!
Suffer now and live the rest of your life as a champion!"

—Mohammed Ali

There are many ways to trade stocks. Some traders rely exclusively on technical analysis. Each night, they scan through hundreds of price charts, searching for just the right combination of technical indicators and price patterns. They run their preset technical scans, isolating stocks making pullbacks, breakouts, relief rallies, and consolidations. They check watch lists of charts for candlestick formations, moving average crossovers, and indicator to price divergence. They scroll up to the weekly chart then down to the hourly chart, making sure there is nothing in either the macro or micro picture that would hinder their technical assessment. This book teaches a better way.

Other traders rely exclusively on fundamental analysis. They spend countless hours poring through reams of company-specific financial data, comparing price multiples with growth metrics, checking their financial rankings relative to industry and competitor standards, all in search of companies on the verge of dynamic growth. They read reports from financial analysts and research services. They listen in on conference calls and speak to investor relations personnel. They tease out from the news cycle any macro-economic change—changes in commodity prices, currency exchange rates, new tax legislation, etc.—that might affect profit margins, and thus net earnings, of the companies they follow. This book teaches a better way.

This book will teach you seven strategic methods for building a winning portfolio of stocks without having to rely exclusively on either of the previously mentioned research methods. Our approach is to combine the two. We have found that technical and fundamental analyses, long thought to be independent disciplines, complement each other's effectiveness when integrated into the same trading system. Furthermore, we have found that the ideal way to manage such systems is to use the volatility-reducing, returns-enhancing power of bidirectional positioning (i.e., being long and short the market at the same time). The trading systems taught in this book are thus structured in this two-fold, market-neutralizing way: They utilize both technical and fundamental analysis, and they come in two versions, long and short. They are also fully automated, taking advantage of preprogrammed scanning services for true ease of use.

These new systems offer traders the following potential benefits:

- *Never again will you have to spend long hours scanning through charts to find the best setups.*
- *Never again will you have to spend long hours reading through financial reports to find the best companies.*
- *Never again will you have to guess at future market direction to figure out whether you should be long or short the market.*
- *Never again will you have to figure out when to put on or take off hedge positions.*

Imagine the following scenario: It is a Sunday night and you go to your computer to see what trades you need to make the following day. You log in to your technical scanning software and open the encoded filter you are currently using. With two or three clicks of the mouse, a list of 14 stocks pops up on your screen. These satisfy the technical parameters of the long side of the system. With a couple more clicks, you run the short screen for the same system, and 11 more stocks pop up that satisfy the parameters of the short side of the same system. Your next step is to open a web browser and go to two websites that offer fundamentals-based research. You run the remaining 21 stocks through the predetermined grid on one website, then the other. You quickly see that of the 11 remaining longs, only 5 pass muster on the first site, and of those, only 3 pass through the grid of the second site. Of the 9 shorts, only 4 pass both fundamental grids. You are now left with

7 ideal candidates, 3 longs and 4 shorts, that have passed the full range of your system's filters.

Your next step will be performed on Monday morning. A good hour or so before the opening bell, you log in to your trading account platform. Once you are in, you see that you already own three of the seven stocks that came through your trading system's grid (two longs and one short). You already own these three stocks because you performed the same selection process last week and, of the stocks you entered positions in, three of them still satisfy the system's parameters. You now have your trading map for the day: Prior to the open, you will put in orders to close the positions from last week that did not show up in your selection process this week. Last week, they were great candidates. Due to changes in price momentum, valuation, or perhaps a contrary earnings estimate revision, they are no longer ideal. At the same time, you will also enter pre-open orders for new positions in the four stocks of the seven passing candidates that you were not already in from last week.

Your next step is to determine your position size. You check your current account balance. With uninvested cash and open positions included, you see that here at the end of another week of trading, the balance you have dedicated to this particular system is just short of $28,000. You smile because you started trading this system with $20,000 just a few short months ago. Yeah! This week, starting from Monday's open, you are going to hold a total of seven positions (four new, three from last week). You also know that market conditions currently dictate an even 50:50 split between longs and shorts, so 50 percent of your allotted capital, including margin, will go into three long positions ($9,333 in each) and 50 percent into the four short positions ($7,000 in each). You then enter three different sets of orders into your trading platform, all set to execute at the open:

- "Market on open" orders to either sell (longs) or cover (shorts) those positions from last week that did not pass your screening filters this week
- "Market on open" orders to buy (longs) or sell (shorts) those new stocks that passed through the filters
- "Market on open" orders to rebalance the three holdover stocks from last week so that your capital is distributed as directed among the longs and shorts, selling or adding shares as needed

At this point, you would repeat the same sequence with any other system or systems you are trading. You happen to be trading four of the systems taught in this book concurrently, with a healthy overall balance spread evenly into each one. If you had only been trading the one system, you are done for the week (or two weeks, or month, depending on how often you choose to rebalance your portfolios). The screening process for this system took you about

15 minutes. Because you are trading four systems at once, you are normally finished with your weekly routine in about an hour (longer if, like me, you get caught up reading headlines and commentary). Tonight you will sleep soundly, resting in the knowledge that you have used the absolute best available information to specify the best possible stocks, and that you have positioned your money in them in such a way that whether the markets go up, down, or sideways next week, you are more likely than not to come out ahead. Trading simply does not get any easier than this!

You have absolutely no hesitation in trading your account in this way because you know, based on 12 years of historical testing and several years of real-money experimentation, that the systems you are trading (along with the others taught in this book) have an amazing profit potential over time. It gives you tremendous confidence to know that this particular set of systems has been generating an average of 1.72 percent return per week, or 144 percent annual return with compounding. Because you have played around with the spreadsheets, you know that this rate of return will transform the $28,000 you currently have in this system into a nice nest egg of nearly $700,000 in six years (and that is *after* paying tithes and taxes). Trading four systems at once, each with a different but substantial profit potential, you figure you should hit your first million within five years! Despite a fragile economy, you can rest secure knowing that your ability going forward to generate substantial income is virtually guaranteed.

I am very familiar with this routine. It is one you will see me perform every week. Those years of experience, that nice weekly profit, and those projected rates of return are all mine! Now, with this book in your hands, they can all be yours as well!

Trading success beyond your wildest dreams may seem like a pipe dream. Those who have attained it are easily dismissed as the lucky few. The truth is otherwise. You can be a successful trader. It is not rocket science. That doesn't mean it is easy; consistent trading profits withhold themselves from all but the most persevering and patient. But in this book you have a guide, and in me you have both a coach and a cheerleader (only I'm not going to put on a dress and wave pom-poms!). If someone like me with no financial background, no MBA, and no real interest in what makes businesses tick can "trade for a living," anyone can! Let's get to it!

PART ONE

alpha:
PRELIMINARY
CONSIDERATIONS

CHAPTER 1

WHY NEUTRALIZE THE MARKET?

Don't judge each day by the harvest you reap but by the seeds that you plant.

—Robert Louis Stevenson

If *buy-and-hold investing* were an S-class Mercedes (looks great in the driveway, but it's expensive when it breaks down), and *short-term trading* were a BMW Roadster (fun to drive, but the daily maintenance is really annoying), then the kind of trading taught in this book would be something like a Toyota Highlander. It's not the sexiest car on the block, but it will let you sleep at night. Our strategies are performance-oriented without sacrificing efficiency and reliability.

Our trading approach seeks an effective synthesis of two, seemingly incompatible, financial goals: lower volatility *and* higher returns. Normally, investments promising lower volatility are rather stingy when it comes to returns (think annuities and municipal bonds). Conversely, investments that promise outsized returns can take you on wild, stomach-churning, roller coaster rides on both sides of the black line (think managed futures). Our trading approach, on the other hand, offers the best of both worlds. First, when you adopt the approach taught in this book, you are positioning your trading portfolio to greatly reduce its overall volatility. You are building into your portfolio what financial professionals call a degree of "noncorrelation." This means, in layman's terms, that when following our approach, your trading positions shouldn't suffer quite so much from the roller coaster swings experienced by the rest of the market; that a graph of your trading returns over time will look more like the drive from Kansas City to Denver than from Denver to Salt Lake City. Of course, like any form of trading, our trading strategies carry risk; they can lose money for a season; but as long as the basic principles outlined in this book are followed, you should find that your losses are generally not the sort that keep you up at night, let alone threaten to wipe out your trading career; and that the drawdowns, which are inevitable, are welcomed as strategic points of entry for new capital.

The other financial goal our trading approach aims for is what is considered to be the holy grail of all professional money managers: the much sought-after, but excruciatingly elusive, "double alpha." In financial terms, *alpha* refers to the net-positive return achieved by an investment or trading strategy after factoring out the expected return of the relevant benchmark index. Most money managers, investment advisors, mutual funds, and many hedge funds use a longs-only approach to generate alpha. This is to say they seek to maximize alpha when the markets trend up and minimize the loss of alpha when the markets trend down. A strategy seeking *double alpha*, however, expects to realize benchmark-beating returns, even net-positive returns, in both up and down markets. As we will see, the trading strategies taught in this book are set up with that expectation.

Many hedge funds seek double alpha by focusing on long positions during bull markets and short positions during bear markets, with some mix of the two during periods of market transition. This works well as long as the fund manager knows when we are in a bull market, when we are in a bear market, and, most importantly, when we are transitioning from one to the other. Therein lies the problem: Skilled stock pickers are not always so skilled at market prognostication.

William O'Neil, founder of *Investor's Business Daily* and author of the bestselling trading book, *How to Make Money in Stocks* (McGraw-Hill, 2009), writes, "If you are wrong about the direction of the general market, and that direction is down, three out of four of your stocks will plummet along with the market averages, and you will lose money big time." I agree. This is why in my first trading book, *Trend Trading for a Living* (McGraw-Hill, 2007), I taught readers a simple system that can be used to determine which of five general market types (strong or weak bull, strong or weak bear, and range-bound) we are presently in. In a seminar based on the book, I teach a more complex system for doing the same thing. But here is the catch: It is easy to determine market direction when the markets are already trending, but not so easy when the markets are transitioning between trends. Those periods of transition can last for weeks, if not months. It is during these whipsaw periods of market confusion that many double alpha seekers who rely on accurate market timing (knowing when a market has "topped" or "bottomed out") can become severely frustrated. The old trader's adage that "you'll go broke trading tops and bottoms" certainly has merit.

If only there was a way to generate net profits in all market conditions! If only we could find some way to neutralize market directionality, removing it from the equation altogether, so we could simply focus our efforts on stock selection! That is what this book is about. By neutralizing your exposure to either technical or fundamental pressures exclusively, and by neutralizing your exposure to either bullish or bearish market direction exclusively, you can trade with the expectation that if the rules are closely followed, you should, over time, show net gains in all market conditions. That is the premise of this book. *Market-Neutral Trading* is about anxiety-free trading. No more worrying about overextended technicals or problematic fundamentals; no more worrying about the market topping or bottoming out; no more worrying about putting on or taking off hedge positions; you can even trade these systems (all but one at least) without worrying about greedy market makers running your stop-losses. The trading systems taught in this book can enable anyone who uses them to trade stress-free, and profitably, in all market conditions.

THE POTENTIAL OF DOUBLE ALPHA

A stock trading system is a step-by-step methodology used by traders to find and execute opportunistic trades in equity shares. From among the thousands of securities on offer, a stock trading system looks for those stocks that satisfy specified parameters that historically have been predictive of future price movement. Any robust trading system will also indicate to the trader when it is best to enter the trade and what the most profitable method for exiting the trade is.

There is a lot of variety in the way stock trading systems are configured and applied to the markets. Some of them can be truly mystifying, especially for anyone unaccustomed to the rigors of financial data analysis. All such systems, however, have two very simple things in common. They all seek to reduce, if not eliminate altogether, the kind of impulsive, fly-by-the-seat-of-your-pants trading that causes many inexperienced traders to crash and burn. And they all seek to outperform a relevant index of securities over time. In other words, they are all going after more and more alpha with less and less financial risk.

Stock trading systems are generally categorized by reference to two key sources of input: parameter type and directional type. In the first instance, a trading system's scans are typically built using either technical parameters or fundamental parameters. Technical parameters measure the relationship between current stock price and its past price movements, assaycd over a specified time period (from minutes to months). These are quantified primarily in the form of price charts overlaid with a variety of mathematics-based oscillators. Technical parameters are further supported by analysis coming from things like geometric price patterns, Japanese candlesticks, and cumulative volume balance. Technical trading systems can be distinguished by various types of price movement—e.g., momentum, reversal, breakout, etc.—but they all tend to ignore information about the underlying company in order to focus exclusively on the day-to-day movements in share price.

Trading systems built on fundamental parameters look beyond the price chart to the underlying company. They use things like price-to-earnings ratios, changes in cash flow, earnings estimate revisions, and quarter-to-quarter sales growth to determine the most likely path of a company's earnings prospects, and on that basis, its most likely share price trajectory going forward. Fundamental trading systems come in three basic types—growth, value, or some mix of the two—and tend to be further distinguished by company-specific descriptives, like market cap, industry, and sector. The common bond of all fundamental trading systems is that they largely ignore stock price in order to devote their full attention to the underlying company itself.

Both technical and fundamental trading systems have their place. Each can perform well for a season. But there are times when, for largely fundamental reasons, a stock's share price decouples from and overrides the technicals of the price chart. There are also times when, for largely technical reasons, a stock's share price can trade up or down in ways that contradict the underlying fundamentals of the company. When either of these disconnects happens, trading systems built on technical or fundamental parameters alone will undergo that most dreaded of all trading experiences: the drawdown.

The second key vector governing the construction of stock trading systems is a primary, if not exclusive, focus on either the long or the short side of the market. A longs-only trading system looks for stocks that, for technical or fundamental reasons, are positioned so that upside momentum over the near term is expected. All mutual funds are structured, at least functionally, as "longs-only" funds. It is true that in recent years a few so-called active-extension mutual funds have been launched.[1] Sometimes called "130/30 funds," these put a small percentage of their holdings into short positions (RegT rules limit their short exposure to 33 percent), but they also are required by law to leverage the longs side of their portfolios to render a net 100 percent longs exposure, so, in effect, they continue to function as longs-only funds.

Conversely, shorts-only trading systems look for stocks that, for technical or fundamental reasons, are positioned so that their prices are expected to come under pressure over the near term. While shorts-only mutual funds are currently not allowed, and only a handful of funds among the universe of hedge funds are truly shorts-only,[2] the number of "inverse" exchange-traded funds (ETFs) grows almost daily. An inverse ETF is a true shorts-only portfolio that will show capital appreciation only if the underlying index or industry falls in price. Today there are dozens of inverse ETFs—unleveraged, 2× leveraged, and 3× leveraged varieties—in each of dozens of different asset classes. With a simple click of a mouse, you can position yourself 100 percent short a wide variety of U.S. and foreign stock indexes; individual commodities like gold, silver, oil, natural gas, beef, and pork; foreign currencies and exchange rates; business sectors like financials, real estate, and retailers; market volatility; and even carbon emissions.

We then have four basic categories of trading systems—technical-long, technical-short, fundamental-long, and fundamental-short—each of which will have its appointed time in profit-heaven. It probably goes without saying that the longs-only systems tend to perform well during bull markets, while the shorts-only systems tend to perform well during bear markets. Anytime the system is out of sync with the overall market, however, the inevitable result is, again, the dreaded drawdown.

So here is a thought: What would happen if we built a set of trading systems that integrates both technical and fundamental indicators? Wouldn't that, at least to some extent, help us avoid the decoupling problem mentioned earlier? For example, wouldn't shares of a stock with strong technical momentum run less risk of an implosion if their company also had strong fundamentals? Conversely, wouldn't your profit potential on a stock with great fundamentals be enhanced if you could time your entry to buy it at price support, or after a pullback to oversold levels? The answer to both these questions is a confident, "Yes it would!"

Here is another thought: Suppose we built an amazingly profitable, longs-only trading system that integrates both technical and fundamental parameters. What would happen if we then reversed those parameters to their opposites to give us a shorts-only screen built on the same theme? For example, suppose we built a longs-only screen centered on analyst upgrades (fundamental) and relative strength (technical) that back-tested really well, and then we reversed those parameters—analyst downgrades and relative weakness—to give us a shorts-only screen. Do you think it possible that this inverse, shorts-only screen could also be profitable? The answer to that question is, again, a confident, "Yes, it is possible!"

In fact, and here is the real surprise, it turns out that with the right system (or systems), both the longs-only, techno-fundamental system and its inverse, the techno-fundamental shorts-only system, are quite often profitable *over the same market period.* On a week-to-week basis, we will normally see one side of the system outperforming the other and yielding a net profit. We will, as we would expect, see our longs rising faster than our shorts in a bullish market and our shorts falling faster than our longs in a bearish market. But when we look at longer time frames—quarter to quarter or year to year—we often see both sides of the system showing a profit, regardless of the overall market direction. Thus, you would see your account grow when the market goes up. And when the market goes down, you would also see your account grow. This is the real beauty of the kind of trading approach we are outlining in this book: You can be profitable on both sides of the market, regardless of market direction. Thus, by neutralizing the market's tendency to reward either fundamentals or technicals and either longs or shorts, we are able to be positioned to profit in all market seasons. This is true "double alpha"!

WHAT WE ARE PROPOSING

As defined in this book, my trading methodology involves using one or more step-by-step stock selection processes, coupled with a unique strategy for putting those stocks to work in the market. Our approach requires that you trade one or more trading systems that screen for stocks triggering *both* technical *and* fundamental indicator values. Each of the trading systems we teach here comes as a paired set: It has both a longs-only screen and a shorts-only screen. A position sizing and apportionment strategy also will be recommended. This involves putting a percentage of your account balance (most often, it is 50 percent) into the longs side of one or more of the systems, then a complementary amount of capital—the precise percentage depends on the market—into the short side of the same system(s). In this way, you are exposed to both sides of the market in stocks whose fundamental and technical types, in both long and short versions, have proven profitable in all kinds of market conditions.

This book teaches seven fully replicable trading systems. Imagine the possibilities that come with this type of trading:

- You have no need to discern whether the markets are trading more in line with the technicals of the index price charts or the fundamentals of the companies that make up the indexes. You know that your systems are a synthesis of technicals *and* fundamentals, thus reducing the risk that you have misread the market.
- You are never worried about when the current bull market will top out, or whether the current market correction is at a bottom. You know your trading systems can make money in both up and down markets. You have a system (described later) for managing your capital apportionment among both longs and shorts, so you can rest assured that you are always in a position to profit no matter what the market is doing.
- You will never again get stopped out by market makers greedy for new shares just before they let the order flow take the price higher. Nor will you ever see your target price hit just moments before the stock skyrockets without you. Instead, you will let the system itself tell you exactly when you

should exit your trades. Every exit will, in most cases, come with a replacement stock the system has determined to be a better candidate. Thus, you have the confidence that at every period of "rebalancing" you are improving your profit potential and reducing your risk.

- You will never again spend hours and hours studying price charts or flipping through reams of company balance sheets, searching for your next trade. Once you input into your scanning software the parameters we define in this book, you will, with a few mouse clicks, generate two lists of stocks: a longs list and a shorts list. Further testing of the stocks on those lists will tell you exactly which among them are the best candidates to trade.

Let me add one more benefit to the systems outlined in this book: You do not have to be a PhD economist or a certified market technician in order to understand, run, and manage them profitably. All you need to know are the rules for each of the trading systems as outlined here. I have read several of the classic books on investing—like Ben Graham's *The Intelligent Investor* (HarperBusiness, 2005), Martin Zweig's *Winning on Wall Street* (Warner Books Grand Central Publishing, 1997), and Peter Lynch's *One Up on Wall Street* (Simon & Schuster, 2000)—as well as many books on technical analysis (too many to list). Invariably, once my reading comes to an end, I am left asking, "Now what?" I think I am right in saying that most of the books published on investing and trading, including many of the classics, suffer from a singular fault: They are long on theory but woefully short on practical application. This book seeks to remedy that. Here you have outlined, in very practical, step-by-step terms, how to trade seven profit-proven, techno-fundamental, market-neutralizing trading systems.

To be sure, I have not reinvented the wheel here. In explaining the seven systems included later I offer nothing very original. Rather, I merely gathered together the most effective pieces from some of the most profitable fundamental and technical trading systems, testing and tweaking them for consistency and outperformance, and then broke them down step-by-step so you will know how to run them as market-neutralizing, long-short trading systems. Some of those pieces come from familiar sources; others have been dug out of dusty dissertations and forgotten journal articles. Either way, within the trading systems described here is embedded the hard-won wisdom of a number of very smart people. We are their happy beneficiaries.

My role in this book is merely to present an integration of trading wisdom, structured in the form of distinct trading systems, along with guidelines for position management. No one should ever mistake me for a guru! I'm just an ordinary guy with an extraordinary passion for learning, and then teaching to others, what works in the stock market.

NO MORE HEDGING

Thus far, we have learned that the trading methodology taught in this book consists of using an integrated system of technical and fundamental parameters to find the best long and short stock pairs for trading. The kind of trading described here does not find its maximum profit potential by determining general market direction; pinpointing stock price pivot points; or staying one step ahead of sector rotation, earnings announcements, corporate buyouts, analyst upgrades, Food and Drug Administration (FDA) approvals, and the like. Rather, the profit potential in our trading approach lies in the simple identification of those stocks that, for specified fundamental and technical reasons, are expected in the near term to outperform the market and those that are expected to underperform.

We have also learned that to properly neutralize market risk, we not only need to integrate technicals and fundamentals, but we also need to position ourselves to profit from the two primary market directions, bullish and bearish. Our strategy, as will be explained, is to let the market itself dictate what percentage of our capital we will put to work on each side, long and short; but we will always be

100 percent invested, and always to some degree both long and short at the same time. The default setting as we run each system is to invest half of our capital into the long set of stocks, while the same amount of capital is put to work in the short set of stocks (those less risk-averse may use margin to add leverage). The minimal expectation is that the outperformance of the long portfolio over the short portfolio during rising markets and the outperformance of the short portfolio over the long portfolio during falling markets will render the account as a whole profitable over time. The maximal expectation, which historical performance demonstrates to be a reasonable one, is that both sides of the system, long and short, will be profitable over time, regardless of general market direction.

It needs to be said that the kind of long-short pairing taught in this book is different from the hedging of positions. Hedging is used to minimize potential loss in long positions when market conditions turn unexpectedly volatile. Hedges come in a variety of forms. Inverse ETFs, call writes, a short basket of stocks from the same industry as the longs, buying puts on commodities essential to the businesses we are long, forex shorts to protect profit margins against a currency devaluation—all these can serve as hedges. For example, if you buy $5,000 worth of shares in each of four Dow stocks—say, American Express (AXP), Caterpillar (CAT), Intel (INTC), and Exxon (XOM)—with the markets trading near resistance, you might hedge those positions with a $20,000 short position in DIA (the ETF for the Dow Jones Industrial Average), or a $10,000 purchase of DXD (the 2× leveraged short ETF for the Dow), or even the purchase of a set of puts on DDM (the 2× leveraged long ETF for the Dow). In this example, because you are long individual stocks, you would expect, should the market break through resistance, that the hedge would return a loss, only less of a loss in absolute terms (because it is an index and, thus, theoretically less volatile) than the anticipated profit of the four Dow stocks. If your fears materialize and the market pulls back, you would expect to earn a small profit to partially offset the loss in the four stocks. The hedge is, therefore, a kind of two-edged sword: It can help to minimize your loss should the trade not work out, but it also takes a chunk out of the profits if the trade goes in your favor. In other words, hedging is like paying an insurance premium: It is a pain to pay it each month, but you are glad to have the coverage when disaster strikes.

The trading we teach here, on the other hand, operates from a very different mindset. If hedging is about paying a premium to buy down the risk inherent in your market exposure, our trading is about reducing risk without having to pay a premium. Hedging is motivated by the fear of substantial losses. Our trading is motivated by the quest for double alpha gains. Hedging is most commonly used during market downturns. Our trading can profitably be done in all market conditions. Hedging requires the need to predict when the markets will reverse to the downside (to put on the hedge) and then reverse back up again (to take off the hedge). Our trading has no such need. You take the same equally weighted long-short approach, regardless of market direction.

Let us now drill down a little further into the way our trading systems are structured. At the heart of each system in this book is the nature of the relationship between the securities that are paired together, long and short. This relationship can be characterized in one of two distinct ways. The first type of system centers its search for candidates primarily, though not exclusively, on fundamental parameters. In these systems, technical parameters play a more supportive role. The stocks that rise to the top of these systems are bought and the stocks at the bottom are sold short. In this way, you might have stocks that are primarily paired according to things like opposing growth rates, critical valuation ratios, analyst estimate revisions, or other fundamental criteria. There are four trading systems based on these types of fundamentals-based screens. They are described in Chapters 7 through 10.

The second type of system centers its search for candidates primarily, though not exclusively, on technical parameters. In these systems, fundamental parameters play a more supportive role. Here, the stocks that appear at the bullish end of a predetermined technical scan are bought and the stocks sold short are those that appear when the parameters of that same scan are reversed (there is one slight exception to this rule). In this way, you might have stock pairs that are put together, long and short, because one is oversold and one is overbought, or one is breaking out of a bullish consolidation while the other is breaking down from a bearish consolidation, or one is showing accumulation at an area of price support, while the other is showing distribution at an area of price resistance. The trading systems that use these technicals-based scans are described in Chapters 11 through 13.

In either case, every trading system explained herein uses a common method of position management. All seven systems are designed to be traded from both the long and short side, with an equal amount of capital devoted to each system (if trading more than one) and a specified amount of capital—we will explain a simple method for determining this amount—to the long and short sides of each system. Each side of the system may or may not have an equal number of positions, but each position is equally weighted with respect to capital invested. Each portfolio, long and short, is then rebalanced at regular intervals. In most cases, weekly rebalancing will yield the strongest returns. Thus, once each week on a specified day, you would run the scans of each of the systems traded and replace any stocks that no longer qualify with stocks that pass the screen. Less active traders can still attain solid, market-beating returns with bimonthly or even monthly turnover of positions.

Each of the systems taught in this book, whether based primarily on fundamentals or technicals, is fully explained. I've tried to make each of the steps for trading the systems as clear as possible so that they can be replicated by newbies and professionals alike, by the part-timer with a $5,000 account, as well as the professional with $50 million under management. To run each system, you will need certain supporting software and/or online screening tools. These tools are listed and explained in Chapter 4. In each of the system-specific chapters, you will learn how to use these tools to automate the search process to the point where your regular routine of finding new pairs to trade is reduced to a few minutes of mouse-clicking. With one prominent exception, all the tools you need are reasonably priced or free; they are all user-friendly, and more than adequate for our purposes here.

THE MOST IMPORTANT BENEFIT

I have served as a private trading coach to traders and investors for over 11 years (you'll read more about this in Chapter 5). During that time, I have worked with several hundred clients. Whenever I work with individual traders, whether they are first-timers or experienced professionals, I put them through a trading profile inventory. The results of this inventory give me a good idea what type of trader I'm working with, where strengths and weaknesses lie, and thus how to tailor my coaching to best meet his or her needs. While this more detailed information is useful, I have discovered over the years that nearly all the clients I work with fall under one of two categories: Either they don't know enough about trading to make it work for them; or they know too much about trading, which causes them to be indecisive and unable, even unwilling, to follow any one system consistently.

All things considered, those in the first category are easiest to work with. Their lack of trading "baggage" makes them far more teachable and willing to follow the rules of successful trading. Let me tell you about one client who clearly fell into the latter category (which is where I locate myself too). Let's call him Joel. Joel and I met in the conference room of an airport hotel. Joel had flown all the way from Seoul, Korea, and, despite his jetlag, he was alert and eager to get to work. On the surface of things, Joel had all the makings of a trading wizard. He had an Ivy League degree in business; he was clearly bright and a quick learner; and he was the eldest son of a successful private equity investor who had been grooming Joel to take over the business. Joel's problem was that he didn't want to work for his dad. He wanted to make his living trading.

One year prior to our meeting, Joel's father had given Joel a million-dollar trading account to get him started. This was pocket change to the father, but to Joel, it was his chance to pursue his dream. Equipped with a top-notch business education and quality experience gleaned from the years spent at his dad's side, Joel put the money to work in the markets. Unfortunately, things didn't go quite as planned. By the time Joel came to me, his account was down over 70 percent. He was desperate. From Joel's profile inventory, I learned that he was making a number of critical mistakes, not the least of which was allowing himself only four to five hours of sleep each night as he scanned the global news for trades. To make things worse, Joel's trading profile showed me that he was trading way out of his comfort zone. His temperament was better suited to a rules-based systematic approach that focused on large-cap stocks. In his erratic haste to recoup trading losses, however, Joel had become a futures-fueled adrenaline junkie. His style was more of a fly-by-the-seat-of-his-pants approach as he chased after every fast-moving commodity and forex pair.

I told Joel I could help him turn things around, but that he would have to radically change his methods. I also added that if he did change, he would be a much happier, and likely more successful, trader. My approach was simple: I would teach Joel a clearly defined, long-short stock trading system, and that his first task was to work it with a small amount of what money he had left for three months. After that, assuming he was profitable, I would slowly move him back into the futures markets as long as he continued to reach very reasonable profit targets. Joel gave me his assent; or at least I understood his lack of complaint as a form of compliance. So, for the next three hours, I carefully outlined one of my trading systems that was a good match for his profile. After a lunch break, we spent another two hours working through various scanning techniques, discretionary sorting methods, position management, crisis response strategies, and live chart examples of the system at work. All the while, Joel seemed to me to be very engaged. I was giving him my best stuff; my impression was that he was fully on board.

At the end of our allotted time together, I asked Joel whether he had any questions. I'll never forget his response. "I only have one question," he said. "Can you tell me if natural gas is going to keep going up?" It turned out that Joel was long his entire account in natural gas futures contracts. He was showing a nice profit, and there was no way he was going to close it out to trade anything as pedestrian as what I was suggesting. So after all my work, Joel really didn't want to learn a better way to trade. He only wanted to know whether he was in the right trade.

Since Joel had flown a long way and was paying a considerable fee for my advice, I agreed to look at the chart of natural gas (NG). It was quite plain to me that the recent breakout in NG (this was late 2011) was probably a "head-fake"; i.e., it was likely to reverse course very soon. While the price had indeed risen to print new two-month highs, several of the technical indicators had not done so, suggesting that this rally was not sustainable compared to others in the past. I, therefore, suggested to Joel that he cut his position size in half and put a stop-loss at his entry on the rest. He said a polite "no" to both suggestions, then flew over 20 hours back home. Less than three weeks later, natural gas was down over 20 percent, a loss that would have wiped out his account—futures contracts are highly leveraged—and then some. I never learned whether Joel cut that loss, but I suspect he is now fully committed to working in his father's business. I also suspect that this may well have been his father's plan all along!

This sad but true story is one that is too often repeated among traders, even experienced ones. I've even seen a version of it in my own trading over the years. Contained in this story are the four most common causes of all trading failure:

1. *Not using a systematic entry-to-exit trading program*
2. *Not using reasonable position sizing*
3. *Not accounting adequately for market risk*
4. *Refusing to be mentored by a more experienced trader*

The demons lying behind these causes are legion. They include adrenaline addiction, an unwillingness to admit to mistakes (what the Bible calls "pride"), fear of success, a "poverty" mindset—i.e., a condition of believing one "deserves" financial failure, which is caused by deep-rooted shame—lack of self-discipline, stubbornness (more "pride"), and sheer rebellion against any form of authority (again, "pride"). While exorcising such things is a complex and often lengthy process, their effects, at least in terms of trading, can largely be mitigated by following a clearly laid-out trading system with a proven track record and by willingly submitting oneself to a trading apprenticeship under a trusted mentor.

We will say more about the importance of being mentored later. Here it can be said that systematic trading (as opposed to Joel's "seat-of-the-pants, fueled-by-adrenaline" kind of trading) neutralizes three of the four causes of trading failure: It offers a series of entry-to-exit trading rules; it determines in purely objective fashion how to size every position; and with continuous long-short exposure, market risk is not only accounted for, it is also harnessed for profit. Trading a well-researched, real-money tested, long-short system (or systems) can help many traders get past their stuck places of mediocrity and failure to find at least a modest measure of trading success. For some who really take to it, it can be a very powerful and reliable generator of wealth. For more on this topic, keep reading.

CHAPTER 2

Going Beyond
Technical Analysis

*Do not go where the path may lead; go instead where there is
no path and leave a trail.*

—Ralph Waldo Emerson

I have been a trader of stocks, stock options, and stock index
futures since 1996. My journey through several years of
research and experimentation (including many failures) to
where I am today has been narrated in two previous books,
Trend Trading for a Living (McGraw-Hill, 2007) and *Micro-
Trend Trading for Daily Income* (McGraw-Hill, 2010). In all
these years of trading, my focus has been on short-term
trading using a series of (mostly) self-developed systems
that rely exclusively on technical analysis. In October 2002,
I launched Befriend the Trend Trading (www.drstoxx.com),
a stock pick advisory and trader training service. We began
publication that year of our flagship advisory, *The Trend
Trade Letter*, which offers daily market guidance and specific trading recommendations. This was followed in 2007
by our most profitable advisory, *The ETF-Reversal Letter*,
and in 2010 by our service for smaller account traders, *The
Cheap Stocks Letter*. The systems I have developed over

these years of trader training and advising continue to serve me and my clients well. My experience, therefore, confirms what many stock traders hold to be true: that the technical analysis of price charts works well as a stand-alone predictive tool. To paraphrase comedian Garrett Morris's "Chico Escuela" character from *Saturday Night Live* (back in the years when it was mostly watchable), "[Technical analysis] been berry berry good to me!"

There is always room for improvement, however. Even the most robust technical trading system can experience times of poor performance. This was especially true of my trading during the crash of 2008–2009. During those tumultuous months of unprecedented market volatility, technical analysis was rendered virtually worthless as the markets moved in lock-step with an increasingly hostile news cycle. Beautiful chart setups, profitable under most market conditions, would turn ugly very quickly. Oversold technical indicators flashing buy signals kept getting more and more oversold. Market sentiment charts would hit key bullish reversal levels, only to plunge through to set new historic lows. When we finally did get some reasonable signals to go short (overbought in the downtrend), the markets would squeeze higher still. It was a very frustrating time for technical traders who had in view any time frame longer than the next few minutes of market action.

During the last weeks of the crash and for the several months of fearful trading that followed it (remember the May 2010 "flash crash"?), I found myself struggling as a trader. Of course, I had traded through market downturns before. Every trader and investor, no matter how accomplished, has muddled through periods when nothing is working. Every trading success story is punctuated by such chapters. Those that are ultimately successful are those who respond appropriately; they reduce size, manage the risk, and wait patiently for things to turn around. But at the risk of violating a maxim of one of my heroes, Sir John Templeton, this time, *things really were different.* In the past, whenever I saw a string of losses coming from one of my systems, I simply changed systems. I would switch from buying breakouts to buying pullbacks, for example. Or, I might key support and resistance off of Bollinger Bands instead of trend and channel lines. But in that confusing, "new normal" of a market after the crash, what used to work in the past was no longer working now.

My struggles were compounded by the fact that I was not just trading for myself. I was supposed to be providing daily trading guidance for our several hundred subscribers. They were looking to me to lead the way through this muddle of a market, and I was not so sure I knew the way. For the most part, and only by the grace of God, we managed to stumble our way through without too much damage. Our stock newsletters eventually returned to form enough to show a modest profit over the period. But it was not an easy ride.

What I didn't know then that I know now is that those months of uncertainty were a kind of divine setup. I was being prepared for one of the most powerful revelations of my trading career. It all started when those challenging market conditions caused me to lose confidence in chart reading as my primary form of analysis. Chart reading had been my bread and butter. It formed the basis of all my seminars, my published writings, and, indeed, my own trading. But in these new post-crash market conditions, chart reading alone was not working; at least, it was not working in a way that I could stomach. I felt that there was something missing in my approach to these new market conditions. I didn't know what that something was, but I knew I desperately needed to find it.

THE 500 STOCK EXPERIMENT

Initially, I was determined to prove myself wrong. My intuition was telling me that technical analysis alone was not enough to pull consistent profits from the "new normal" of the post-crash market. My reason, however, told me that it was enough; I just needed a new system. So I did then what I often do when faced with a serious challenge. I cleared my desk, put a yellow legal pad in front of me, took out a pen, and prayed. After a few moments of silence, words and phrases began to flood my mind. I quickly scribbled them down. This is what I wrote: "500 stocks . . . five years . . . 50 percent return . . . one month . . . common grid." Putting this together, I decided to scan the market for 500 stocks over the previous five years—a period that included years before, during, and after the 2008 crash—that have returned at least 50 percent within 20 trading days (one calendar month). My task was to scrutinize each chart, looking for any kind of recurring grid of indicators and price patterns evident just prior to breakout. If I could isolate this grid, then I could build a scan for its component parts. Thus, I would have my new system: one that was able to locate stocks poised on the verge of massive breakouts.

I began by building a watch list of 500 historical charts that at some point in the past five years showed a one-month return of at least 50 percent above the close of the previous month.[1] In any given month, there are about 10 such stocks—more during bull markets—that are reasonably liquid (trading over 100,000 shares per day) and not penny stocks (priced over $3 per share), so I had a sufficient number of charts to work with. Moreover, this was an ideal market period to study since it covered time before, during, and after the market crash.

Once I had my watch list of historical charts, I then built a chart template that included candlesticks, several moving averages and technical oscillators, and two volume-based indicators. My plan was to note in a spreadsheet what price patterns were evident and what values the indicators were in the days and weeks leading up to each of the 500 bullish breakouts. My assumption was that after several thousand data points had been entered, a recognizable, statistically significant pattern would emerge.

Of course, I was highly motivated to conduct this research. I knew that if I could identify a price, indicator, and volume pattern that consistently preceded a one-month return of 50 percent, I would have in my possession the most powerful stock trading system ever! So over several weeks, I spent many late nights and early mornings poring over each of the 500 charts I had collected. For each chart, I looked for one of a dozen common chart patterns—gleaned from Bulkowski's excellent *Encyclopedia of Chart Patterns*[2]—along with the pre-breakout values of nine technical parameters, which I carefully logged in a spreadsheet. The parameters I used were all common to technical analysis: moving average crossovers, moving average slope, moving average convergence-divergence (MACD), commodity channel index (CCI), stochastics, relative strength indicator (RSI), Bollinger %B, on-volume balance (OBV), and relative volume. For each of these I recorded several closing values over the 40 trading days prior to the breakout. The spreadsheet was programmed to calculate the rate of change of those values over several time periods. After about two months of work, I was done with the analysis. It was time to assess the data.

Sure enough, once the 500 charts had been analyzed and statistical tests run, several price and indicator patterns began to emerge. Of those, one pattern clearly dominated the charts on my watch list. I called it the *baseline pattern*. Comprising nearly a third of the various chart patterns I surveyed, the baseline pattern is seen when, after a long and steep selloff, share price trades up and down within a fairly tight price range before consolidating near the top of that range. In my study, this price pattern was most often coupled with a certain minimum percentage increase in volume, making it evident that shares were being accumulated by professional traders in anticipation of a big move. My study suggested that any close above the trading range would likely precipitate an extreme bullish move upward. A typical chart bearing the baseline pattern is seen in the 2012 breakout of UNXL (Figure 2.1).

In the chart, shares of UNXL traded within a relatively quiet range for several weeks until late November 2012. At that time, the company began issuing press releases about several new contracts they had secured. The news pushed UNXL's stock price through resistance and above its trading range. The move emerged slowly for several days, then

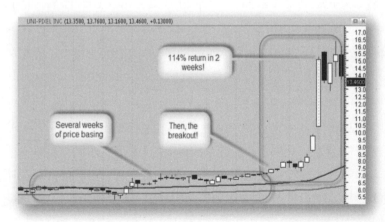

Chart courtesy of MetaStock

Figure 2.1   Three-month chart of UNXL.

gained momentum and volume. By mid-December, UNXL was trading over 100 percent above its breakout pivot.

UNXL's chart was typical of quite a number of the 500 charts I scrutinized over two months of research. Of course, there were also many outliers. There were charts that gapped up 50 percent or more in a day following a corporate buyout. There were charts that plunged during a sharp selloff, or that gapped down sharply on bad news and then mysteriously reversed higher for a 50 percent move off the lows. There were charts that rallied 50 percent only after hitting new annual highs. And there were a number of charts that offered no discernible pattern at all, yet they still managed to pop 50 percent or more within a month's time. But 159 of the 500 charts I evaluated conformed more or less to the baseline pattern. So my next step was to build a set of scans that would find stocks making this pattern.

It was hit or miss for a while, but after several days of experimentation, I had a set of scans that nicely isolated both the price and indicator configurations of the baseline pattern, along with the technical triggers that were required for best entry. Thus, any stock that passed the multifilter scans would qualify as a candidate for entering a long position at the next market open. As for an exit strategy, my research indicated that the trade would have the best chance of working if held for one full month, regardless of price action. If at any time during the month the price hit a 50 percent return from entry, the position should be closed. If after 20 trading days the position failed to reach

50 percent return from entry, it should also be closed. No stops were to be used since there was quite a bit of volatility expected prior to and during the breakout move.

My excitement over this new system was by now at a peak. There was, however, a kind of unspoken suspicion lurking in the recesses of my mind that something was not quite right with my research methods. Those of you familiar with this kind of retrogressive back-testing will have already spotted the fatal flaw. The problem, of course, was that my analysis focused on 500 charts that were selected because they were already "winners." What my research didn't tell me, because it wasn't designed to tell me, was just how many stocks making a baseline pattern go on to become winners. Hence, there was a faulty inference, an unwarranted leap of logic, at the heart of it all. I had wrongly assumed that most charts completing a baseline pattern would make 50 percent in a month simply because most stocks making 50 percent in a month do so from a baseline pattern. That is like saying, "Every time it rains, the grass gets wet; therefore, when the grass is wet, I know it just rained." It is one of the most common "freshman" mistakes made in a college logic class, and in my haste to grab quick profits I, a professor of philosophy no less, had just made it!

On any given trading day, there are dozens if not hundreds of stocks showing the same baseline pattern I had isolated. But of the 3,000+ stocks trading over $3 per share with 100,000 average daily volume, only a handful go on to return 50 percent or more within a month. And of those, at least according to my research, only one out of three will do so from the baseline pattern. Thus, while a baseline breakout is certainly a tradable bullish technical pattern, and while it may well have a better chance than other patterns of yielding a 50 percent monthly return, it should not be expected to do so. The odds of that happening are pretty slim: about 1 in 30, I figure, maybe less.

My suspicions that I was working with a bogus trading system were confirmed by real-money trading. Over a period of four months, I put on a total of 32 baseline pattern breakout trades. My position size was small, but my plan was to reinvest all profits—which I imagined would be massive—back into the system with the next set of trades. On each position I set a 50 percent limit order to close, an MOC (market on close) order to close after 30 days, and an OCA (one cancels all) conditional on both. Then I waited. As each day passed, the realization grew ever clearer: The system was not working. None of the 32 positions came anywhere near a 50 percent return. Some of the stocks did manage to close the month with a profit; the rest closed down, way down, or way, way down. In the end, I lost money and wasted time; but at least I learned what does *not* work in the markets.

THE TURN TO FUNDAMENTALS

At this point in my quest for a more robust trading approach, I took up the timeless wisdom to "humble thyself." I declared my ignorance and so put myself on an intentional self-directed course in what has been successful in the market. For my teachers, I turned to a set of books that had been sitting on my shelves for years but that I had never read. These books all shared one common trait: They were the biographies, memoirs, and market strategies of the all-time greats of fundamentals-based investing. These were books by Ben Graham, the all-time great value investor; Graham's protégé and the most successful investor of the modern era, Warren Buffett; the manager of history's most successful mutual fund, Peter Lynch; Martin Zweig, whose weekly commentary, *The Zweig Forecast*, was for 30 years one of the most successful market letters ever published; and William O'Neil, founder of *Investor's Business Daily* and developer of the famed CAN-SLIM growth stock system. My study also took me to a number of key papers published in peer-reviewed economics journals. Of these, two papers were seminal: one by former Chicago Business School professor (now at Stanford) Dr. Joseph Piotroski, and one by Dr. Len Zacks, an MIT-trained mathematician and founder of Zacks Investment Research. All of these authors (with the exception of Piotroski, who remains in academia) were guys with decades-long careers in the money management business, who had amassed huge fortunes for themselves and their clients, and who year after year attained market-beating performance. They had weathered through the recessions by being the first to get defensive, and they were often out in front of each new uptrend.

The more I read, the brighter the little light over my head began to shine. The more that light shined, the more it revealed the bleak, dark hole at the center of my trading methodology. Learning from the "gurus" of the investing world made me realize that something essential was missing from my orientation to trading. There was a unique understanding embedded in their trading decisions that gave them a certain posture of confidence that my systems simply could not provide. In my estimate, the key to this edge, which the gurus had and I did not, boiled down to this: They knew the companies they invested in very well. I, on the other hand, didn't know them at all. I knew their charts: the mathematical relationships between various price points, their volume patterns, their areas of support and resistance. This statistically significant information was what fueled my trading decisions. Still, at the end of the day, those all-important decisions on which our trading success depended floated on a foamy web of lines, bars, and numbers. The gurus, on the other hand, stood on a much firmer foundation. While I was buying *shares*—never a more notional entity has man created than the publicly traded "stock share"—they were buying machines, product lines, essential services, and supply chains, along with hard-working employees and the geniuses who manage them.

As a market technician, my only concern was the chart, not the company. In most cases, I knew little about the businesses whose shares I was trading. I never knew whether the uptrend I was buying was not hiding a major cash flow problem about to implode or whether the downtrend I was shorting was not about to squeeze higher because of an earnings revision. Those kinds of questions weren't even on my radar. Technical analysis trains the trader to focus on the past movements of share price. It empowers its proponents with valuable knowledge of the road a company's shares have traveled over time. From that vantage point, the technician peers into the future to predict what that road will look like going forward. Not so the investing gurus. Their focus is on the present: They have one eye on the present state of the companies they invest in—their assets and liabilities, management strengths and weaknesses, the currency of their business model, etc.—and the other eye on the present state of the national and global economies. Through this comparison, I began to realize just how speculative my trading decisions had been and how much more grounded, more justifiable, more *explainable*, are the decisions made by the investing gurus.

Imagine a weekly management meeting at one of the larger hedge funds. The founder is there, seated at the head of the table, looking wise and relaxed as he gazes at the young analysts before him. One by one the analysts take turns highlighting the strengths and weaknesses of the fund's current holdings, as well as possible future investments. PowerPoint presentations and pie charts fill the large screen behind them. Nervous excitement fuels their brief but detailed presentations. They speak with great confidence about things like forward-looking earnings projections, valuation ratios relative to peers in the industry, the impact an upcoming debt payment might have on margin rates, and so on. Finally, the one market technician at the table stands up to speak. He scrolls through a series of charts, pointing out a head-and-shoulders top here, key levels of support and resistance there. After five minutes, you can see the eyes of the other analysts glaze over as the founder tries in vain to stifle a yawn.

The contrast between technical analysis and fundamental analysis cannot be more clearly drawn than at an analysts meeting.[3] The analysts operate in a "thick" economy of linguistic markers, gleaned from Nobel laureates wearing bow ties and tweed jackets at places like Harvard, Wharton, Sloan, and Kellogg. The technicians, by comparison, work with a much "thinner" tradition. Their knowledge is a more recent product generated by computers that fine-tuned the trend and pattern analysis invented by Edwards and Magee in the mid-twentieth century.[4] While technical indicators have been added over time, they are but new variations on the same theme: the price chart.

Here is the key issue behind this comparison. Technical analysts know a company's stock price chart very well. To be specific, they know the chart's past and on that basis predict the future moves of a stock's price per share (PPS). The essential relationship on which decisions are made is the mathematical relation between a future possible PPS and the definite past PPS. But once the move is made from prediction to taking a position, with all the risks that that move entails, this essential relationship changes. For the technician actually in a position, the essential relationship is now between the definite past PPS and the present PPS, represented by the flickering tick at the "hard right edge" of the chart. Every up or down tick changes the nature of that essential relationship, based as it is on computer-generated mathematical models. In other words, what was once support can become resistance, or a bearish head-and-shoulders pattern can morph into a bullish double bottom. The only thing a technician can do is to put on a stop-loss and hope for the best.

Fundamental analysts, on the other hand, stand in a very different relationship to their trading decisions. Like technicians, they are also predictors, but of people, not price charts. As a recent candidate for president famously retorted to a heckler during a campaign speech, "Businesses are people too, my friend!" So when PPS turns against its predicted direction, the fundamental analyst starts working the phones. She speaks with investor relations, middle management, vendors in the supply chain, and friends at other investment firms who follow the company. She makes a site visit and meets with the CEO, CFO, CIO, and COO to see what can be determined. She brings the wealth of her financial knowledge to each of these conversations to see what lines up and what doesn't. On this basis—face-time with real people in real time, not with computational math in past time—she'll decide what to do going forward.

I don't mean to disparage technical analysis and the traders who use it exclusively. It still butters my bread every day. I use it, teach it, and trade with it. Each of the systems described later has a technical component; for some, technical analysis is the primary component. But week after week of reading from the giants of the investing world led me to believe that I could gain a real edge, and certainly a lot of *confidence*—the real fuel driving competent trading decisions—by adding at least an entry-level education in fundamental analysis to my arsenal of trading tactics.

All fundamental analysis boils down to this: a reasoned assessment, from a nearly infinite number of angles, of a company's earnings prospects going forward. The gurus know that when a company's earnings prospects fail to match up with where the market is offering its shares, the market is wrong, not their analysis. They know it is only a matter of time before the market catches up to what they already know. The beauty of fundamental analysis is that it offers a clear picture of where the company is now, along with a concise indication of where price *should be* relative to that picture. If a company's stock price more or less matches the underlying fundamentals of the company, the guru investor will call it a "hold" and will likely move on to better prospects. But if there is a mismatch, he or she becomes keenly interested. This is what gives the guru the confidence to buy into deep drawdowns, to sell into momentum madness, and to hold through the long slog of price consolidation.

PUTTING THE "VEST" IN INVESTMENT

It is no coincidence that the word "invest" comes from the Latin verb meaning "to clothe." We see the same root in "vest" (sleeveless sweater), "vestry" (wardrobe), and in the "vestments" worn by priests. This seemingly trivial bit of etymology discloses an important point: Once you buy a company's shares, you become intimately connected to the company itself. The verbal intentionality located in the act of investing is to clothe yourself, so to speak, in the company's ethos, its values, its mission in the world, if only for a few days. To flesh out the analogy further, we probably should be buying stock shares the way we buy our clothes: Our focus should be on what fits, what feels comfortable, and what is in line with our character and values. Few see trading as an integrity issue, but that is exactly what it is. The point bears repeating: Once you move beyond chart analysis to take on a trading position, your money, and you by extension, stand in relation to the company, with all that that relation implies, not to the chart. For good or for ill, what we invest ourselves in, we become.

The investing greats understand this. They know that investing is a form of relationship, an intimacy, and as such is governed by the same rules that attend relations between people. There is a "getting to know you" stage; there is "due diligence" done, which may lead to "friendship," even "courtship," and occasionally, when all lines up properly, "marriage." There are also disappointments, estrangements, trial separations, and sometimes divorces too. In short, what the investing gurus know that we technical analysts have for too long dismissed is that to invest your money wisely in the market, you need to be intimately acquainted with what you are investing in. It follows, then, that if I wanted to trade with the same confidence that they operate with, I would need to break out of my comfort zone (technical analysis) and begin employing a form of analysis that would take me past the chart and into the company that underlies it.

CHAPTER 3

Moving Toward a Synthesis

Failure after long perseverance is much grander than never to have a striving good enough to be called a failure.

—George Eliot

After passing through several months of concentrated study, I felt ready to make a major shift in my identity as a trader. I had traded for 16 years as a technicals-only chart reader. Now I was preparing myself to step into the trading arena as a business-oriented, drill-down-into-the-financials stock picker! In the course of what had become a rather lengthy period of study, however, I ran into a major obstacle. My study of the investing greats, and of market theory in general, brought me to two key ideas about stock market investing that nearly derailed my whole trading career.

SIDETRACKED BY A RANDOM WALK

What I learned during those months of study was that market theorists generally fall into one of two camps: Some believe that the market tends to "discount" or price in a company's financial information correctly and efficiently as soon as it becomes available (this is called "efficient market theory"), while others believe that there are elements of inefficiency at work in the discounting process that can be exploited for gain. This is obviously a crucial divide. It goes right to the very heart of market analysis as a viable profession. For if the stock market is truly *efficient*, then predicting future price movements on the basis of a company's earnings prospects becomes a pointless endeavor. If all fundamental data is accurately assimilated into the present price of a company's stock, then a company's earning potential is already reflected in that price; thus, there is no way to outperform the overall market on that basis. The best an investor can do is to leverage gross domestic product (GDP) growth by investing in a handful of strong, stable blue-chip stocks or, if lower risk is desired, to buy a passively managed index fund. If, on the other hand, the markets are truly *inefficient*, where price does not always match the underlying fundamentals, then there is room to capture alpha. There is the possibility through accurate company analysis and market timing to exploit the gap between the current price and the price investors will eventually pay for the company's earning potential (or lack thereof).

I also discovered a second major division among those who study stock market investing. Some believe, as I always have, that there is a genuine edge to future market prediction. The assumption of these "market timers" is that "history tends to repeat itself." They hold that price and earnings momentum, whether up or down, are more likely than not to continue their trends going forward. In other words, if a stock is rising in price, it is more likely to continue rising than to fall; or if company X is showing a significant quarter-on-quarter earnings decline, it will likely continue to decline in the coming quarter. On the other hand, there are theorists who argue that consistent market prediction is not possible using either technical or fundamental analysis; that changes in stock prices over the near term are purely random events. These so-called random walk theorists claim that stock price distribution models show no consistent signs of predictability; that just because a stock went up last week, last month, and last year, there is no more than a 50:50 chance it will continue to rise going forward.

Here is the bottom line: Both the efficient market theorists (EMTs) and the random walk theorists (RWTs), albeit for different reasons, contend that outperforming an index benchmark—i.e., the quest for alpha—is no more possible for a highly paid analyst than for a monkey throwing darts at the *Wall Street Journal*. EMTs and RWTs are very smart people. Some of them are Ivy League professors of finance; some hold important posts in government and industry; some are even Nobel Prize candidates.[1] Who was I to take the other side of that trade? To be sure, standing with me were legions of fund managers, certified market technicians, independent traders, armchair investors, and other species of alpha hunters. We all believe analysis—either technical or fundamental—can provide a market-beating edge. But on what grounds? This was the question I desperately needed to answer.

For many decades, the EMTs and RWTs were a rather inconsequential subculture among financial professionals.[2] They remained cloistered behind ivy-covered walls, communicating with each other only in the indecipherable code of applied mathematics. All that changed in 1973 with the publication of Burton Malkiel's classic, *A Random Walk Down Wall Street*. As an economics professor at Princeton, Malkiel had the academic chops to give the book real gravitas, but his folksy spin on the whole analyst's game of chasing alpha made it accessible to the general public. To date, the book has sold over 2 million copies (unheard of for an economics book) and has been updated a number of times since its original publication. In *A Random Walk Down Wall Street*, Malkiel successfully harnesses both EMT and RWT to forward a coherent set of reasons why it is impossible to outperform the stock market. I like to simplify this EMT-RWT synthesis—derived from Malkiel's book, but also from other sources—as follows:

- *In theory at least, all current financial information about a company (X) is available to financial analysts in some form or other, which they then use to determine the intrinsic value of X.*
- *The intrinsic value of X, once made known to the public through pronouncements like upgrades, downgrades, and reiterations, very quickly gets baked*

into the price of X's shares. Thus, the current price of X's shares reflects X's intrinsic value a majority of the time. Put differently: The window of opportunity within which pricing discrepancies can be exploited is very narrow.

- *But as it turns out, analysts are human; some of them aren't the brightest cats in the game either. Sometimes they get the intrinsic value of X wrong. Moreover, even if the analysts do their work well, company X may have been wrong (either accidentally or deliberately) in the calculations of the fundamentals it made public. Analysts, in other words, might be working with faulty information without knowing it.*

- *This then puts in motion the following cycle: New financial information about X eventually comes out that contradicts what the analysts said about X, or what X said about itself, which in turn causes the public to either buy up or sell off the shares of X. This rapid flux in price was largely unpredictable. It was a random occurrence based on faulty information that no one knew was faulty until new, more correct, information surfaced.*

- *The problems don't end there, however. Unforeseen setbacks can happen to company X at any time— e.g., weather-related disruptions in X's supply chain, ethical scandals among X's executives, or geopolitical skirmishes intensifying in regions serviced by X—that cause unpredictable changes in X's intrinsic value.*

Moreover, the general economy can also experience fluky instability that can lead to unpredictable changes in X's earning potential.

All of this brings us to the following inescapable conclusion:

- *While current share price of any publicly traded company can be rationally explained given what is known about the company's financials, there is no reliable way to predict share price going forward; there are simply too many variables that can cause stock prices to fluctuate in ways that were not expected. In other words, the only information we have of a company's valuation is past information. And when it comes to stock market predictions, what is past is not always prologue.*

Malkiel concludes, though a fair bit more eloquently, that both technical and fundamental analysis are a complete waste of time.[3] Both technical analysts and fundamental analysts believe they are able from past information to map out the most likely future of a stock's price per share (PPS)—up, down, or sideways. But the EM/RW theorist insists that there is no edge to that predictability without taking on increased risk, which, in turn, wipes out the edge. As Malkiel puts it, the probability of a company's shares

moving up or down is as calculable as the statistical distribution of 1,000 coin tosses.[4] Each new price point, he
insists, is neither the product of price momentum continuing from the current trend (as per the technicians), nor an
extension of earnings potential carrying over from previous
earnings growth (as per the fundamentalists). It is merely
the efficient assimilation of 100 different information vectors, some of which were unknowable ahead of time. In
other words, as Malkiel famously states, "A blindfolded
monkey throwing darts at the stock listings could select a
portfolio that would do just as well as one selected by the
experts."[5]

So where did this assessment leave me? After all, I
was making a pretty good living predicting the future price
trends of the stock market. Was it all just a fluke? Eleven
years of profitable performance on over 3,000 trades, all
published and open to public scrutiny on our website: Was
that all simply a product of fortuitous chance? What about
the hundreds of traders I've trained over the years, some of
whom are now trading professionally: Did they just happen to catch me on a lucky streak? I could certainly affirm
the key insight of these analysis deniers: that sometimes
when it seems like you have the perfect trade on, something
comes out of left field that causes you to say, "Whoa, I sure
didn't see that coming!" But what trader is not aware of
these risks? What investor does not know going in that you
have to risk striking out if you ever want to hit a home run?

THE NECESSITY OF RISK

The more I read Malkiel and the proponents of EM-RW theory, the more I began to smell the stench of the very thing I was seeking to dispel from my trading life (and from my life as a whole): *the fear of taking a risk.* Fear of risk too often prevents traders and investors from making ultimately profitable trades. Or, as was the case with Joel, it causes us to hold on too long to ultimately unprofitable trades. EM and RW theories are ripe with the fear-based counsel that it is better to retreat to the safety of passively managed index funds than to risk the random elements that affect individual stocks. I stand opposed to this counsel. I believe that to orient oneself so as to avoid risk is to gravely miscalculate the human capacity to transform *risk* into *opportunity.*

I am reminded of a parable that illustrates the importance of taking risks, even financial risks. In Matthew 25, Jesus tells the story of a very wealthy CEO who went away on a business trip. Before leaving, he called three of his employees and gave each of them a very large sum of money. To one fellow, he gave five "talents" of gold (at today's prices, about $6 million); to a second, two talents ($2.5 million); and to a third associate, one talent ($1.2 million). He then gave them this single instruction, "Go and *trade* what I've given you until I return."[6] After some time passed, the CEO returned and called the three men together to see how they fared while he was away. The one who was given five talents showed his boss a 100 percent return. Through trading, the $6 million entrusted to him had become $12 million. "Well done, good and faithful servant," says the CEO, "... come rejoice with me over your success!"[7] The second man, when queried, also showed a 100 percent return. He received the same approbation. Then the third man, head hung low, stepped forward. "Sorry boss," he says. "I was afraid that if I lost any of your money you would be upset with me. So I put it in a tin can and buried it in my back yard. Here, you can have it back." Jesus called this third man "wicked" and "lazy"; he was fired on the spot. The money given him was taken away and handed to the man with $12 million of assets under management.

The CEO in this parable, of course, is God, whom the Bible depicts as the true source of all wealth and prosperity (see Deut. 8:18). He gives to each of us a measure of that wealth—not just money but spiritual, physical, and intellectual capital as well—and expects us to steward it in ways that line up with both His character and with the plans He has for our lives. Successful stewardship, however, requires us to assume some measure of risk. Just like what the CEO gave to his employees, what God gives us can get stolen, lost, or otherwise devalued through unforeseen events. But the good steward is the one who willingly assumes those risks. Two of the three did and so received approval. The one who allowed fear to influence his decisions, however, did not.

The moral of the story is this: Yes, Malkiel is right to point out that the risks involved in trading and investing cannot always be determined ahead of time and certainly need to be accounted for; but what he won't tell you is that there are also risks that go with doing nothing out of fear; in many cases, they are far worse. At the time of this writing, the call of the RW-ET crowd to stick to passively managed index funds has been wrong for 13 years running. $1,000 invested in the S&P 500 from January 1, 2000, was only worth $970 on January 1, 2013; even less if inflation is taken into account. On the other hand, during those same 13 years some amazing fortunes have been made by risk-taking stock pickers using time-tested strategies. Consider the following returns gleaned from the American Association of Individual Investors' database of various strategies over the same period (Table 3.1):[8]

TABLE 3.1   Passive vs. Active Investing—Comparison of Returns (1/1/00 to 1/1/13)

INVESTMENT STRATEGY	STARTING $	ENDING $	ANNUAL ROI	TOTAL ROI
S&P Index Fund	$1,000.00	$970.00	−0.2%	−3.0%
John Templeton	$1,000.00	$3,500.00	10.1%	250.0%
Joel Greenblatt	$1,000.00	$3,600.00	10.2%	260.0%
Warren Buffett	$1,000.00	$3,650.00	10.5%	265.0%
Peter Lynch	$1,000.00	$4,000.00	11.2%	300.0%
Martin Zweig	$1,000.00	$9,900.00	19.3%	890.0%
William O'Neil	$1,000.00	$16,600.00	24.7%	1,660.0%

All of these active EM/RW denying strategies rely primarily on fundamental analysis. Templeton looks for undervalued growth; Greenblatt's "magic formula" buys cheap companies with a high return on investment; the "Buffettology" approach screens for monopolies selling at a bargain; Lynch's focus is on fundamentally sound but undervalued stocks whose goods and services have wide appeal; Zweig looks for low PEG ratios (price/earnings to growth) with insider buying and price momentum; and O'Neil buys companies with strong earnings momentum, rising accumulation of shares, and new price highs. It is of interest to note in passing that the two strategies showing the strongest returns, Zweig and O'Neil, each have a technical component; that is, they are techno-fundamental synthesis strategies.

TWO ACADEMIC PAPERS THAT SAVED MY TRADING

Following this educative but ultimately fruitless discursion into EM/RW theory, and with even more certainty that a synthesis of both technical and fundamental approaches was the key to finding double alpha, I continued my quest. By this time I was getting desperate. Like many traders after the 2008–2009 crash, my trading during the first leg of the recovery seemed always to be set against a background of worry. Every negative piece of news, every close in the red, every call from the talking heads that "we haven't seen the worst of it yet," would cause me, in kneejerk fashion, to throw on a slew of shorts for fear of another meltdown. That kind of fear-based trading is never healthy, even when it works out. In my case, it rarely did.

Hindsight made it clear that while I was reading every technical sell signal as a sign of impending doom, smarter heads were busy stockpiling fundamentally sound, under-valued companies. They had backed up the proverbial truck and were using the dips to load up for the inevitable recovery rally. I should have been with them. Instead, I stood among those handing them the shares. The investing gurus knew what I hadn't yet learned: that there are time-tested ways to determine the true valuation of companies on which basis alone confidently held positions can be taken, even when the general market structure is contrary. They knew that determining what to buy when everyone is selling requires going beyond the charts to assess the underlying health of the companies themselves. Some of the terms and tools these fundamental analysts used were still quite foreign to me. Still, I felt certain that going further down the path they trod was the right way to go.

It was around this time that my research led me to two academic papers, both of which completely revolutionized my understanding of the markets. While published in obscure academic journals by authors who at the time were relatively unknown, they have since been canonized as valid inductees into the financial research hall of fame. One article has influenced a number of fund managers and financial analysts who use the author's "F-score" metric to determine the financial health of companies. The other planted the seed for what is today one of the investing world's most influential research institutions. Each paper is grounded in doctoral-level, peer-reviewed research; each lays out a solidly reasoned, statistically supported argument for its financial evaluation model; and each in its own way says a decided "No!" to both EMT and RWT.

The first paper I came across was published by a then-obscure business school professor named Joseph Piotroski. Professor Piotroski's 2002 paper, published in the journal of the University of Chicago Graduate School of Business, was titled "Value Investing: The Use of Historical Financial Statement Information to Separate Winners from Losers." Starting with highly ranked book-to-market companies (a value metric), Piotroski suggested further screening using nine fundamental measurements—the details of which we will explain in Chapter 7—to determine the operational health of these companies going forward. Those that register positive for all nine parameters rise to the top of the list. These are the strongest-value stocks, fundamentally speaking, that are currently trading. Stocks that fall to the bottom of the list, i.e., those that only qualify on one or two parameters, are more likely than not on their way to harder times, if not full bankruptcy.

Most importantly, this purely fundamental ranking system really works.[9] Professor Piotroski's research demonstrated decisively that, with all due respect to

Professor Malkiel, with the right system, it *is* possible to outperform the markets over time. Professor Piotroski's little article, later expanded with further research by dozens of disciples, left two gaping holes in the sinking ship of EM/RW theory:

> First, I show that the mean return earned by a high book-to-market investor can be increased by at least 7.5 percent annually through the selection of financially strong high BM [book-to-market] firms. Second, the entire distribution of realized returns is shifted to the right. Although the portfolio's mean return is the relevant benchmark for performance evaluation, this paper also provides evidence that the left tail of the return distribution (i.e., 10th percentile, 25th percentile, and median) experiences a significant positive shift after the application of fundamental screens.

To put this in layman's terms, what Piotroski is saying here is that by simply running value companies through a series of tests and buying only the winners, one can *both* significantly outperform the market *and* reduce the severity of drawdowns during down market periods. Moreover, and here is where it gets really interesting, Professor Piotroski demonstrated that if you concurrently buy the best stocks and short the worst ones, that alpha edge jumps from 7.5 percent to a whopping 12.4 percent! If you could have recorded the sound going off in my head when I read this part of Piotroski's discussion, you would have heard something akin to a small nuclear explosion. What Piotroski was here outlining, in terms that even I could understand, was a systematic, easily replicable way to achieve double alpha. His approach to neutralizing the markets through buying fundamentally sound companies and shorting unsound ones was earning an average annual ROI of 23 percent from 1976 to 1999. These were, admittedly, unusually bullish years. Still, passively managed index investors following the Malkiel crowd earned only 11.6 percent over the same period, and with far greater portfolio risk. So, thus far, it is University of Chicago 1 and Princeton University 0.

The second article, "EPS Forecasts—Accuracy Is Not Enough," was published in a 1979 edition of that unrivaled paragon of great bedtime reading, the *Financial Analysts Journal*. The author was Dr. Len Zacks, an MIT-trained mathematician and founder of Zacks Investment Research. Dr. Zacks claims nothing less for himself than being the one who discovered "the most powerful force impacting stock prices." We will get to the particulars of his thesis in Chapter 8, but the gist of his findings is this: It is not the actual growth of earnings (or lack thereof) over time that drives a company's near-term stock price changes; what drives a stock's price up and down in the near term are the anticipatory revisions analysts make to the company's earnings estimates. Once analysis is done on the consensus of those revisions—Zacks uses a proprietary system for evaluating the quality and quantity of estimate revisions—what results is a very effective tool for identifying the most likely winners and losers over the next few weeks of trading.

Dr. Zacks eventually worked his theory into a stock-grading system that stands today as one of the most widely used portfolio assessment tools. Those stocks rising to the top 5 percent of all publicly traded companies are given a rank of 1, or "strong buy," while those in the bottom 5 percent are ranked 5, or "strong sell." The 20 percent of stocks just below the top tier are ranked 2, or "buy," while the 20 percent of stocks just above the bottom tier are ranked 4, or "sell." Stocks in the middle tier, roughly 40 percent of all publicly traded companies, are given a rank of 3, or "hold."

How well does this research-based system work? The following chart tells the story (Figure 3.1). Here is how only those stocks qualifying as rank 1, "strong buy," fared by comparison to the broader market over a 25-year test period: By holding only Zacks Rank 1 stocks, you could have improved your returns more than 3,600 percent!

Table 3.2 shows the breakdown by Zacks Rank over the same period. Note that in only 3 of the 25 years of recorded data did the rank 1 stocks fail to outperform the S&P 500. The average annual alpha was +16.3 percent per year! Moreover, the rank 5 stocks underperformed the S&P 500 60 percent of the time by an average annual alpha of −7.7 percent. This not only demonstrates the power of Dr. Zacks's earnings estimates revision method for ranking stocks—it also gives one more nod toward the

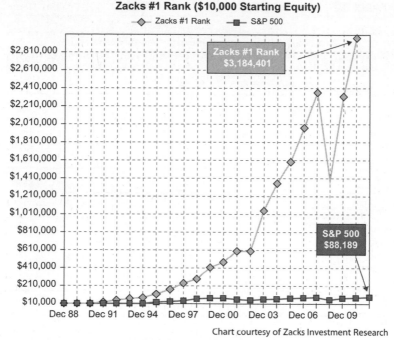

Figure 3.1   Returns for Zacks Rank 1 stocks (1988–2012).

idea we have been building here: that double alpha can be obtained across various market conditions by simply taking a successful longs-only system and reversing the parameters.

Though I needed no further proof than this to demonstrate the power of a solid fundamentals-based trading system, I found additional confirmation on the website of the American Association of Individual Investors. This site ranks 76 fundamentals-based stock screens by performance, with monthly rebalancing, over several different look-back periods. In both the 5-year (Table 3.3) and 10-year periods (Table 3.4), the Zacks method of ranking stocks by their

TABLE 3.2   Returns by Zacks Rank (1988–2012)

	Zacks Rank Performance Summary—Monthly Rebalancing					
YEAR	#1 RANK	#2 RANK	#3 RANK	#4 RANK	#5 RANK	S&P 500
1988	39.18%	29.69%	20.79%	19.13%	18.39%	16.20%
1989	39.58%	26.84%	15.85%	9.55%	–5.10%	31.70%
1990	–2.64%	–13.69%	–21.32%	–23.85%	–34.71%	–3.10%
1991	81.36%	56.80%	45.98%	36.60%	34.35%	30.40%
1992	40.97%	29.63%	18.04%	12.24%	17.31%	7.51%
1993	45.26%	26.86%	14.78%	8.59%	9.54%	10.07%
1994	12.73%	5.15%	–3.56%	–11.14%	–10.90%	0.59%
1995	52.56%	46.84%	30.63%	17.35%	9.11%	36.31%
1996	40.93%	28.60%	16.07%	7.71%	8.02%	22.36%
1997	43.91%	33.87%	22.93%	10.17%	3.05%	33.25%
1998	19.52%	12.92%	–3.47%	–8.77%	–14.84%	28.57%
1999	45.92%	35.53%	31.02%	18.46%	17.69%	21.03%
2000	14.31%	–1.47%	–17.75%	–19.52%	–3.95%	–9.10%
2001	24.27%	11.70%	14.09%	17.93%	20.20%	–11.88%
2002	1.22%	–14.51%	–19.39%	–23.50%	–17.59%	–22.10%
2003	67.03%	71.02%	66.69%	57.34%	55.99%	28.69%
2004	28.71%	23.26%	18.51%	11.92%	16.63%	10.87%
2005	18.80%	12.01%	6.54%	–1.31%	–5.08%	4.90%
2006	27.31%	26.63%	18.09%	15.17%	16.88%	15.80%
2007	19.71%	5.42%	–4.34%	–13.06%	–23.90%	5.49%
2008	–40.41%	–43.48%	–48.70%	–45.75%	–50.95%	–37.00%
2009	65.85%	82.46%	78.42%	59.91%	49.18%	26.46%
2010	28.98%	35.04%	27.89%	29.28%	27.18%	15.06%
2011	–10.21%	–4.87%	–13.56%	–18.57%	–21.39%	2.11%

TABLE 3.2   Returns by Zacks Rank (1988–2012) *(Continued)*

Zacks Rank Performance Summary—Monthly Rebalancing						
YEAR	*#1 RANK*	*#2 RANK*	*#3 RANK*	*#4 RANK*	*#5 RANK*	*S&P 500*
2012	24.40%	17.26%	16.65%	6.78%	8.27%	16.00%
2013	13.27%	10.73%	8.63%	6.80%	7.95%	10.61%
Annual Average	**26.60%**	**18.71%**	**10.12%**	**4.32%**	**2.16%**	**9.93%**
2013 returns are for the period of Jan. 1–Mar. 31, 2013						

Chart courtesy of Zacks Investment Research

earnings estimate revisions and buying only the top tier outperformed all other systems. Also of note is that the Piotroski method of ranking stocks according to F-score came in third in each year out of the 76 systems tested.

So here were two cross-verified examples of trading systems that blew away the efficient-market/random-walk hypothesis that no form of analysis can consistently produce alpha. With the strong returns shown also by other fundamentals-based systems from investing gurus like Martin Zweig and William O'Neil (see Figure 3.1), I now had several trading methodologies on which to base further research. All that remained now was to synthesize these systems by adding the right mix of technical components, test the inverse of the synthesis to make sure each system could produce a profitable set of short candidates, and then develop further systems, long and short, to ensure that I had a sufficient arsenal for profiting from all market conditions.

TABLE 3.3   Top Three Trading Systems on AAII.com (5-year average annual ROI)

SCREEN	YTD	3-YEAR	5-YEAR	10-YEAR	INCEPTION	RISK	STYLE
1. Est Rev: Up 5% Introduction to the use of earnings estimates.	28.8%	22.9%	23.1%	29.9%	28.6%	1.76	Earnings Estimates
2. Est Rev: Top 30 Up Introduction to the use of earnings estimates.	21.9%	20.7%	20.5%	29.3%	25.7%	1.85	Earnings Estimates
3. Piotroski: High F-Score A study of low price-to-book value stocks to see if it's possible to establish basic financial criteria to help separate the winners from the losers.	91.7%	42.7%	20.4%	28.5%	26.2%	2.02	Value

Chart courtesy of the American Association of Individual Investors

TABLE 3.4 Top Three Trading Systems on AAII.com (10-year average annual ROI)

SCREEN	YTD	3-YEAR	5-YEAR	10-YEAR	INCEPTION	RISK	STYLE
1. Est Rev: Up 5% Introduction to the use of earnings estimates.	28.8%	22.9%	23.1%	29.9%	28.6%	1.76	Earnings Estimates
2. Est Rev: Top 30 Up Introduction to the use of earnings estimates.	21.9%	20.7%	20.5%	29.3%	25.7%	1.85	Earnings Estimates
3. Piotroski: High F-Score A study of low price-to-book value stocks to see if it's possible to establish basic financial criteria to help separate the winners from the losers.	91.7%	42.7%	20.4%	28.5%	26.2%	2.02	Value

Chart courtesy of the American Association of Individual Investors

That was a tall order. Fortunately, the hard work had already been done. The next step on my journey toward building a set of alpha-busting, market-neutralizing trading systems was to find the right screening and testing tools. That is the subject of our next chapter.

CHAPTER 4

New Tools for the Trader's Toolkit

What's important is that you have faith in people, that they're basically good and smart, and if you give them tools, they'll do wonderful things with them.

—Steve Jobs

In today's anemic economy, many people have started small businesses in their spare time in order to supplement the income of their day jobs. Some spend their weekends scouring the flea markets for things to fix up and sell on eBay. Others throw in with this or that multilevel marketing (MLM) scheme, coaxing their friends into buying cosmetics, jewelry, berry juice, or some other product we presumably cannot live without. Still others risk borrowed money on a franchise or the development of a product they one day hope to pitch to the buyers in Bentonville, Arkansas (home of Walmart).

Why these people don't consider trading stocks is beyond me. As I said in my first book,

Trading is the ideal home-based business. There is no inventory to store in warehouses, nothing to ship, no bothersome customers, no cold calling, no gimmicky marketing. . . . There is no Walmart down the road to undercut your prices. There are no franchise fees, no staff to employ, no lawyers to keep on retainer. . . . Trading has as low a set of barriers to entry as any business could possibly have.[1]

A friend of mine is a busy professional who, in order to support his growing family, has turned to investing in real estate. He buys old homes on the cheap, works late-night and long weekend hours fixing them up, and then rents them out by advertising on Craigslist. What little time he has beyond his full-time job and getting his homes ready to rent is filled with chasing down delinquent payments and responding to maintenance emergencies, which, because his homes are really old, are a frequent occurrence. I once asked if he might let me train him to trade stocks. "Me, trade stocks?" he replied. "I can't do that." "Why not?" I asked. "That's way too much work!" he said. (Can you hear the *da-bum-bum* rim shot as I say this?)

Trading stocks is not difficult. While a mental challenge, it is not rocket science. To trade stocks well, you do not need a Harvard MBA, a finance PhD from Wharton, or an uncle in the business. Having above-average intelligence is not essential and may, in fact, be a hindrance. Being both intuitive and decisive (a rare combination) can quicken your path to trading greatness, but there are other paths. Being numerate, knowing your way around Micro-soft Excel, and having a passion for the never-ending flow of market news—none of these things, while helpful, can ensure your trading success.

There isn't even a standard psychological profile per-fectly fitted to successful trading. Despite what the books on trading psychology tell you, you do not have to be calm and level-headed (think of Jim Cramer's constant rants on CNBC!) or coolly rational and detached (think of the coldly calculating George Soros, the man who purportedly "broke the Bank of England"). There is only one essential trait all traders must have, whether they ride the emotional roller coaster along with their holdings or not: determined persistence to stick with it through thick and thin. There will be a lot of both. Get over it!

LET'S GET VERY PRACTICAL

Beyond dogged determination, what else is required to trade stocks profitably and sustainably? Let's get very practical for a few pages here. To become a successful stock trader—which in my terms means you are one whose goal is to integrate profitable trading into a holistic, purposeful plan of life, even if you are not there yet on either front—you absolutely must have the following tools in your possession:

- *An online margin account*
- *Sufficient trading capital*

- *A set of proven trading systems*
- *Scanning software with data-feed (real-time preferred)*
- *Current, company-specific fundamental data*
- *A power-packed PC with a large monitor or monitors*

Even the most determined "Secretariat" trader won't get out of the gate without a margin account at a deep-discount online broker. I can personally recommend only one online broker: Interactive Brokers (IB). IB has been around as many years as I've been trading. It has a high-end, professional-grade trading platform; decent, real-time charting (free); fast executions; routing that actively seeks price improvement between bid and ask; and, most importantly for our purposes here, among all the deep-discount brokers IB keeps the largest inventory of shares to short. In addition, IB has extremely low commissions ($0.005 per share or less) and well below industry-standard margin rates (another plus, since margin is used for shorting). Any other reputable firm that has all these things should also be a good fit for you. IB is simply the firm I am most familiar with. I've used a number of online brokers over the years, including E-trade, Scottrade, and Goldman Sachs Execution and Clearing. All things considered, I prefer IB.

Starting capital is the largest barrier to entry for most people wanting to launch a trading business. The most common question asked by those seeking my coaching services is this: What is the minimum amount of money needed to trade? My response is always the same: The minimum needed to trade is the minimum needed to open a trading account. At Interactive Brokers, this is $10,000 for a margin account. There are other discount firms with lower minimums. Some firms have set their minimum to open a margin account for stocks at $2,000. Be careful, though. Firms with low account minimums will sometimes make up for the lack in capital by charging higher commissions and margin interest. I've also seen online brokers give me lousy fills on market orders—e.g., a "market on open" order that fills above the official open price—or charge hidden fees on limit orders. Still, it is possible to launch a successful trading career with less than $10,000 in your account. I myself started with only $2,000 back in 1996. Of course, there were plenty of false starts and ups and downs. I don't ever want to imply that stock trading provides an unswerving trajectory to early retirement. But again, determined persistence—and a willingness to refund your account as needed—certainly can pay off over time.

This leads me to a second question I'm often asked: How much money is needed to trade for a living? My answer to this question is never very welcomed. I tell them that to support a family with consistent income through trading alone and with enough capital to draw on during the sluggish months, they will need something north of $500,000 in their accounts. A $500,000 account and an average net return of 2 percent per month—not impossible by any means—will sustain an annual six-figure salary (after tithes but before taxes). Those who wish to trade merely to *supplement* their income, however, can start with much less. A $25,000 account, the minimum needed to do any day trading, can add $5,000 or more to an annual income; enough to pay down debt, fund an extra vacation, or build toward a down payment on property. Those who start with less than $25,000 will have to defer their financial goals until a trading process of small position sizing and sustained success builds up their accounts to size. The truth is that whether you start with $2,000 or $2 million, your trading is going nowhere if you don't have a robust, tradable set of systems in place.

Thus, the second essential element of profitable hybrid trading is a varied set of systems that have passed the test of time over different market conditions and that include the clearly specified steps needed for finding, filtering, entering, and exiting new trades. This book supplies all those things: Here, you will find a set of trading systems for finding and filtering new trades, along with the rules for entering and exiting them. The seven trading systems described here are divided into two primary types: four that focus on fundamentals but also use a technical filter, and three that focus on technicals but also use a fundamental filter. Smaller account traders should begin by trading one system from each group. Those with larger accounts can jump right into trading all seven.

The systems described here have set filters or other forms of evaluation that require services that are used to find viable candidates matching the systems' fundamental and technical parameters. If you have never used a screening tool before, here is how they work. They scan the universe of publicly traded stocks—either in real time during market hours or in delayed fashion after the close, depending on which service you choose (real time is more expensive, of course)—and filter them through a variety of preset parameters. These preset parameters are configured according to the trading system you are using. Once these parameters are coded into the screening software per the system being used, a simple run of the scan will produce a list of stocks that satisfy the requirements of the system.

You will use these services regularly—daily, weekly, monthly, etc.—depending on how active a trader you want to be. The good news is that the fees associated with most of these services are reasonable, and some are even free. Regardless, you can't trade the systems in this book if you can't find the stocks that satisfy their requirements, and you can't do that without one or more of the screening services described here.

It is rare to find a single screening tool that filters for both fundamental and technical parameters. Since both are required for our systems, there will, therefore, be occasion for us to use more than one screening service. Sometimes we will use one service to weed out high-probability technical setups, long and short, and then another service to run those stocks through a set of fundamental tests to determine which of those on the short-list are best to trade. At other times, we will use one service to scan for the best (and worst) stocks on a fundamentals basis, and then a second service that will tell us exactly when they are ripe for entry based on certain technical parameters.

In addition to screening software, you will need a charting package that offers a full range of technical indicators, shows the price action clearly, and allows for a number of user-configured stock watch lists. Supplying your charts with a real-time data-feed provides the best trading environment, but it is not necessary to trade the systems in this book. We will, for the most part, be running our system scans after the markets close and then entering any new positions at the next market open. To save on overhead costs, it is completely possible to benefit from our trading systems with end-of-day or delayed data. Even better: We will show you one service that combines one of the most powerful technical screening tools currently available with an excellent set of real-time technical charts, all for a very reasonable monthly fee. More on this later.

YOUR PC TRADING STATION

I want next to talk about the last item on our list of essential tools for hybrid trading: your desktop PC. Much has been written lately about "the death of the PC" amidst today's explosive growth in secondary devices like tablets and smart phones. As of this writing, PC sales have been flat since 2009, while sales of iPads and Androids have skyrocketed. The use of PCs to access the Internet is expected to decline over 7 percent this year as online browsing is being done more and more by mobile devices.[2] But none of this means that the traditional PC will go away anytime soon. Much to the chagrin of the "death to Wintel" crowd, the PC is here to stay. Here is why:

There are two essential components a PC has that smaller mobile devices do not have: keyboards and monitors. Keyboards are needed to write, conduct research, and crunch numbers with accuracy and speed. Monitors are needed to view documents, browsers, and software platforms clearly and efficiently. These are all work-related tasks. They are also trading-related tasks. Smart phones and tablets are great for playing games, posting to Facebook, and reading your e-mail; but as long as people have to work and trade for a living, there will be PCs. The size, power, and capabilities of PCs will most certainly change over time. In the future, we may well have even more efficient ways of translating thought into written text and numeric code. But until then, every productive workstation will feature a keyboard of some kind and a large display of some kind (see Figure 4.1 for an idealized view of a proper trading station).

Some of my subscribers do manage to trade on their phones. Even I occasionally use my broker's mobile app to adjust stops or to add a few shares on an expected dip in one of my core positions. I do not hold anything against anyone who feels comfortable trading on a tablet or smart phone. I just can't do it myself. Maybe it is my eyesight dimming as I age, but I find I need more visual acreage to work with. To be sure, whenever we travel, which we do frequently,

Picture courtesy of Super PC

Figure 4.1   The dream workstation with multimonitor setup.

I carry a laptop for trading purposes. I've traded on laptops in cafes and coffee shops from Seattle to Singapore. But to follow what we are doing here in this book, I suggest you use a larger platform.

To make the most of your time, and to minimize frustration, you will want to run these market-neutralizing systems on a PC running the latest Windows operating system with at least two monitors attached (21" or larger preferred). Yes, there is the Apple option. While the most essential software applications we will use for hybrid trading are only offered in PC format, there are ways of running Windows-based programs on a Mac. For example, Apple has a program called Boot Camp that allows users to install Windows on their Mac in a separate partition of the hard drive. But spend a few minutes reading the feedback on any trading software user forum and you will see that Apple fans are less than thrilled with the level of compatibility they get from it. Bugginess, strange work-arounds, and loss of functionality seem to be the norm with any of these PC–Mac synthesizers. So let's assume for the sake of argument that you are working with a PC. The question remains: Which one is best?

Here is my suggestion: If you are happy with your current machine; if it has not been acting buggy; if it has plenty of space left on the hard drive; if you have its RAM capacity maxed out to at least the current entry-level minimum (4GB as of this writing); if you have a video card installed that gives you sharp images on your monitor without much pixilation at the highest resolution, then by all means, stay with what you have. Just get it regularly cleaned and dusted, delete old files and unused applications on a periodic basis, and it should continue to serve you well for many months to come. If, for any reason, you are not happy with the box you are working on, however, I suggest you consider an upgrade. I like to trade with a new workstation every three years or so, and this is what I do.

First, I recommend staying out of the big-box stores. Forget Best Buy, Costco, Sam's Club, or any other bricks-and-mortar retailer for your trading box. These stores are fine for most electronics and appliance purchases, but they are really not equipped to meet your particular computing needs as an active trader. Sometimes you can get a good deal on monitors in such stores. They will lure you in with cheap liquid crystal display (LCD) prices in order to sell you the box as well; but I would avoid adding on the machine. My advice is to go in for the glass but leave without buying the box.

As a trader, your computing needs will surpass what the brand retailers can do for you. The best way to fulfill those needs is to have a PC custom built. To do that properly, you should find a couple of local PC shops and give them a call. Explain to them that you are looking to build a computer specifically for online trading. Explain to the proprietor that throughout the day you will have a number of streaming data applications and web portals open, that you will be crunching a ton of financial data, and that you will be running real-time scanning software—all at the same time! Tell him or her that your most pressing needs are for fast, stable processing speed; lots of RAM space; a huge hard drive; high-pixel resolution support; and a multi-mon-i-tor configuration. As of this writing, mid-range specs for a trading machine that meets these requirements are more or less as follows: The Intel Quad Core i3 processor, 8GB RAM, 1TB hard drive, and a 1GB graphics card with dual-monitor capacity (you can always upgrade the card or use a video graphics array [VGA] adapter for more monitors) to which you will be plugging in at least two 20″ monitors.

As you call each shop, it is best to ask the manager the following question first: "Have you ever built a computer for a finance professional?" (If you say "trader," they might think "baseball cards"!) If the answer is "no," find another shop. If the answer is "yes," then lay out the specs I listed earlier and ask him or her to give you a price quote. You may want to upgrade the various components if finances are not an issue—e.g., to the Core i5 or i7 (there is not much difference in performance, and even the i3 is plenty fast), to 16 or even 32GB RAM, etc.—but I would avoid going any lower than the mid-range specs. As of this writing, the quote you are given should come comfortably under $1,500 for the box alone, not including the monitors and dual mount, or well under $2,300 for the full package. If you want a tri- or quad-monitor system, you may be quoted as high as $3,000 to cover the monitors and upgraded graphics card.

Once you have a quote from the first shop, call another local shop to compare prices. Be sure to specify the exact components so you get a fair comparison. Prices will vary depending on brand name, so be sure to duplicate the brand names listed in your first quote. Your next step, and likely your final step, is to take the specs to an online computer retailer. Several PC retail sites cater to the trading and financial community. The one I recommend using is Super PC (www.multi-monitors.com). Other online PC retailers like Super PC cater to traders (e.g., Tiger, Falcon), but Super PC has the largest inventory of custom-built, multimonitor machines. Super PC also consistently has the lowest prices, and with free shipping you'll even save the time and gas costs you would have spent buying locally. Super PC services a wide variety of financial and professional organizations, including several branches of the U.S. military, the Department of Justice, the Federal Deposit Insurance Corporation (FDIC), and blue-chip companies like Archer Daniels Midland (ADM) and General Electric (GE). Despite the heavy lifting those big contracts require, Super PC remains focused on equipping those in the finance professions. Their service department is very knowledgeable and will work with you as you put together your dream machine. They also are very cost conscious and are quick to recommend less expensive options without sacrificing the power you need as a trader. E-mail me at drstoxx@drstoxx.com with the subject heading "Super PC discount" and I will send you a coupon code for a nice reduction off your next purchase.

In the end, you may end up buying from your local shop. It may be that your local shop has the best price. Keep in mind that Super PC offers to match any price, so if you prefer one of their models, put them to the test! Still, there are advantages to going local, not the least of which are the lack of shipping delay, the ease of getting it serviced as opposed to shipping it across the country, and if you find the right shop you'll get a pretty cool place to hang out and talk the latest tech trends. Who knows, you might pick up a good stock idea that way!

One last word of caution before we move on. Many new traders are forced to live on a tight budget as they build their capital base. I've been there myself and know how difficult a season like that is, especially if you are supporting a family. Those in such a situation, however, may find themselves tempted by some of the deep-discount computers that can be found online. *Caveat emptor*: buyer beware! Many of these discounted boxes are refurbished models, filled with used and "open box" parts. The manager of our local shop has told me horror stories of stockbrokers coming to him with fried-out motherboards after only a few weeks on a machine bought online. If you are lucky, you may get a decent machine free of problems. But quite often there is a good reason why these parts have been returned. My suggestion is to buy from Super PC or from a trusted local shop. If you have any questions, e-mail me at drstoxx@drstoxx.com.

FUNDAMENTAL SCREENING TOOLS

Working our way up the list of essential trading tools, we next come to those services you will use for current, reliable, company-specific fundamental data. We can divide our needs for this data into two basic types: We need a screening tool that will let us scan through all publicly traded stocks using specified fundamental filters to find lists of stocks that meet our criteria, and we also need a resource supplying fundamental analysis on specific stocks that will tell us what kind of shape an individual company is in. There is some really good news on both these fronts: Most of what we need for our trading purposes in this book can be found for free from various online sites. Let's start with the screening tools.

One resource that I recommended in my previous books, and can still recommend, is the free screening tool from Yahoo! Finance. You can find it by going to www.finance.yahoo.com. Once there, pull down the Investing menu and select Stocks. Then, under Research Tools, click the Stock Screener link. This will open up a small dialog box with an option for downloading their free screening tool. Be sure to select the Java-based advanced tool, not the basic version. Yahoo! Finance's screener is quite extensive, with criteria that include all the standard fundamental parameters, such as growth metrics, valuation ratios, earnings estimates and revisions, dividend yield, margins, leverage, profitability, and so on. You will find a few technical parameters as well, including price momentum, relative strength, moving averages, and beta. You can save your personally configured screens for later use, and can export the results to either e-mail or a spreadsheet for further research. A simple click on the company symbol will take you to the company's Yahoo! Finance page, giving you access to company profiles, upcoming announcements, headlines, and those amusing if not always helpful message boards. Figure 4.2 shows the Yahoo! Finance stock screener in action as it filters out all but the most liquid, volatile small to midcap sized stocks.

There are some drawbacks to using Yahoo!'s screener, however. It is not the most user-friendly or the most aesthetically pleasing of tools. It is functional, yes, but it certainly will not be winning any design awards. More importantly, it does not include in its database any exchange-traded funds or foreign stocks, and its options

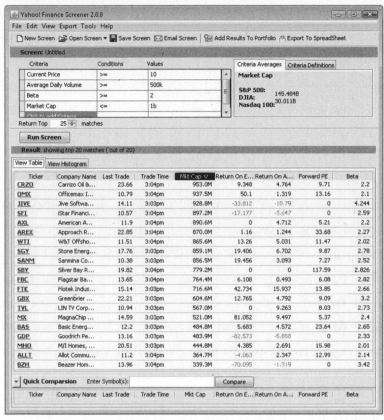

Image courtesy of Yahoo! Finance

Figure 4.2   Yahoo! Finance stock screening tool.

for the Index filter only list the Dow Jones Industrial Average and the S&P 500. So, for example, one cannot screen only for NASDAQ or Russell 2000 stocks. But it is free, and with trading tools, as with life in general, when you pay peanuts, you tend to get monkeys.

For our purposes here, a far more functional tool is Finviz.com, a full-service yet (mostly) free financial research site that offers one of the web's best techno-fundamental screening tools along with a top-notch news feed, futures, and forex data, and a portfolio tracker. On its home page you will also find bullish and bearish hotlists (a good place to look for trade ideas); lists of stocks printing computer-detected chart patterns; a "heat map" for the S&P 500; a list of recent insider transactions; upcoming earnings announcements; and commodities, forex, and bond data. Moreover, as you drill down to look at specific companies that come up in your scans, Finviz supplies you with just about all the fundamental data you need to make a reasonable assessment of their financial fitness. It is truly a one-stop shop for traders looking for their next trade.

After registering for a free account with Finviz.com, you will want to bookmark the site's home page (www .finviz.com). We will be using this page as part of our stock selection process for one of the trading systems described later. The company-specific data available on Finviz includes over 70 fundamental and technical metrics. Moreover, a number of parameters are rarely found, sometimes never found, in any of the free screening services. These include beta (measures a stock's volatility relative to the S&P 500), insider transactions (measures net of buying and selling activity by company insiders), float short (measures the percentage of publicly owned shares that are held short), analysts' recommendations (consensus of financial analysts on whether the stock is a buy, hold, or sell), price target (average one-year consensus of analyst estimates), and relative volume (ratio of today's volume vs. a three-month average of daily volume). Imagine screening for stocks that show the following parameters:

- *Beta > 2.0*
- *Insider transactions > 0*
- *Float short > 15%*
- *Analysts' recommendations = Buy or better*
- *Relative volume > 1.0*

I do not recommend this screen as a stand-alone system, of course, but it is a good way to show why Finviz .com is such a powerful tool. This simple screen will return stocks that are currently trading at twice the volatility of the S&P 500 in which there is more buying of shares than selling by company insiders, that should rise strongly on any upswing because there is a significant percentage of shares that need to be covered by short sellers anxious to avoid further losses, that receive a "buy" or "strong buy" rating from a consensus of financial professionals at the large investments banks, and that are likely gearing up for a significant move because they were trading today at a higher volume level than the three-month average.

Again, I do not recommend this scan by itself, but to illustrate some of the Finviz.com features. I ran the scan on April 24, 2013, and found three stocks that fit these criteria (see Figure 4.3). With a simple click of the mouse,

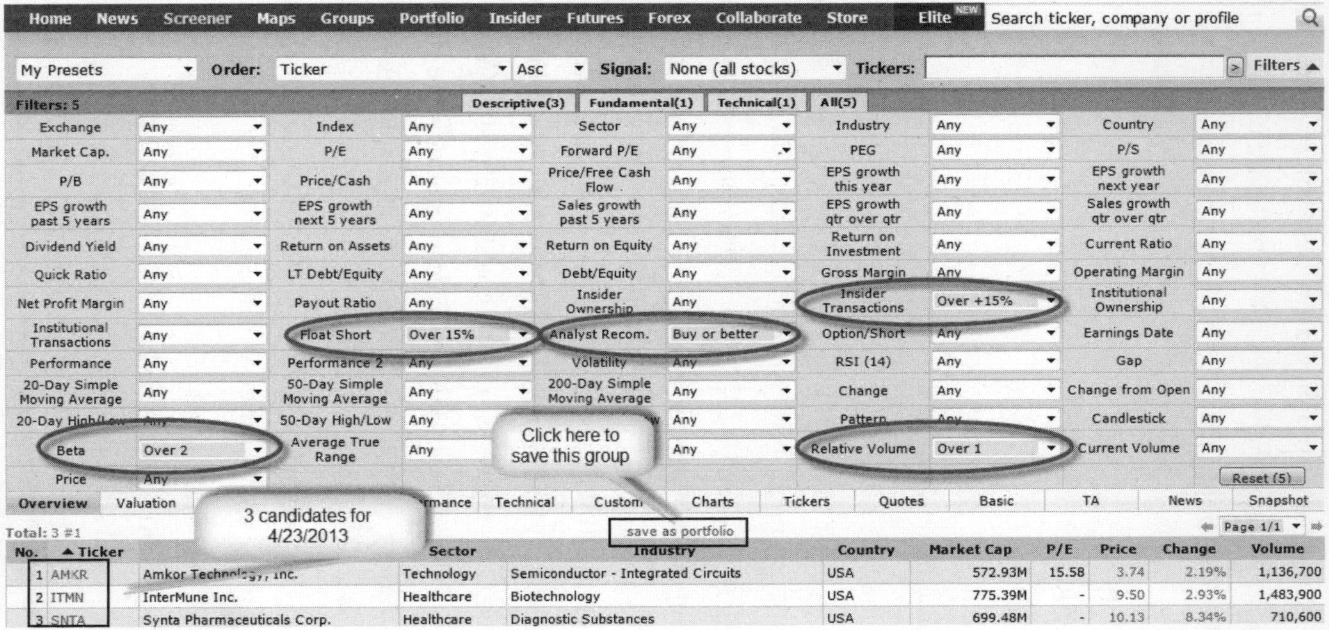

Figure 4.3 A sample scan using Finviz.com.

Image courtesy of Finviz.com

I saved this group to a portfolio that will automatically track the returns of each stock over time as if they were part of a $100,000 portfolio. The entry price is automatically entered as the last closing price if the scan is run outside of trading hours, or the intraday last price (delayed data for free users) at the time the scan was run if it was run during market hours. Current returns are automatically updated throughout the trading day.

Here is what one of my portfolios looks like in Finviz.com (see Figure 4.4). This portfolio is one of several where I deposit stocks that pass through my various scans for further research. One nice feature of Finviz's portfolio tracker is that when you hover your mouse over the ticker symbol on the left, a three-month thumbnail chart pops up. Click the symbol, and you will get a full-sized, 10-month chart complete with moving averages, computer-generated trendlines and price patterns, and key levels of support and resistance (see Figure 4.5). This gives me a quick glance at how the stock has been faring in recent trade. Note the list of headlines for each of the stocks in the portfolio. A simple click on the headline will take you to the original article. Note also the updated returns, both since the portfolio was created and for the day. One last feature to point out is that when you click the Open In Screener link, your stocks open up in a grid that, with another mouse click, can be sorted according to a variety of fundamental and technical values, enabling the best candidates in each category to rise to the top.

Portfolio — Watch List of Possible Longs ▼

view | edit | delete | create new | open in screener

▲No.	Ticker	Company	Price	Change%	Volume	Transaction	Date	Shares		Value	Gain$	Gain%	Change$
1.	GLW	Corning Inc.	13.13	2.42%	11,486,100	Buy	03-26-13	1,537	13.01	20184.47	184.47	0.92%	476.56
2.	NAVB	Navidea Biopharmaceuticals, Inc	2.43	0.41%	556,900	Buy	03-26-13	8,197	2.44	19918.03	-81.97	-0.41%	81.97
3.	KERX	Keryx Biopharmaceuticals Inc.	8.31	-0.12%	3,938,200	Buy	03-26-13	2,874	6.96	23879.31	3879.31	19.40%	-28.73
4.	SRPT	Sarepta Therapeutics, Inc.	30.92	-4.92%	3,338,200	Buy	03-26-13	576	34.75	17795.68	-2204.32	-11.02%	-920.86
5.	ARQL	ArQule Inc.	3.05	4.45%	454,100	Buy	03-26-13	7,605	2.63	23193.92	3193.92	15.97%	988.59
Total	5 Stocks			0.57%						104971.42	4971.42	4.97%	597.52

Today's gains

Overall gains since inception

An awesome news feed that is updated in real time and from a variety of reliable sources

24-Apr-13 08:45AM NAVB Navidea Biopharmaceuticals Announces Underwritten Sale of Common Stock Business Wire
08:08AM GLW BRIEF-Corning shares up 2.4 percent in premarket trading at Reuters
07:45AM GLW UPDATE 1-Corning profit beats on strong demand for Gorilla Glass at Reuters
07:12AM GLW InPlay: Corning beats by $0.06, misses on revs; raises qrtly dividend to $0.10 from $0.09, announces $2 bln buyback Briefing.com
07:11AM GLW Corning profit rises on strong demand for Gorilla Glass at Reuters
07:10AM GLW Corning Announces Increased Quarterly Dividend and New $2 Billion Share Repurchase Program Thomson Reuters ONE
07:07AM GLW Corning sees Q2 Telecommunications sales up 20% sequentially theflyonthewall.com
07:07AM GLW Q1 2013 Corning Incorporated Earnings Release - Before Market Open CCBN
07:02AM GLW Corning Announces First-Quarter Financial Performance Thomson Reuters ONE
12:03AM GLW CORNING INC /NY Files SEC form 8-K, Results of Operations and Financial Condition, Financial Statements and Exhibits EDGAR Online
23-Apr-13 02:58PM SRPT A Biotech Firm's Ultimate Decision: To Finance, To Find A Partner Or To Go Bankrupt at Seeking Alpha
01:54PM SRPT Are These Billion-Dollar Biotechs Overvalued? at Motley Fool
10:38AM SRPT Analyzing Market Efficiency: Why Future Catalysts Imply Sanuwave Still Has Room To Double at Seeking Alpha
08:30AM ARQL ArQule, Inc. to Present at Needham 12th Annual Healthcare Conference Business Wire
22-Apr-13 05:00PM KERX Keryx Biopharmaceuticals Inc. (KERX): Today's Featured Health Care Winner at TheStreet
03:02PM KERX Keryx, Zerenex, And IP Protection: A PropThink Conference Call at Seeking Alpha
10:31AM SRPT 5 Hot Stocks: Facebooks Home Fails To Dazzle, Check Points Lukewarm Earnings, and Six Flags Sets A Record at Wall St. Cheat Sheet
10:24AM KERX Want to Invest in Biotech? Think Like a Venture Capitalist at Motley Fool
04:59AM KERX Keryx BioPharmaceuticals: A Favorite Of Mine In The Pharmacology World at Seeking Alpha
01:02AM SRPT Coverage initiated on Sarepta Therapeutics by Needham Briefing.com
21-Apr-13 05:15AM SRPT 5 of Last Week's Biggest Losers at Motley Fool
20-Apr-13 06:24PM SRPT Here's What This 2,115% Gainer Has Been Buying at Motley Fool
18-Apr-13 01:40PM NAVB Navidea Biopharmaceuticals Announces that Results of NAV4694 Clinical Trial Published in the Journal of Nuclear Medicine Business Wire
09:15AM NAVB XenoPort: A High Probability Run-Up Trade at Seeking Alpha
17-Apr-13 07:07AM ARQL Early-Stage Clinical Data Highlights From AACR 2013 at Seeking Alpha
16-Apr-13 08:37PM KERX These Cutting-Edge Science Stocks Are Soaring at Motley Fool
06:17AM NAVB Three Biotech Stocks With Low Price But Great Potential at Seeking Alpha

Figure 4.4 A sample portfolio in Finviz.com.

Image courtesy of Finviz.com

AMZN [NASD]
Amazon.com Inc.

Courtesy of Finviz.com

Figure 4.5   A sample technical chart in Finviz.com.

FUNDAMENTAL DATA ON COMPANIES

This brings us to resources that will fill our need for fundamental analysis on specific companies. We will use these resources to determine which of the stocks that show up on our system scans are in the best (and worst) financial shape. As mentioned earlier, Finviz is a great resource for this purpose and will be used in the Pullback/Relief Rally system described in Chapter 12. It is an especially ideal resource for those who are new to fundamental analysis. When you plug a company into Finviz, any metric that demonstrates financial strength by historical standards—e.g., a price-to-sales ratio below 1.0 (which shows good value) or a projected increase in fiscal year earnings per share (EPS) over 25 percent (which shows solid growth)—shows up in green.

Any measurement thought to demonstrate fundamental weakness shows up in red. Values between the extremes show up in black. Thus, Finviz can give us a quick visual read on fundamentals without having to understand exactly what the numbers themselves mean.

Another site you will want to bookmark is VectorGrader (www.vectorgrader.com). While some features of this site are reserved for paying members, what it offers for free is of great help to us. If you go to the home page and scroll down, you will see a link entitled New Piotroski Scores. Click that, and you will be taken to a blog describing the Piotroski F-score and what each of the nine components of the ranking system is looking for. You will have to click a couple more times to find the actual grader itself, but if you get lost, e-mail me (drstoxx@drstoxx.com) and I will send you the link.

What this awesome tool gives you, entirely for free, is the exact Piotroski F-score for any stock. Plug in QCOM and MSFT and you will get an exact numerical value from a range between 0 and 9. We will learn more about this scale and the nine separate tests that comprise it later in the book (Chapter 7). In general, the higher the number, the more likely the stock is to outperform the market; the lower the number, the greater the risk of loss. The two stocks just listed have Piotroski F-scores of 5 (QCOM) and 7 (MSFT). What this ranking tells us is that, according to Dr. Piotroski's research, MSFT is a better trade—more stable, less likely to implode—than QCOM. That is how we will use this tool. When we run the Blue Sky/Blue Sea system (Chapter 11), we will take the stocks our technical scans turn up and use VectorGrader to filter out the best Piotroski F-score for our longs and the worst F-score for our shorts.

To show you what a Piotroski F-score looks like, here is VectorGrader's F-score for Apple Computers (AAPL), which as of this writing ranks 7 out of 9 (Figure 4.6):

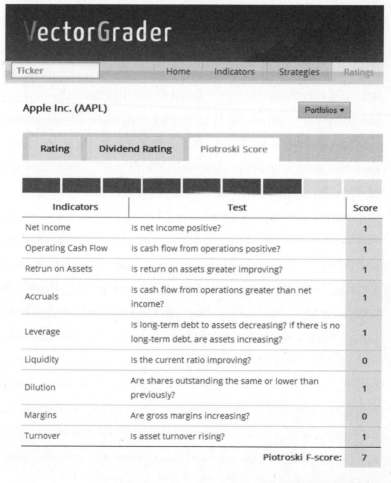

Indicators	Test	Score
Net Income	Is net income positive?	1
Operating Cash Flow	Is cash flow from operations positive?	1
Retrun on Assets	Is return on assets greater improving?	1
Accruals	Is cash flow from operations greater than net income?	1
Leverage	Is long-term debt to assets decreasing? If there is no long-term debt, are assets increasing?	1
Liquidity	Is the current ratio improving?	0
Dilution	Are shares outstanding the same or lower than previously?	1
Margins	Are gross margins increasing?	0
Turnover	Is asset turnover rising?	1
	Piotroski F-score:	7

Courtesy of Vectorgrader.com

Figure 4.6 A sample Piotroski F-score for Apple Computer.

A third site you will want to bookmark is the Portfolio Grader, a fundamental analysis tool offered by Louis Navellier, one of the great masters of growth stock analysis. We will be using this tool in the Mean Reversion system described in Chapter 13. While the Portfolio Grader is free, you will need to register with the site in order to build and access portfolios of stocks. Navellier is CEO and founder of Navellier and Associates, a money management firm with several billion dollars in assets under management. Navellier publishes four separate investment letters, each with a growth stock focus. Navellier's Portfolio Grader is the only site I know of that tracks eight key fundamental growth metrics—including sales, cash flow, return on equity, and estimate revisions—on an A (best) to F (worst) scale, and at the same time lets you see the evolution of overall grades over the past 12 months. This allows us the coveted ability to track the growth of earnings (or lack thereof) of individual companies, without having to flip through page after page of past financial statements. A typical Portfolio Grader report looks like the following analysis of SanDisk (SNDK), a maker of data storage devices (see Figure 4.7).

There is one more site you will want to bookmark before going any further. It's not free, but it is cheap (currently less than $15/month; cheaper still in longer-term subscriptions). We will be using this tool to run two of our systems: O'Neil's CAN-SLIM system (fundamentals-based, Chapter 9) and the Blue Sky/Blue Sea system (technicals-based, Chapter 11). Investors.com is the online site for

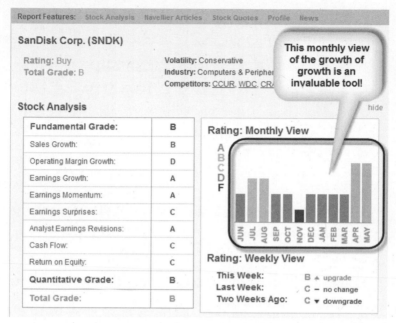

Courtesy of Navellier Growth/Investor Place

Figure 4.7   A sample Navellier's Portfolio Grader for SNDK.

the daily print publication *Investor's Business Daily* (IBD).
By paying the monthly fee, you will have access to IBD's
proprietary grading information of every publicly traded
company listed with the major indexes and exchanges.
We will be using the grading tool known as the Stock
Checkup, which more or less translates William O'Neil's
famous CAN-SLIM trading system into a numerical value
on a scale of 1 to 100. Stocks scoring at the top end of that
range are the strongest stocks trading in terms of various
fundamental and technical parameters, including earnings
growth, margin rates, and relative strength. For an example of what Investors.com offers by way of analysis, see the
analysis of Qualcom (QCOM) in Figure 4.8.

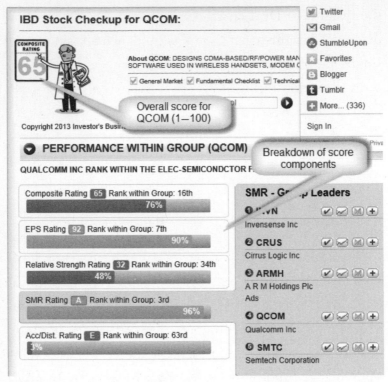

Courtesy of Investors.com

Figure 4.8   A sample of stock analysis in Investors.com.

FEE-BASED FUNDAMENTAL DATA SCREENING SERVICES

There are two fee-based screening services that will be needed to trade three of our fundamentals-based systems (Chapters 7, 8, and 10). You needn't use both, which is fortunate since one is considerably more expensive than the other. Let's start with the more expensive service. Zacks Research, which we introduced in the previous chapter, is a professional-grade equities research portal built around the insights of Dr. Len Zacks. As noted, Dr. Zacks's fundamental insight—that earnings guidance revision is the single most powerful driver of stock price over the short term—was transformed into a proprietary system for grading stocks on a sliding scale. This scale, when combined with other key measurements of fundamental value and growth, has a remarkable record as a predictor of near-term price movement. We have already seen the results. Here, I want to introduce Zacks Research's primary screening tool, the Research Wizard (see Figure 4.9).

Zacks's *Research Wizard* (RW) is built around the Zacks Rank, the aforementioned rating scale. A Zacks Rank of 1 puts a stock, among all stocks followed by major analysts, in the top 5 percent of stocks likely to raise earnings guidance in the near future. A Zacks Rank of 5 puts the stock in the bottom 5 percent. In addition, the RW has a large number of other fundamental parameters—growth metrics, valuation ratios, leverage, turnover, liquidity—as well as a handful of technical (momentum) filters that serve our techno-fundamental approach well. There is also the option to create your own filter expression from a wide variety of variables, calculation operators, and functions.

Imagine that you could isolate all the stocks ranked at 1 and then filter out only those that are showing both significant earnings growth and are still relatively undervalued. Then imagine that you could back-test that screen to get the filter set just right to maximize returns while

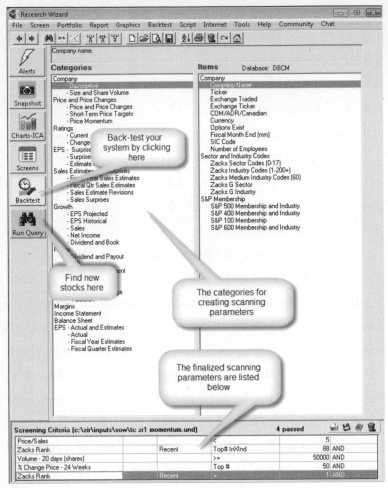

Courtesy of Zacks Investment Research

Figure 4.9   Research Wizard Scan editor.

minimizing drawdowns. Finally, imagine that you could do the same thing on the short side as well, with stocks at a rank of 5 that are showing negative growth and are overvalued. In doing this, you have just neutralized the market! This is exactly what the RW enables you to do (see Figure 4.9).

I have been using Zacks's RW for several years now, primarily as a systems development tool. It is my first "go to" destination whenever I get an idea for a new fundamentals-based trading system. RW has more than 100 predefined scans built into the product, many of which have been featured in the "Screen of the Week" column on www.zacks.com. For a $199 annual fee, you can have access to passing candidates for most of these scans through the Zacks.com website. I have personally back-tested many of these scans over historical periods ranging from 3 to 12 years. To be honest, I have had difficulty finding more than a handful that consistently outperformed the overall market (and that in a mostly bull market). There were a few, however, and these performed amazingly well. To build my own set of scans, therefore, I took the best pieces of the best of these more robust scans and combined them with several proprietary parameters I created using RW's Calculation Expression editor. After several months of playing around with all this—trading systems developers will tell you that the "playing around" is the fun part!—I came away with three separate systems that were off the charts successful. I show you the results of my work with the RW later. The basic structure of those three systems is fully disclosed here in the Carr Hybrid system (Chapter 10).

The RW is far from a perfect research tool, however. One major flaw with the software is that while it updates its data daily (a real plus), it only does so overnight. This means that the stocks that pass the filters from today's trading can only be entered at tomorrow's open. This in itself is not an issue; the same is true for all but a handful of real-time scanning services that are able to run on intraday data. The problem with RW is that the back-testing feature only calculates returns from a Friday closing price. Since stocks that passed the scan on Friday can only be entered at Monday's open, all back-tested returns include price movement from Friday's close to Monday's open, which cannot be captured by traders using the service. I can say from several years of using the RW that this difference is critical. In some of my back-tested runs, it meant the difference between a market-beating gain and underperformance.

I tried solving this problem a couple of different ways. The general idea was to try to approximate Friday's closing price as much as possible as the entry price for any newly passing stock and as the exit price for any stock that needed to be replaced (the three systems I developed were most profitable using a weekly rebalance period). My first attempt at a solution was a simple one: After running the scans over the weekend, I simply placed "market on open" orders in Monday's premarket for all passing candidates that I did not already own from the previous week's scans. Any stock I did already own that failed to pass this week's scans would then be sold or covered at Monday's open. In this way I was assured of always being in the same stocks that factored into the back-test results, just not always at the same entry and exit prices. Unfortunately, as I said earlier, that difference proved critical. While sometimes I experienced price improvement on the Monday entry as longs gapped down and shorts gapped up, the weekend lag proved to be far more of a handicap. My real money returns never matched the back-tested results over the same test period.

My next attempt at a solution was more complicated. This time, I placed "market on close" orders set to execute on Friday on all open positions. This left me fully in cash over the weekend. Then, for all stocks that passed the weekend scans, I would set a limit order exactly at Friday's closing price for entry on Monday morning. In this way I could completely eliminate the lack of capture of weekend price movement since my entry and exit prices exactly coincided with those of the back-tested results. Unfortunately, this solution created two problems. First, there were additional commission costs incurred by exiting each Friday and then re-entering each Monday, as a number of positions did not need to be replaced since they passed the filter in both the past and present holding periods. Second, by entering new positions on Monday morning only at Friday's closing price, I invariably failed to get into those positions that gapped (up for longs, down for shorts) at Monday's open and never looked back. More often than not, these were the most profitable positions for that week. Indeed, there were periods when I sustained a loss while the RW back-test feature recorded a gain simply because I was left out of one or two key positions.

Apart from the back-testing anomaly, the other issue with the RW—for some it is a deal-breaker—is that it is relatively expensive. An annual subscription to the nightly data upload and the full range (12 years) of historical data costs $3,000 per year. If you manage a $300,000 account, this is a reasonable 1 percent annual administrative expense— less than what many mutual funds charge. But on a $30,000 account, paying a 10 percent premium is really not an option. Fortunately, there is a lower pricing option. If you can get by on only six years of price data, you can knock $1,200 off the price, which brings the charge down to a more reasonable, though still pricey, $150 per month, paid annually. I suggest you go to the website for the RW (www.zacksrw.com) and call the number at the bottom of the screen. Tell them that you read about the RW in *Market-Neutral Trading* by Dr. Carr. Don't be shy about asking for a discount. They should oblige with a substantial cut off the first year's fee. The sales reps at Zacks are also active systems developers who know the RW product very well. They can show you a number of tricks to get the most from this powerful research tool.

With the caveats behind us, let me go on to say that the RW is definitely a tool to consider putting in your trading arsenal, especially if you enjoy systems building. It will certainly help you identify nice trading opportunities, some of which are destined for true greatness. Consider the following back-test I ran in the RW over a five-year test period, from May 2008 to May 2013. To attain these results, I back-tested a rather simple, longs-only scan I built in RW based loosely on the research of Dr. Len Zacks as described in the previous chapter. This particular scan also contains a proprietary valuation filter that keeps us out of stocks deprived of cash flow, along with a set of relative strength filters to ensure that the stocks that pass the scan show long-term strength but are at or near oversold levels. Note that the lower line in the chart (see Figure 4.10) is that of the S&P 500 over the same period.

This simple system produced (in theory, at least) a nearly 200 percent return on investment (ROI) over five years during a period when the S&P returned only about 30 percent. That is some pretty healthy alpha! Keep in mind that our test period includes the bulk of the 2008–2009 market crash. For the first 10 months of our test, the S&P was in strong sell mode, ultimately losing 46 percent into the nefarious 666 intraday print of March 2009. What makes our returns especially remarkable is that from the lowest trough of our test (December 2008) to the end of the run, our system produced a net return in excess of 700 percent ROI!

We can do better. What would happen, for example, if we took that same system, but this time we limited our selections to only small-cap stocks (<$1b market cap)? This way, we know that we are putting our money into those sectors in our economy with the greatest growth potential. Furthermore, what if we screened out all stocks except those that carried a Zacks Rank of 1? As described in the last chapter, a Zacks Rank of 1, according to Dr. Zacks himself, would instantly put our passing candidates into the top 5 percent of all publicly traded stocks according to their degree of increase in earnings estimates. With these two additional filters in place, we now get a return on investment that looks like this (Figure 4.11):

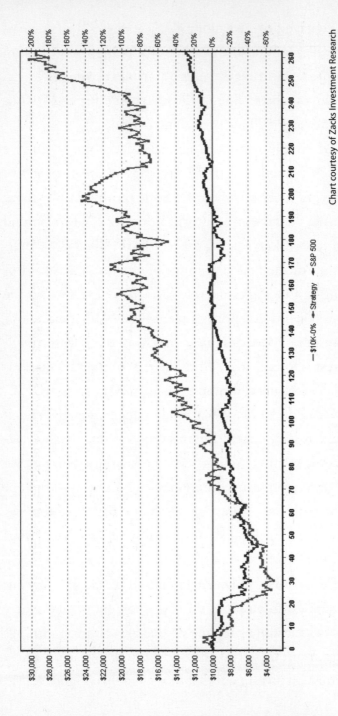

Figure 4.10 Five-year back-test of Earnings Estimate Revision (EER) system—longs.

Chart courtesy of Zacks Investment Research

— $10k-0% — Strategy — S&P 500

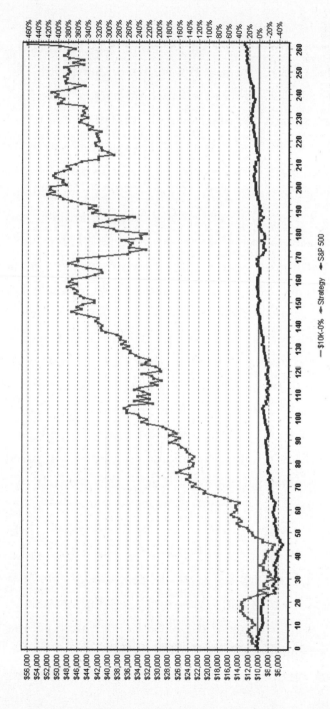

Figure 4.11 Five-year back-test of EER system with Zacks Rank 1 added—longs.

Chart courtesy of Zacks Investment Research

— $10K-0%   — Strategy   — S&P 500

With these two additions, we've more than doubled our ROI to nearly 460 percent, or more than 14 times the return of the S&P. Not bad! But we can do better still. For one last tweak, let's find out what would happen if we took the revised system just described, but this time we limited our selections not to oversold charts but to stocks showing the strongest price momentum. These are stocks that are no longer flying under the radar. Their rising earnings potential has been spotted by professional money managers who have been accumulating shares on the dips. Hedge funds are also getting on board, causing these stocks to break out of their long-term price channels. Their CEOs are making appearances on CNBC, *Investor's Business Daily* is featuring them in its "New America" column, and Jim Cramer is giving them a "booya" buy-buy-buy. All that attention is causing the momentum indicators to run vertical. This, along with the previous filters mentioned, puts such stocks on our short list of trading candidates. How do these growth + value + momentum candidates perform compared to their oversold peers filtered out in the previous two screens? Take a look at Figure 4.12.

This is an amazingly strong outperformance, with nearly 70,000 basis points of alpha over a five-year period. Moreover, as you can see from the left side of the chart (Figure 4.12), our system's dip into the red during the market crash was not as deep as the S&P's, despite a greater peak-to-trough drawdown. This is the kind of outperformance that will cause Wall Street to come calling with

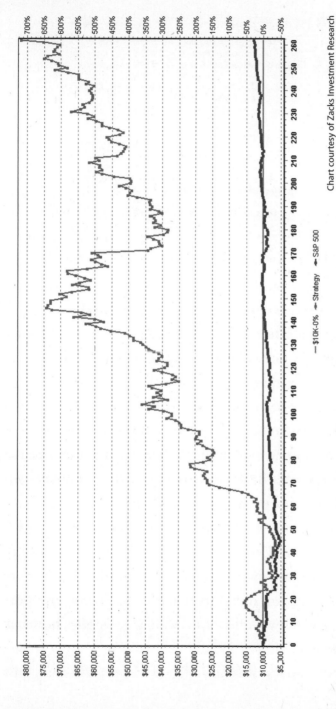

Figure 4.12 Five-year back-test of EER system with momentum filter added—longs.

— $10K–0% ◆ Strategy ◆ S&P 500

Chart courtesy of Zacks Investment Research

STATISTICS ex.: $10,000 start	Strategy	S&P 500
Total Compounded Return %	717.7%	28.7%
Total Compounded Return $	$81,769	$12,870
Compounded Annual Growth Rate %	51.7%	5.1%
Win Ratio %	58%	56%
Winning Periods/Total Periods	151 of 262	147 of 262
Avg. # of Stocks Held	3.0	
Avg. Periodic Turnover %	52.9%	
Avg. Return per Period %	1.0%	0.1%
Avg. Winning Period %	5.0%	2.1%
Largest Winning Period %	23.5%	12.1%
Avg. Losing Period %	-4.4%	-2.3%
Largest Losing Period %	-27.5%	-18.1%
Max. Drawdown %	-58.3%	-50.9%
Avg. Winning Stretch (# of Periods)	2.5	2.1
Best Stretch (# of Periods)	10	7
Avg. Losing Stretch (# of Periods)	1.8	1.7
Worst Stretch (# of Periods)	6	6

Courtesy of Zacks Investment Research

Figure 4.13 Five-year back-test of EER system with momentum filter added—longs.

seven-figure salary offers, even if you live in the middle of corn-picking nowhere (as we do!). Here is the breakdown of the returns for the third variation of our three Earnings Estimate Revision hybrid systems (Figure 4.13).

This last set of numbers is worth a closer look. As we drill down among the line items, we see that our most profitable trading system of the three just described is also dangerously volatile. It is a system capable of dramatic out-performance, but to get there, one would have to sit through some very painful drawdowns. The worst week saw a loss of over 27 percent! During the market collapse of 2008–2009, this portfolio of longs would have lost nearly 53 percent of its trading capital. Investors might be forgiving, given the overall market's volatility. Less willing to forgive, however, were those who got in about three years into the test period when the fund was at a new high of 650 percent ROI, only then to see it plunge to below 300 percent, a loss of nearly 60 percent. Given the problems associated with using the RW that we mentioned earlier, real-time trading returns would likely have been worse than that.

This is where the market-neutralizing orientation of our trading systems comes into play. What would happen if we took these three successfully back-tested longs systems and reversed their parameters from bullish to bearish? For example, what if, instead of looking for increases in earnings estimate revisions, we screened for decreases? What if, instead of looking for undervalued companies, we screened for the overvalued ones? What if, instead of looking for stocks with a Zacks Rank of 1, we took only those with a Zacks Rank of 5? How would those stocks have fared in a back-test of the system as a shorts-only portfolio over the same look-back period? Quite well, it turns out. All three longs systems, when reversed to the short side, proved profitable. Of the three systems described, the second system, which adds Zacks Rank and relative strength filters (see Figure 4.12), performed the best. Take a look at these returns (Figure 4.14).

There are two critical things to note from this chart. First, we see how the periods of most intense drawdown in the best-performing longs-only portfolio (Figure 4.12) are well matched by periods of strong returns in the shorts-only portfolio (Figure 4.14). This nicely illustrates the double alpha potential of a market-neutralizing trading approach: When one side of the equation is lagging, whether long

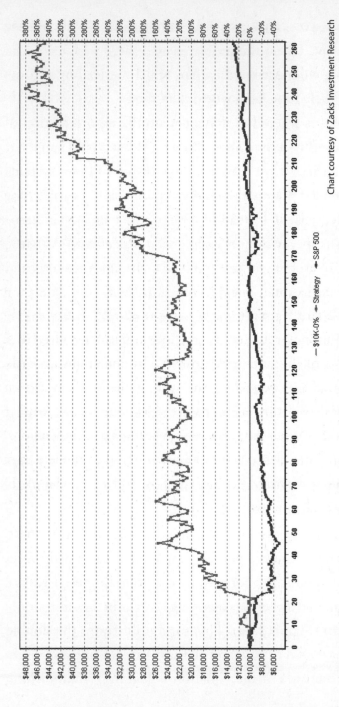

Figure 4.14 Five-year back-test of EER system with Zacks Rank 5 added—shorts.

Chart courtesy of Zacks Investment Research

— $10k-0%   — Strategy   — S&P 500

or short, you can look to the other side to make up the difference.

Second, if we consider that short sales in any account are always done on margin to attain a total ROI for a long-short portfolio of equal capital weight in each, we can simply add the returns of the short portfolio (about 340 percent) to the return of the best-performing long portfolio (about 700 percent). Thus, with the whole of our trading capital invested in the two best-performing systems, we are looking at something north of 1,000 percent return over five years, minus fees, margin interest, commissions (in total, roughly a 5 percent annual charge if you use the right broker), and the aforementioned lag of real-money returns relative to the back-tested results. This is a phenomenal performance by anyone's standards. Again, it bears repeating that you will not likely match that kind of return using the RW as your sole screening service. But even half that return for a purely mechanical trading system, especially when compared to the less than 30 percent return of the S&P 500, is worth a good look. In Chapter 10, you get that look.

FUNDAMENTAL DATA SCREENING SERVICES—STOCK INVESTOR PRO

The other fee-based service that traders using my systems should consider is offered by the American Association of Independent Investors (www.AAII.com). When you just look at the name, the American Association of Independent Investors sounds like a trade organization or lobbying group in Washington, D.C. It is not. It was founded back in 1978 by Dr. James Cloonan as a venue for conveying investing wisdom from top-notch financial professionals to lay investors. AAII.com's mission is built upon Cloonan's stated belief that "individual investors armed with effective investment education materials and a bit of dedication could outperform the popular market averages."[3] In the three decades since its founding, AAII.com has grown to over 150,000 members, with expert contributors ranging from Ivy League professors of finance to world-class portfolio managers. AAII.com has become for many a go-to portal for investing ideas and education.

Much of AAII.com's online content is available for free. There are weekly articles on various investing topics from guest contributors, and a daily blog with current stock research posted by the AAII.com team. There is the frequently referenced AAII Investor Sentiment survey. This survey offers a weekly glance at whether the average "independent investor" is presently feeling bullish, neutral, or bearish about the overall market. The AAII Investor Sentiment survey has been quite successful as a contrarian indicator; that is, when the masses are feeling strongly bullish, the market tends in short order to put on a correction, and vice versa. So successful is this survey that you can even find a technical indicator based on it in some charting packages. Called the "AAII Bulls minus Bears

Index," the survey's weekly results are plotted as a line chart and then because it tends to be very volatile, it is smoothed as a moving average. The idea is to go long at historically extreme levels of bearish sentiment and short at extreme levels of bullish sentiment.

Also available for free on www.AAII.com is a list of more than 70 stock investment strategies. These strategies are based on the systems created by some of the all-time greats in the investing world. For each system, there is an explanation of the selection thesis on which it is based. One can also see monthly updates of returns. Included among these systems are Joseph Piotroski's F-score, Len Zacks's Earnings Revision system, and William O'Neil's CAN-SLIM. To get access to a list of passing stocks for each of these screens, you will need to become a paying member. The bad news for paying subscribers is that the lists of passing stocks are only updated monthly and only then after about half the month has passed. The good news is that the entrance fee to gain that delayed access is a very reasonable $29 per year, $99 for four years, or $290 for lifetime access.

For the purposes of this book, there is no need to pay for access to the www.AAII.com site. Instead, you will want to purchase a license to use AAII.com's excellent fundamentals-based scanning service, *Stock Investor Pro* (SIP). With SIP, weekly updates of all publicly traded companies are fed automatically into one of the most powerful—and most affordable—fundamentals-based scanning services available. One of the best features of SIP is that the service comes preloaded with every one of the 70-plus professional systems tracked on the www.AAII.com site. This means that, with the click of a mouse, you will know each week which are the best stocks to buy according to Piotroski, Zacks, or O'Neil; or indeed, dozens of other investment gurus. As just mentioned, each of these systems has its returns recorded on the AAII.com site, with year-to-date, 3-year, 5-year, 10-year, and since-inception returns listed, updated monthly. The systems we are highlighting in this book are taken from those that have risen to the top of those lists.

In addition to giving users access to professional-grade trading systems, SIP allows users to custom build just about any fundamentals-based system imaginable. SIP has an editing tool that allows users to create their own system screens, including (like RW) the option to build custom parameters by connecting two or more individual parameters together with a wide variety of mathematical functions and conditionals. The screen editor houses a massive list of more than 2,000 data fields—far more than what is available in the RW—of which many are adjustable to a nearly infinite degree of precision. There are several technical parameters as well, making the SIP an ideal tool for our market-neutral trading systems.

Once a list of passing companies is generated, you can enter these at the next market open. If the list is too long, there is a function in SIP that ranks the list according to various metrics (see Figure 4.15). Among these are valuation

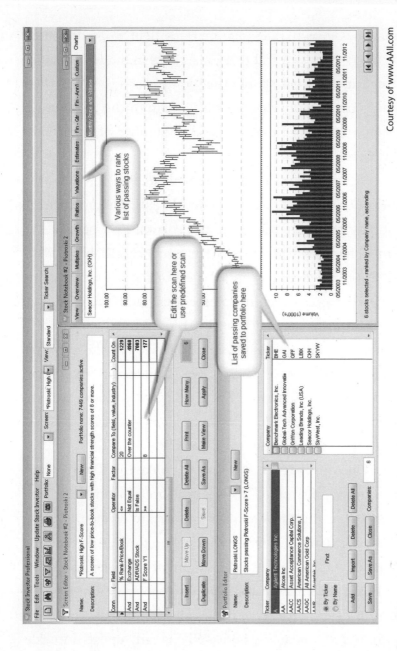

Courtesy of www.AAII.com

Figure 4.15 AAII.com's Stock Investor Pro.

multiples, growth rates, margin rates, debt-to-equity ratios, earnings estimates and revisions, ranks in industry, relative strength, and a variety of other comparison variables. This makes our job of selecting the "cream of the crop" much easier when more than a tradable number of stocks pass the screen.

SIP comes as a software download, which is unlocked with the purchase of a key code. Weekly data updates are run automatically each time the software is opened. The annual fee for full access to SIP is a very reasonable $198 or $298 for two years (cheap!). Access includes a set of online tutorial videos, which introduce users to the full range of scan editing in the SIP, as well as how to use the product to perform company-specific data analysis. For those new to fundamental analysis, these tutorials alone are more than worth the entrance fee. They will give you an excellent introductory-level education in fundamental analysis as you also get up to speed on using the SIP.

One drawback to SIP is that, unlike the RW, it has no back-testing feature. This is a deal-breaker for those who want to use this book as a springboard to create their own trading systems. Certainly, there is no greater thrill in the sport of trading systems development than seeing a near-vertical performance chart pop up after running a long-term back-test. Moreover, RW allows for daily screening with nightly updates, whereas SIP is only updated weekly. For the truly ambitious (and deep-pocketed), these two differences give the edge to RW in a head-to-head comparison with SIP. But if you factor in the huge difference in price, the greater range of fundamental filters that SIP has to work with, and the fact that with this book in hand you already have a set of thoroughly tested systems—and thus no real need for a back-testing feature—the overall edge may well have to be given to SIP. Again, you will not need both RW and SIP to trade the systems in this book, but you will need a fundamentals-based screening tool of some kind and these are two that, having used both for years, I can recommend.

THE DR. STOXX TREND TRADING TOOLKIT

There is one last product—another screening tool—to consider adding to your kit. RW and SIP are screening tools that focus primarily on fundamental analysis. This tool serves as a nice complement by focusing primarily on technical analysis. While not a requirement to trade the systems discussed, it will be featured prominently in several of them. It has a distinct advantage over similar products. While the Research Wizard and Stock Investor Pro require you to program my system descriptions into their software, this tool has already done that for you. It took nearly two years of daily work to develop, but all the sweat and effort were worth it. With this tool on your PC, along with either the RW or SIP and the free websites mentioned earlier, you will be able to trade every system described in this book.

In my first book, *Trend Trading for a Living* (McGraw-Hill, 2007), I told my readers that I used www.stockcharts.com exclusively to do my technicals-based stock research. Since the publication of *Trend Trading for a Living*, a new product has come online that is easier to use; more robust; and, unlike www.Stockcharts.com, it comes with professional-grade charting, back-testing tools, and news feeds (the new "Eikon" interface). This new product is offered on the MetaStock research platform. Launched over 30 years ago, MetaStock is today one of the most widely used research tools among market technicians, day traders, futures traders, and trading systems developers. For the past two years, the code writers at MetaStock have been programming the trading systems from *Trend Trading for a Living*, along with three other of my systems, into their scanning and charting software. The result of all that work is one of the largest and most comprehensive products MetaStock sells, the Dr. Stoxx Trend Trading Toolkit (TTTK).

The TTTK is a new plug-in (or "add-on" in MetaStock-ese) for the MetaStock software. It has preprogrammed all my *Trend Trading for a Living* systems, two day trading systems from *Micro-Trend Trading for Daily Income* (McGraw-Hill, 2010), and a recently developed long-short mean reversion system. This last system is unique to the TTTK and is, to date, my most profitable system. I use it regularly in my own trading account, the results of which you will see in Chapter 13. The MetaStock TTTK contains this scan fully programmed. A single run of the scan will yield a daily list of both long and short candidates for consideration. Of the three technical-based systems in this book, it is the one that most purely neutralizes the market.

After many long months of back and forth tweaking the Dr. Stoxx Trend Trading Toolkit, testing and perfecting and testing some more, the final result was launched in April 2013. The TTTK includes all of the following (see Figure 4.16):

- *Eleven scans from* Trend Trading for a Living
- *Nine expert advisories from* Trend Trading for a Living *(these highlight technical setups in real time)*
- *Six chart templates matched to the various setups they support*
- *Two expert advisories from* Micro-Trend Trading for Daily Income

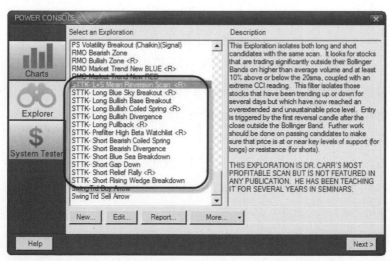

Courtesy of Thompson Reuters

Figure 4.16   The Dr. Stoxx Trend Trading Toolkit—explorations.

- *One Mean Reversion system scan (long-short)—a NEW system!*
- *One prefilter scan for creating watch lists of the best-trading stocks*

The good news about the TTTK is that it is surprisingly affordable. When I first used MetaStock back in the late 1990s, it cost $1,500 up front for the software license and then a sizeable monthly fee for the data-feed. Today, the software license is much more reasonably priced. There is a small, one-time fee for the add-on itself (e-mail me at drstoxx@drstoxx.com for a discounted offer), but once that is paid, your monthly fee for the data-feed is just a shade more than what you would pay for a StockCharts subscription. Moreover, if you want to use StockCharts, you will have to code in the screens yourself. With the Trend Trading Toolkit, no coding is needed. It has all been done for you by some of the smartest guys in the business. All the technical systems I teach are ready to go right out of the box. Simply click the mouse a couple of times, and you will have a fresh list of stocks that pass all the technical filters I've developed and use each day. Moreover, there is no way to optimize my systems in StockCharts because it has no back-testing feature; MetaStock has one of the most versatile back-testing features available.

My favorite feature of the TTTK is the Expert Advisor. This feature prints real-time alerts on any chart you select, or on each chart in a watch list, for each of our trading systems. No longer do you need to eyeball your watch list charts, waiting for setups to form. The Expert Advisor will let you know in real time whenever a new signal has formed. Each alert also sets up a commentary window to give you an exact entry price for each alert, along with suggestions for stop and target prices based on the historical testing of the system. The Expert Advisor has encoded all the systems from *Trend Trading for a Living*—including four versions of the "Coiled Spring" setup—along with my favorite day-trading setups from *Micro-Trend Trading for Daily Income*: the long-short "Afternoon Reversal" setup and the long-short "Bread and Butter" setup. In the following chart you will see three Expert Advisor alerts for my "Coiled Spring" system as described in *Trend Trading for a Living* (Figure 4.17).

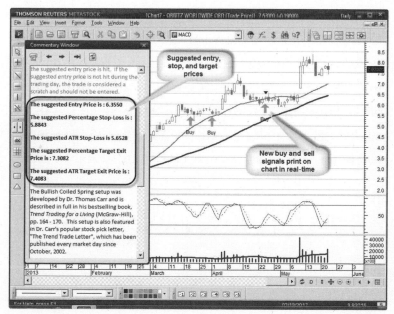

Courtesy of Thompson Reuters

Figure 4.17   The Dr. Stoxx Trend Trading Toolkit—chart with Expert Advisor.

The last thing to say in support of using the MetaStock Trend Trading Toolkit to trade the systems in this book may, for some of my readers, be the most important. I know from some of the e-mails I receive that there are those who use my systems to trade things other than U.S. stocks and exchange-traded funds (ETFs). They trade index futures, commodities, and forex; or they trade stocks on exchanges outside the United States. Trading is such a global phenomenon now that it is possible to make a living from trading anywhere in the world and at any time of day or night. MetaStock is positioned on the frontlines of that growth, thanks to its inventory of market data from every global trading bourse and of just about every conceivable security type. Want to trade the Bombay Stock Exchange or the Stock Exchange of Thailand? Want to sell crude oil in Jakarta or buy the Yuan in Shanghai? You can; and you can use the Dr. Stoxx Trend Trading Toolkit on all of them. In the TTTK, you will find a set of 13 proven trading systems, all coded to identify tradable setups in any security that can be charted, including forex, futures, and the index e-minis.

WHERE DO WE GO FROM HERE?

In sum, to trade our systems properly, you will need to add several of the aforementioned services to your trading platform. Doing so will raise your overhead costs to some degree. In case you are now thoroughly confused, let me summarize what was said in this chapter in this way:

- *Your most economical setup is to equip yourself with Stock Investor Pro to filter out lists of trading candidates based primarily on fundamental parameters and then use a free charting package like Finviz to measure the technicals of your short list to arrive at your best trading options, both long and short. You will not be able to trade all the systems in this book, but your overhead costs will be a very reasonable $20 to $40 per month. This is probably the best choice for those trading accounts sized under $25,000.*

- **[RECOMMENDED]** *Your most robust but still affordable route is to get the Dr. Stoxx Trend Trading Toolkit from MetaStocks and then add a subscription to Stock Investor Pro. With this package, you will have the option of front-loading your systems with a primary focus on either fundamentals (using SIP) or technical (using TTTK), plus you will have full access to MetaStock's professional-grade charting package. With this setup, you are able to trade all seven of the systems in this book, and because these two screening tools are preprogrammed, you will also be trading with the confidence that you are getting into stocks that exactly fit the systems described in this book. Your monthly overhead costs will be in the $75 to $225 range (the higher end is for real-time data), which is very* *reasonable for anyone trading an account greater than $25,000. Again, you will not need real-time data unless you plan to day trade or like to time your entries and exits using intraday technicals.*

- *Your most versatile but costliest route—and the best choice for those who want to use this book as a guide toward creating their own systems—is to pay for the full Research Wizard package (with 12 years of price data) along with MetaStock's Trend Trading Toolkit so as to harness the power of their powerful back-testing features, fundamentals-based and technicals-based, respectively. For this package, you will be paying between $225 and $500 per month. Even at the lower end of that range, you will need an account larger than $50,000 to be able to absorb the overhead costs without putting too much of a dent into your returns.*

If you are still confused, do not despair. In the following chapters you will find clearly defined steps you can take to screen for and trade stocks that match each of the systems, regardless of what trading toolkit you set up for yourself. We have taken care to make sure that traders of all account sizes and trading experience can harness the power of these systems to neutralize the markets. After a brief but important interlude, we will next turn to the trading systems themselves.

You may be tempted at this point to move directly from here to Part III of this book. Please don't. At the risk of sounding melodramatic, I consider this next section to be the most important part of the book. To skip past the next two chapters, while tempting, is to position your trading on shaky ground. In Chapter 5 I will explain the *sine qua non* of successful trading. If you can avail yourself of this, you will possess the skills to turn even a mediocre trading system into a profit-making machine. If you do not have it on your side, even the most robust system can cause your hard-earned capital to dwindle ever downward. Then, in Chapter 6, I am going to pull up a chair next to my trading desk and invite you to sit down with me as I take you step by step through a typical trading day. Chapter 6 will show you what it looks like to take the one essential thing described in Chapter 5 and put it to work in the markets.

PART TWO

intermission:
THE ONE THING
NECESSARY

THE TWO TYPES OF TRADING FAILURE... AND HOW TO AVOID THEM

CHAPTER 5

Failures are fingerposts on the road to achievement.

—C. S. Lewis

I want you to start making money with the systems in this book. This means we will need to move on from our more preliminary discussion about trading tools to the trading systems themselves. These provide your personal interface between the phenomenal money-making potential of the markets and your own private trading account. But we must not get ahead of ourselves. It would be imprudent to jump into the practicalities of systems trading without first laying out the one thing that makes all robust trading systems work consistently.

What I am about to say here is controversial; you may disagree with it. Heck, I might disagree with it myself at times. But that is okay. Disagreement on a matter, the philosophers like to tell us, does not make the matter any less true. They also tell us that recognition of the truth is the first step toward aligning yourself with it. So please read the following to see what resonates with the wiring of your faculties of recognition.

SYSTEMS TRADING ALONE IS NOT ENOUGH

In this pause in the narrative I am going to make every effort to be as straightforward as I can. It is said that someone who can take complicated things and make them simple is called a genius, while someone who can take simple things and make them complicated is called a professor. As a former professor of 16 years, my tendency is to over-complicate things a bit. I will try not to do that here. This is too important.

Before we go any further, I need to be very honest about something. It can be said that behind every successful trader lies a string of trading failures. I am no exception to that rule. I have not always been a successful trader. I don't mean that I've had a few drawdowns in my account. I mean pack-up-the-bags, close-up-shop kind of failure. I mean seeing my account get so small I can only buy penny stocks and way-out-of-the-money options kind of failure. Remember Joel from Chapter 1? There but for the grace of God went I, not too many years ago. Thanks be to God for turning my trading around! How did that happen? Keep reading.

My trading failures can be divided into two basic types. I'll call these the "Joel type" (not to pick on Joel, but he's so archetypal) and the "not-Joel type." The "Joel type" is probably the most common type of failure among the traders I work with as a trading coach. Joel got into trouble because he was trading on a whim in a very unsystematic fashion. Joel-type traders trade on hunches, educated guesses, hot tips, and the like. Hooked on adrenaline, they jump on anything that is moving fast. They put on stop-losses and then remove them when the price gets too close. The not-Joel-type traders trade in a more mechanical fashion. They follow the rules of their trading systems religiously, fearing lest any "sin" of disobedience ruin their profit-making potential. The not-Joel-type traders trade without thinking critically about what they are doing. They put complete faith in the system programmed into their screening software and in the success of its back-tests. Whatever the system says to buy or sell, they do so, no questions asked.

I can say from personal experience that both Joel-type trading and not-Joel-type trading lead inevitably to failure. My first attempts as a trader were of the Joel type. Joel-type failure is usually swift and lethal. I managed to trade over two years that way—nothing but trading news, tips, rumors, etc.—until I ran out of money. Later, I regrouped, got some education, and jumped back in the game. This time I was determined to be a not-Joel trader. Not-Joel traders reject hunches, instinct, intuition, and above all reason; their only aim is to follow the rules of their system. The discipline of following a system curbs a good deal of the risk associated with Joel-type trading. Not-Joel-type failure, therefore, tends to occur slowly over time. I spent the better part of 10 years chipping away at a not-Joel-type masterpiece of trading failure. During that time I lost a lot of money. I lost other people's money, too, because in the middle of that period I was trading a small fund for clients strictly based on my trading systems. Yes, the 2007–2009 market crash was partly to blame for the outsized losses. Still, there is no getting around the fact that blindly following a set of systems was not working.

Here is where it gets interesting. During those years of losing real money, I was making a lot of virtual money for my subscribers. Throughout the nearly 11 years we've been publishing daily stock picks on www.DrStoxx.com (formerly www.befriendthetrend.com), our newsletters were banking nice profits. Our flagship product, *The Trend Trade Letter*, has posted an average annual return on investment (ROI) of over 31 percent since its inception in 2002. The S&P 500 over the same period has managed an average return of only about 4 percent. In fact, from November 2007 through February 2009 the period of the market crash, *The Trend Trade Letter* posted a net-positive ROI of +25.7 percent, and that on mostly long positions (see the "Performance" link on www.DrStoxx.com). The S&P 500 during the same period lost over half its value.

This raises a crucial question: How could I be so successful a stock picker for my subscribers and so unsuccessful a trader when following my own systems? The answer is found in the question: The line of demarcation between trading success and trading failure lies in the critical difference between what it means to pick stocks as opposed to simply managing a system. In my own accounts, I was trading in a very detached, mechanical fashion. If the system told me to buy XYZ because it had passed through five different technical filters, or to sell short ABC because it displayed this or that bearish chart pattern, I simply did so, no questions asked. When the system stopped working, as they all inevitably do, I simply switched systems.

For the newsletters, I engaged in a very different process. It was a process that I have now repeated nearly 3,000 times since the launch of our trading business in 2002. I will describe this process in detail in the next chapter. Here, we need to ask a more fundamental question: Why does this process work so well? My daily routine involves the decidedly not-Joel step of running my system scans each day exactly as the rules dictate. But then I do something in addition to that; something quite "unmechanical"; something, in fact, that has long been considered "taboo" among systems traders. I use "discretion." To the short list of stocks my screens turn up I apply God-given skills of discretionary analysis, skills that have been honed by years of apprenticeship under some of the great masters of the game, in addition to a long slog of real-time, real-money trading experience. This skillset gives me an almost intuitive sense of what, among possible candidates, is going to work best in current market conditions. It empowers me to select from a list of possible candidates only the best; the ones with the greatest degree of probability for success.

These are the stocks our subscribers receive. Therefore, I attribute the essential difference between success and failure as a trader to a very intangible, yet all-too-real process I will call "discretionary trading."

THE JOYS OF DISCRETIONARY TRADING

Discretion (literally, "to judge between things") can be defined as the ability, garnered through learning and experience, to properly assess the fitness of a thing relative to its context. Someone who acts with discretion is someone who knows how to comport himself in ways that are appropriate to the situation; someone who lacks discretion does not. Biblically speaking, discretion is a gift from God; it signifies the skill, divinely imparted, for sensing the rightness or soundness of things.[1] Like the "wise and discerning" Joseph who could interpret dreams and thereby save a nation (Gen. 41), the one with discretion possesses an uncanny ability to size up the situation and, without fully knowing how, render sound judgment. Discretion thus represents an experienced-based, intuitive, largely inarticulate form of understanding what is right, sound, and appropriate, and what is not.

To trade with discretion is, therefore, to trade *selectively* based on an intuitive sense, grounded in training and experience, of what works and what doesn't work, given the stock's technical and fundamental particulars, and in consideration of current market conditions. To put it in terms relevant to our purposes here, discretionary trading is added to and complements the kind of mechanical systems trading outlined in this book. It is to take what is produced by our 100 percent objective trading systems as starting points for further research with a view, ultimately, toward discerning—even (gasp!) *intuitively*—which among competing setups are the "best" and which are all the "rest."

Let's cut to the bottom line. It has been my experience that whenever I trade without a system (Joel-type trading), I lose money. Whenever I trade with a system, but without any discretionary filtering of what the system tells me to trade (not-Joel-type trading), I lose money. When I combine systems, trading with discretionary analysis, however, I consistently make money; sometimes a lot of money. We don't always hang on to that money because my wife, bless her, loves to give it away! But that is another story.

This leads then to the all-important question: How does one come to possess discretion as a trader? Again, discretion empowers in the one who possesses it a preternaturally effective ability to discern what will work best in a given situation. A neurologist with discretion can look at a magnetic resonance image (MRI) of the brain and know instantly what the problem is and whether or not it is treatable. A mechanic with discretion can simply listen to an engine and know whether it is the carburetor or the transmission that is the issue. A trader with discretion, then, is one who is able to look at a set of charts or financial data on the companies—or, in our case, both—and say with confidence that *these* stocks, not *those* stocks, have the best chance of moving in the desired direction.

In each of these cases, what is known in discretionary fashion flows from a convergence within the individual of knowledge, experience, and unique insight.[2] It is not simply a head-thing. You cannot learn discretion in a classroom or from a book. You can learn trading systems that way (hence, *this* book!), but not the discretion needed to make them profitable. The difference is critical.

The question then remains: How does a trader whose hunger for consistent profitability knows no bounds gain discretion? There is only one way to successfully maneuver the world of systems trading through the application of discretion; only one way to assimilate the substance—experience, wisdom, insight, intuition—of the discretionary skillset and make it your own: You need to find a mentor who already has it and sit by their side for a while. You need to find someone who trades with discretion successfully and learn directly from him or her. The only way to become an expert trader is to first humble yourself and ask for help from someone who already is one.

THE NEED FOR A MENTOR

There are two ways to do the mentoring thing: the long, hard, expensive way and the quick, easy, and much cheaper way. The long, hard, expensive way is to find one or more

trading and/or investing gurus who have proven themselves successful and who have been in the business a long
time. Buy and study their books and articles; subscribe to
their newsletters; attend their seminars and webinars; buy
their courses and trading systems; then, after you feel you
have digested all that material, trade using the techniques
you've learned. At first, you will lose money—this is virtually guaranteed. You will likely need to take on extra work
in order to pump new funds into your account to keep it
afloat. Consider it all part of the acquisition process if you
want strong discretionary skills. Sooner or later, if unlike
90 percent of newbie traders you manage to persevere, it
will all click into place: You will begin to trade profitably;
you will take the systems of the masters and trade them
with discretion. So when one of their systems says both
stock A and stock B are buys, you know from looking at the
charts and/or financial data that B, not A, is the better buy;
and it turns out, more often than not, that you are right.

I estimate the cost of this first option, not counting
opportunity costs, to be $50,000 or more, depending on how
much money you started with and how much more you had
to put into your account to keep it solvent. Let me be honest:
The previous paragraph describes my own journey to successful trading; only for me, it cost a lot more than $50,000! I
am sure it also describes the experience of many of you. You
are so passionate about becoming a profitable trader that your
hunger to succeed far outstrips the angst that comes from so
many false and costly starts. Let me show you a better way.

The best way to become successful at applying the kind of discretion needed to trade systems profitably—and by far the cheaper and quicker way—is to be apprenticed or coached by someone who is already trading a set of systems profitably. Like all time-honored skills, trading is a mix of both science and art. You can learn the science from books and seminars. But you can only learn the "art part" through one-on-one or small group coaching in direct contact with someone who knows what he or she is doing. What residency is to the medical specialist and doctoral seminars are to a professor, private coaching with a trusted mentor is to the successful trader.

In truth, this is how it has always been in the trading game. In former times, traders in training served as floor runners, shuttling orders back and forth between the brokerage desks and the open outcry pits. From that vantage point, they developed an intuitive sense for things like order flow, the timing of entries, and position sizing. Once they made it to the trading desks themselves, they brought with them all that discretionary mojo. Electronic trading has eliminated the floor-running gig, but the need to be apprenticed, to learn directly from a mentor, remains. So how does one do that? Other professions have formalized the apprenticeship process. How does it work for traders wanting to be successful?

I assume you do not want to spend 10 years on the buy side of the business at a large mutual fund or investment bank. You are an independent trader trading for yourself, maybe for a few friends and family members, and you want to keep it that way. How then can an independent trader be coached? The answer is that you hire someone who is both a successful trader and does private coaching. If you are not consistently profitable as a trader and want to avoid the long and costly route to trading success outlined earlier, you need to engage the services of a trading coach.

CHOOSING THE RIGHT COACH

Yes, I do private coaching and yes, I work mostly with independent traders. I wear a number of hats at DrStoxx.com, from research analyst in our daily stock pick letters, to trading systems developer for Befriend the Trend Trading, to portfolio manager for Kingdom Capital. I love all these tasks, but the truth is my favorite hat to wear is my coaching hat! Nothing market-related gives me greater joy than seeing someone's face light up once they realize that simply adding a few disciplines to their daily routine, changing this or that in their position management strategy or their stock selection process, can empower them to turn their trading around. But before my phone starts ringing off the hook, let me say that my coaching services may not be the best fit for your trading style. There are a number of well-qualified trading coaches out there, and some of them may be better suited to your needs. With that in mind, let me give you some pointers on how to select the right coach.

1. You want to find a trading coach who is not just a great teacher, but also a successful trader. You will want to see a long-term, publicly accessible record of trading success. Make sure that record shows consistent alpha through a variety of market conditions. Avoid any website that offers coaching but doesn't also have a publicly accessible, up-to-date, trade-by-trade record of past performance, including all losses. You especially want to see exact entry and exit prices and dates, not just percentage returns.

2. You want to find a trading coach who is not just a successful trader, but is also a great teacher. He or she may have a lot of great ideas for improving your trading, but if those ideas cannot be communicated in a way that you understand, you are wasting your time. Avoid trading coaches who speak in generalities. You want clear, specific, step-by-step instruction.

3. You want a coach whose trading style matches your trading style. Don't hire a stocks guy to teach you forex; don't hire a day trader to teach you swing trading. Most trading strategies are transferable to different markets, but the skillsets required to trade them well are not. Locate yourself within the spectrum of trading styles and then go after someone who displays a mastery of it.

4. Trading schools have their place. But sitting in a class with 20 other traders while learning from a team

of "specialists" is a far cry from the kind of one-on-one apprenticeship you need. They also tend to be overpriced, with pressure from management to upsell. Those who teach trading are worth their salt, but fleecing newbies is never justified.

5. If you can, avoid being "coached" by a DVD set or a series of recorded webinars. There is nothing wrong with that kind of content delivery. I sell recorded webinars from my site and will occasionally do a live coaching webinar with an individual or small group if in-person coaching is not possible. But it is not the ideal. The true mentoring experience is only possible through genuine personal contact.

In short, you want to be coached by an individual trader with a proven track record of success and who fits your preferred style of trading. You want it to be a true mentoring experience; that is, you want to sit right beside the trader and observe what he or she does and doesn't do; and you want him or her to observe you as you try out your new skills. The essence of a genuine coaching experience is full exposure to a live-market trading day, with all the stress and information overload that goes with it, while sitting alongside a successful trader doing the stuff it takes to navigate well through that territory. You need to physically see how it is done, and like a good apprentice, you need to try doing it yourself under your coach's supervision.

If you think my coaching services might be a good fit for your trading style, e-mail me at drstoxx@DrStoxx.com and I'll send you my free self-assessment test. This will let me know whether you are best served working with me or with someone else. If I think I can help you, we will work out a time for you to fly to me; if necessary, I can come to you. I normally rent out the boardroom of a hotel near the airport and set up a trading station there. On our first day, we work together on finding and filtering stocks. The second day is devoted to the real-time trading routine as you watch me do what I do every market day. I demonstrate the steps I take to decide what to trade and how to time entries. I show how to manage open positions including positions in crisis, and how to improve the profit potential of your longer-term holdings. After two days of this intensive mentoring, you should be able to walk away with the skills to do what I do on your own. I warn you, my time is not cheap. But it is probably less than you expect, and certainly worth the price considering you will be gaining skills that, over time and with experience, can truly generate big-league wealth.

A SPECIAL OFFER FOR PASTORS AND MINISTRY OVERSEERS

We need to move on, but before we do, I want briefly to share a true story. I am, as most of my readers know, a man of faith; puny, mustard-seed-sized faith, but faith nonetheless.

Today I can say that my relationship to my heavenly Dad is the most important part of who I am. But this hasn't always been the case. Despite being raised in a believing home, and after years of theological study, I lived for quite a while as an atheist; or to put it more precisely, I lived pretending not to care about God because I believed that He didn't care about me. All that changed a number of years ago. I won't give you the details here. Discretion's other meaning is knowing when reticence is a virtue. Let me simply say that God made it clear to me, in the most tangible way imaginable, that He is real, good, perfectly loving, happy, wildly unpredictable in the best sense, and that His plan for my life trumps anything I am able to dream up.

If my life were a price chart, I would have to say that before this experience I was trading well outside the lower Bollinger Band, with historic lows in a number of indicators and no bullish divergence in sight. Following this experience, however, my life has been in "gap up" mode, with all indicators turning sharply to the upside. My marriage has been restored, rifts in my family healed, our finances greatly improved, and in every other important aspect of life—including my trading—I have been functioning on all cylinders. It was as if my brain was rebooted to its default setting, or rather, to the default setting of someone much more deserving.

I owe God everything. Even the skills I trade with every day and have worked so hard to improve and strengthen I now recognize as having come from Him.

I take seriously the admonition in the Bible to "remember the Lord your God, for it is He who gives you the ability to make wealth" (Deut. 8:18).[3] When I learned that God had given me unique skills for trading, I knew that whatever proceeded as fruit from that enterprise rightly belonged to Him. It is always a blessing to give, especially when it hurts. For example, a while back, following a prolonged drought, we had a huge financial breakthrough. God really turned up the spigot on "the floodgates of heaven!" Thanks to our trading profits, we achieved a number of "firsts": For the first time ever, we were debt-free, able to buy a brand-new car, and take two family vacations abroad, all while living on only 40 percent of our income because we gave the rest away (unfortunately, the IRS only allows you to deduct 50 percent for charitable giving!). Our donations helped our church buy its building, rescue 20 young girls from the sex-slave trade in India, house and educate several orphans, and sponsor mission trips to Africa and Asia. It is truly awesome what can be accomplished when life is lived aligned with the plans of heaven!

In that same spirit, and with an enormous sense of gratitude for how much we have been blessed through trading, I would like to make a special offer to pastors, missionaries, and those overseeing any ministry or non-profit organization that serves the less fortunate and brings them the awesome news of Jesus. I was raised in a pastor's home. I am very familiar with the financial struggles faced by many in full-time ministry. It has long been a dream of mine to teach techniques for part-time trading to pastors and ministry leaders as a form of "tent-making." This could potentially free them from having to rely exclusively on tithes and offerings and free their ministries for greater outreach opportunities.

Tent-making as a way to fund ministry operations certainly has strong Biblical precedent. Most of the patriarchs were successful farmers and herdsmen; so, too, was David before being crowned king. Most of Jesus' disciples were fishermen, a trade they likely returned to between missionary trips. The apostle Paul performed his trade—actually making tents—throughout his missionary and church-planting career.[4] It was a vital part of his outreach strategy, for it afforded him the freedom to travel and to distribute money and goods to Christians who had lost their jobs through persecution. His portable trade also afforded him key connections to the business and governmental realms wherever he went. Jesus Himself was a "tent-maker" of sorts. He was trained as a manual laborer—by tradition a carpenter[5]—having apprenticed with his stepfather, Joseph, for 18 years. In addition, early in His public ministry, He helped His disciples catch an enormous load of fish. Scholars estimate that the sale of those fish may have brought in as much as $100,000 in today's money, thus funding the entire gospel operation for at least a year.[6] Why can't pastors today do the same thing with trading?

With that in mind, if you are a pastor, missionary, or ministry leader with an interest in trading and would like to learn to trade part-time, please contact me. I will work out a reduced payment plan so we can get you quickly into tent-making mode with whatever you might be able to spare. You don't want to trade church funds, of course, but if you can cobble together $2,000, as I did 16 years ago, you can get started. Help me fulfill my dream to see every plan of heaven fully funded as I help you set your ministry free to fulfill its divine calling.

CHAPTER 6

A Brief Look at My Trading Routine

Opportunity is missed by most people because it is dressed in overalls and looks like work.

—Thomas Edison

In the last chapter, I made the argument that purely mechanical systems trading, what I called "not-Joel-type" trading, is a losing proposition. Yet following this chapter I am going to introduce you to a set of seven newly developed trading systems. This chapter is an attempt to smooth over that apparent contradiction. As stated earlier, the best way to approach the trading of mechanical systems is to get some coaching from an experienced trader on how best to master the systems themselves. Through good coaching, you should get the kind of "discretion" that can stand above the system and work it effectively; that makes the system your servant, not your master. Short of that, you need some general guidelines. That is what this chapter provides. Here, I want to give you a brief primer on what it looks like when I trade these systems. So come into my trading room, pull up a chair, and watch what I do each market day.

Each system described in this book has both a longs version, for stocks to buy, and a shorts version, for stocks to sell short. On most market days, after running both scans, you should end up with two lists of stocks for further consideration. You will need *discretion* (see Chapter 5) to weed out only the best possible candidates from each of the lists. In each of the following chapters you will find some tips on how to do that. It helps if you also have the kind of market experience and education that allow discretion about how best to mix those longs and shorts together in your portfolio. In other words, given the current market conditions, should you be more weighted on the long side, the short side, or perfectly market-neutral? The default setting, if ever in doubt, is to be market-neutral. The thesis of this book is that to neutralize the market (i.e., minimize risks while maximizing profit potential), you need to attend to both technicals and fundamentals, and you need to be both long and short. In this chapter, I want to give you a simple system you can use to add a little nuance to that thesis.

THE DAILY ROUTINE

My day starts early—normally 5:00 A.M. if not earlier—with a strong cup of coffee and a head-clearing hour of prayer and Bible reading. I then usually do some exercise—running, biking, weights—in order to keep up the pretense that I'm athletic (I'm not!). After a shower, my wife and I spend some time together praying, talking through the day's plans, and strategizing over matters concerning www.DrStoxx.com.

My wife has a business background, but chooses to stay home to homeschool the kids (a full-time job in itself), which means I have an onsite business consultant who works for free—a kind of "business partner with benefits!"

I get to my desk about 8:00 A.M. EST, a full 90 minutes before the market opens. I normally run my system scans the night before as I'm updating our three daily stock pick letters, so all I need to do in the morning is decide which stocks among my open positions need adjusting and which stocks turned up by the scans I might want to add. At this time, I will normally open my Interactive Brokers' Trader Workstation (TWS) to check the account balance, available cash balance, percentage balance of open positions, and any trading gaps appearing among my open positions. This gives me actionable information that I will use to determine how many new positions, if any, can be added to my opens and which opens may need to be rebalanced.

I use several different platform configurations for TWS, depending on the account and the kind of trading I am doing. The one I use most often is a workstation template called Mosaic. I tweak that to fit my personal preferences, but the default template is shown in Figure 6.1.

Let's say that the portfolio window tells me that I have a 20 percent cash position that needs to be put to work. Since I normally hold up to 20 open positions concurrently, a quick mental calculation tells me that I can put on 4 new positions, assuming I can find 4 that I like. The next thing I check is the Rebalance Portfolio window. This window enables me to see what percentage of my total capital I

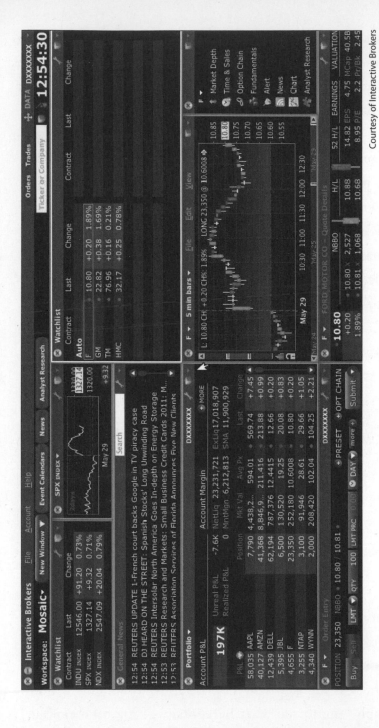

Figure 6.1 Interactive Brokers Trader Workstation.

Courtesy of Interactive Brokers

have invested in each position, long and short. During those times when I am fully market-neutral, I want to see an equal amount of capital in each trade, with an equal amount of capital dedicated to both the long and short sides of the portfolio. In this case, I want to see something close to 5 percent listed for each position. If I see, for example, that a couple of the longs have moved nicely and are up to around 7 percent of my trading capital, but one is down to 3 percent, I'll want to correct that imbalance. To do that, I simply type in the desired percentage (5 percent) in the Rebalance % column for each of the three positions, click the Create Orders button, and then click Submit. The TWS will automatically create three market-on-open orders to sell shares in the two overcapitalized positions and buy shares in the undercapitalized one. The Rebalance window looks like this (Figure 6.2):

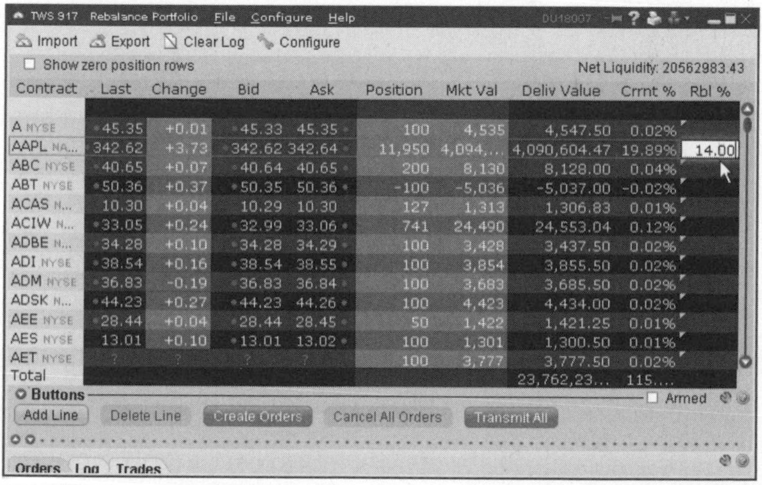

Courtesy of Interactive Brokers

Figure 6.2   Trader Workstation Portfolio Rebalance window.

THE SOAR METHOD

This is then followed by the discretionary part of my routine. A "not-Joel-type" trader never bothers to apply discretion to the system. He or she simply obeys the system's rules, no matter what. As I explained in the last chapter, it has been my experience that I am only consistently profitable when I go beyond the system to engage in a more selective process. Thus, each market day I perform a four-step procedure I like to acronymize (oh, good word!) with the four letters SOAR: Soak, Observe, Analyze, and Recognize.

First, I like to immerse myself in, or "soak" in, any overnight market news so I have a good sense for what traders are focusing on at the open. I then "observe" the technical charts of both my open positions and any new trading candidates my scans turned up. The third step is to "analyze" the fundamentals and news headlines for these new candidates. The final step is to do a "gut check" to see what my years of trading experience "recognize" as the best candidates my system scans are offering me and which of my current positions may need tweaking.

My own *soaking* process begins with a check of any major economic data that has been published since the previous day's close, so I'll check www.Finviz.com for the latest numbers. I want to see how the U.S. futures and overseas markets are reacting. The most important of these include the first Friday jobs report (the nonfarm payroll number), the weekly jobless claims, gross domestic product (GDP) revisions, the two main readings on inflation—the Producers Price Index (PPI) and the Consumers Price Index (CPI)—and the Purchasing Managers Index (PMI). Some of these are so important they can dictate the direction of the tape for several days, if not weeks. I will also check the headlines for our open positions. Overnight news like earnings reports, Food and Drug Administration (FDA) approval decisions, and upgrades and downgrades can greatly influence where a stock will open trading that day. Of course, once the news is out, it is too late to do anything about it, but it helps to know what is causing the move.

The other thing I soak in before beginning my stock selection process, if I haven't done so the night before, is the chart of the S&P 500. This broad market index of the 500 largest companies is the best indicator for the kind of market we are currently in. In my first book, *Trend Trading for a Living* (McGraw-Hill, 2007), I outlined a simple system for determining general market direction using the daily chart of the S&P 500 with two moving averages overlaid. This system specified five basic market types—strong and weak uptrends, strong and weak downtrends, and range-bound—which, in turn, were to guide your stock selection by suggesting a focus on either longs, shorts, or a mix of both. The system described there is still a great way to get a solid feeling for the ebb and flow of day-to-day market momentum. For our purposes in this book, I prefer to use a variant of that system.

Let me remind readers that the seven trading systems in this book are designed to be used in market-neutral fashion, which is to say, with an equal amount of capital devoted to both the long and short sides of the system. This will always be your default apportionment, and certainly the easiest way to neutralize the market. Some, however, prefer to trade with a degree of "discretion" (as defined in the previous chapter) in response to prevailing market conditions. For you, a mix other than the default 50/50 split may be called for. My discretionary process includes a reading of the chart of the S&P 500; a check of investor sentiment; a study of charted market internals, such as tick, trin, A/D (advancing to declining issues), bullish percents, and summation indexes; a consensus of market commentators I follow; and good old, experience-honed intuition that flows from the consensus of all that information in my brain. I cannot give you here the specifics of what I look for in each of those information vectors. However, what I can give you is one of the tools I teach to my clients for gauging potential market direction and thus the ratio of your long-to-short position mix.

MATCHING YOUR LONG-SHORT MIX TO THE MARKET

Feel free to ignore the following if your current method for determining general market direction is serving you well. If that is not the case, I recommend giving this tool a try. To gauge current market conditions, take a weekly (not daily) chart of the S&P 500—I prefer a candlestick chart, but bar and line charts work too—and apply the following indicators to it:

- If you plan to run your scans every day and trade more frequently, apply the *5ema* (exponential moving average) and *13sma* (simple moving average) as overlays.
- If you plan to run your scans weekly or bimonthly, apply the *20ema* and *50sma* as overlays.
- If you plan to run your scans monthly, apply the *40ema* and *100sma* as overlays.

Here are the rules of interpretation that I normally suggest to my clients (I also teach a more nuanced set of rules). Note that to compensate for the historically bullish bias of the market, I have adjusted the ratios to favor longs over shorts. As with any set of trading rules, you may adjust as needed to fit your particular trading style and experience:

- If the EMA is above the SMA and price is above the EMA: *go 70% long, 30% short.*
- If the EMA is above the SMA but price is below the EMA: *go 100% market-neutral.*
- If the EMA is below the SMA but price is above the EMA: *go 100% market-neutral.*
- If the EMA is below the SMA and price is below the EMA: *go 60% short, 40% long.*

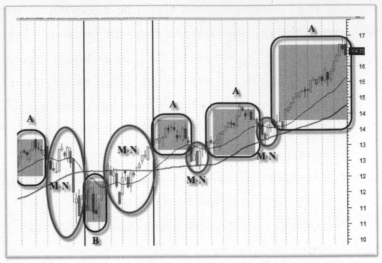

Figure 6.3 SPY with moving average apportionment system.

The chart in Figure 6.3 shows the weekly chart of SPY, the exchange-traded fund (ETF) proxy for the S&P 500, with the *20ema* and *50sma* overlaid. Keep in mind that each bar represents a week's worth of trading. On the chart I've highlighted two crossovers showing three distinct market periods: bullish, bearish, and bullish, respectively. The periods marked "A" are where you would be 70 percent long and 30 percent short. The one period marked "B" would have you going 60 percent short and 40 percent long. The periods marked "M-N" are where you would be split evenly between longs and shorts.

Please note that to avoid too much messiness, there are a few stray candlesticks in Figure 6.3 that I did not mark separately—for example, in the first M-N period on the left. In real trading, these would be weeks where you would consider altering your mix from the previous weeks.

Thus, a thorough "soaking" process should involve an immersion in both macro and micro vectors that converge into an intuitive sense about where the markets are headed over the near term. You will know that you are done soaking when you have a strong "gut" sense of whether the markets are in a good mood or not. This gut sense, in turn, may influence your discretionary selection of new trades as you assess the candidates your scans filter out. It may also impact any positions you are currently holding, since a sudden change in market sentiment may prompt you to lighten longs and add to shorts, or vice versa. I personally like to trade small pieces of my core holdings on a daily basis—the Rebalance Portfolio feature in Interactive Brokers makes this an easy task—in order to reduce risk and enhance profit potential. This means that I bank a little profit after a few winning days and buy those shares back on the dips. For a more hands-off approach, changing the mix of longs to shorts in response to changing market conditions can be done whenever you run your scans for new positions; that is, weekly, bimonthly, or quarterly.

The next step in the SOAR discretionary process is to *observe* your current open positions and to observe any new candidates turned up by your scans. For me, this means a thorough look at the price charts. What little formal training I have is in the interpretation of technical charts, so this is the strongest part of the process for me. To facilitate this step, I keep a watch list of technical charts, with all my favorite indicators on them, of each of my open positions. On these I draw trendlines and S/R (support and resistance) channels, and I highlight points of interest, like price-indicator divergence, price gaps, extreme volume events, and the like. I'll update my notations since my last chart check—e.g., extend the trendlines to cover new price movement, draw in emerging price patterns, etc.—and jot down symbols on a legal pad of stocks I may need to watch closely.

I then set up the same kind of watch list for any potential candidates turned up by my scans, labeling each chart by the system that found it. If the stock came through one of the technicals-based systems (Chapters 11 through 13), then I already know that these stocks have strong technical merit. Still, charts can pass through even the most robust technical scan with technical weaknesses the screen was not able to detect. Stocks that came through our fundamentals-based systems (Chapters 7 through 10) may only have merit in one or two technical categories, if that; they need a more thorough check of the charts. My "observe" process, therefore, has me looking closely at each of these charts one by one. I will immediately delete those that look problematic for whatever reason. Those whose charts I like will be noted on my legal pad for further research.

The third step of SOAR involves *analyzing* the fundamentals of those new trading candidates that passed my "observing" their charts. If the stocks came through one of our four fundamentals-based systems, then I know they have strong fundamentals in the categories screened for. That doesn't, however, preclude them from problems in other categories. For example, a company that recently raised earnings guidance might have just announced a new share issuance that will dilute the company's earnings per share. Or a company showing 25 percent quarter-on-quarter growth in sales might now be facing headwinds because an expected rise in commodity prices is contracting their margin rates. These are the kinds of things you can't screen for, but they will show up in company headlines and analyst commentary. Stocks that came through our technicals-based screens will have had some basic fundamental analysis done that allowed them to make it to the short list. It never hurts, however, to dig a bit deeper to find the strongest possible candidates.

The sites mentioned in Chapter 4—VectorGrader, Investors.com, Finviz, and Portfolio Grader—are instrumental to the analyzing process. Of these, I rely most on Finviz. Using Finviz, I developed a proprietary Piotroski-like, nine-point grading system that I teach in one of my webinars (Figure 6.4). This grading system is used to perform a quick fundamental analysis on possible trading candidates. For example, on a run of one of my system scans at the end of August 2012, I was left with eight stocks—four longs and four shorts—but I only wanted to fill two positions on each side. To find the best four candidates, I put them through my nine-point grader. Each fundamental category has certain

SYMBOL	A	B	C	D	E	F	G	H	I	Grade
HA	2	2	2	0	2	0	0	1	0	9
LMCA	0	1	1	0	2	2	2	2	0	10
DY	2	1	2	0	2	1	2	2	0	12
OXM	2	1	2	2	2	1	1	2	0	13
BAC	2	2	1	2	2	0	0	0	0	9
MT	1	0	1	1	1	0	0	0	0	4
TLM	0	0	1	1	2	1	0	0	1	6
CLNE	0	0	1	0	1	0	2	0	1	5

Figure 6.4   Carr's nine-point ranking system (longs above, shorts below).

threshold numbers that are bullish, bearish, or neutral. If bullish, the stock gets a 2 for that category ; if neutral, a 1; and if bearish, a 0. These nine values are then totaled. The best long candidates have the highest scores (out of a potential total of 18) and the best short candidates have the lowest scores. Figure 6.4 shows how those eight stocks fared (the four stocks on top are long candidates; the four on the bottom are short candidates) (see Figure 6.4).

It is clear from the grid, fundamentally speaking, that DY and OXM are the best long candidates, while MT and CLNE are the best short candidates. In actual trading, I took the two longs and the CLNE short. I chose TLM (a close third) over MT, however, because it had the more bearish chart. The set of charts in Figure 6.5 shows how those four stocks fared over the near term during the same holding period. This demonstrates just how powerful trading a double alpha system can be once you cover all the bases with technical, fundamental, and discretionary analysis.

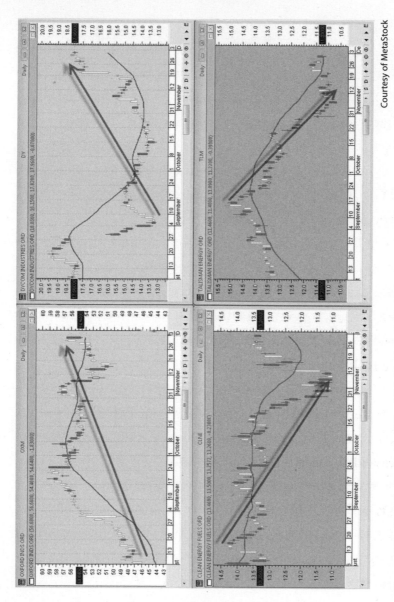

Figure 6.5   Near-term results of Carr's nine-point ranking system.

Courtesy of MetaStock

The final step, *recognize,* is the one where we translate all this information into an action plan for that day's open. Having gone through the first three steps of the four-step SOAR process, you should now know the general market's likely near-term direction going forward. You should also have before you a short list of new trading candidates that have passed the required technical and fundamental filters. What is left now is to "recognize" which of those, if any, you want to enter as new positions.

By "recognize," I mean a kind of final, discretionary "gut check" that results from the analysis work you did in the first three steps of SOAR. For me, recognition comes as a nearly visceral reaction within, a quickening of the senses, a "knowing that I know" what to do next with my portfolio. I call this step "recognition" because, in Platonic fashion, it almost feels precognitive, as if the directions well up spontaneously from some internal source of wisdom. More precisely, "recognition" is the acknowledgement in the conscious mind of the preconscious synthesis of real-world experience with present, reflective analysis on the general market and the trading candidates suggested by my scans. Recognition helps me answer with confidence three essential questions that must be addressed before the market opens:

1. Do current market conditions impel me to change my mix of longs and shorts at all? Or is a market-neutral stance warranted until the next rebalance period?

2.   Of the stocks I am currently holding, are there any that need to be rebalanced, or has anything changed in their charts or fundamental profile that suggests they should be replaced altogether?

3.   If I have extra cash on hand or cash from positions that will be closed, are there any new candidates that stand out for me as ones I want to enter today?

With strong discretionary skills under your belt, you should be able to "recognize" the correct answer to question 1. Your default position in the presence of any uncertainty is always a market-neutral 50/50 mix of longs and shorts. Alternatively, you can use the method explained earlier to determine a more advantageous mix. The systems themselves will help you answer question 2. If any of your current holdings fail to pass through the screen's filters on the rebalance day, it is a good indication that they should be cut from your portfolio. Of course, your discretionary sense can always override the system. For example, if you are in a biotech that has been edging up in anticipation of an upcoming FDA announcement on a drug in its pipeline, it may now be trading at a price-to-sales ratio that prohibits it from passing the systems' valuation filter. But your research suggests the FDA is likely to approve the drug, and if it does, your shares should rally strongly on the news. Your discretionary sense may tell you that it is worth the risk holding a now-overpriced stock until the announcement. Thus, you say no to the system and yes to discretion.

You may be proven wrong, but that works in your favor too because what we learn from our mistakes only serves to strengthen our discretion for future trades.

As for question 3, the system scans taught later are designed to give you a fresh set of stocks, long and short, every trading day. At each new rebalance period, then, you should have a number of trading candidates before you for further discretionary analysis. Your answer to question 3 will be derived from this analysis. It is perfectly fine to say a decided "no" to all possible trading candidates and simply hold what you have, or even to keep a percentage of your capital in cash. A good rule of thumb is: "When in doubt, stay out!" You should reserve new cash for only those stocks that get your heart pumping and your blood flowing; or to put it another way, it is best to enter only those stocks that cause you more concern staying out of them than being in them.

POSITION SIZING AND MANAGEMENT TIPS

Once you have your trading orders for the day, your last task is to decide how many shares to buy and sell. Your default apportionment for this task is always to divide your trading capital into an equal number of positions, work out the percentage allotted to each position, and buy or sell short only that percentage. You will also want to rebalance regularly any current holds that have moved significantly above or below that percentage. In this way, you will be in a constant state of profit reinvestment since the same port-folio percentage on a growing account will naturally mean more cash allotted to each new position. Moreover, you will also reduce risk, at least for your long positions, by taking profits off the table in your winners, and you will poten-tially increase profit potential by adding to those longs that have pulled back under your entry price.

Your short positions are a different matter. When they show a higher percentage than your standard allotment, it means that they have moved against you; you are now underwater in those positions. This is a common occur-rence in strong bull markets. While it is perfectly reasonable to add cash to long positions that are underwater—after all, these are strong trading candidates both technically and fundamentally—there are many reasons you do not want to add to losing short positions. I normally reduce the size of losing short positions at rebalancing and maintain the size of winning short positions even though they now show a percentage allotment below the average. To fill in that gap, which can be significant in strong bear markets, I prefer to add new short positions. The odds of winning always favor a fresh setup than one that has already moved significantly in your favor.

Most of you can figure out what works best regarding how many positions to keep open concurrently (thus, what percentage of your trading capital to allot to each position), as well as how many systems you will spread those positions over. In general terms, the larger the number of positions (and thus the smaller the percentage of capital in each) and the greater the number of systems those positions come from, the lower the risk; the smaller the number of positions and the fewer the number of systems, the greater the reward. Thus, your own personal mix depends on your risk tolerance.

If it helps, I teach my coaching clients that everyone should trade at least two systems—one from the fundamentals-based list and one from the technicals-based list—and that at least eight positions be held concurrently, which would normally mean two longs and two short positions per system. All the systems described here are scalable, however. If you are trading $100 million and need to hold a large number of positions to avoid becoming part owner of any one company, you may do that. The systems are flexible. Simply trade all seven systems and screen for, say, the "top 10" or "top 12" longs and shorts in each. In this way, you'll have 70 to 100 stocks to consider each time you rebalance.

ON TO THE SYSTEMS THEMSELVES

What remains now is to introduce you to the trading systems themselves. The foregoing information has equipped you to get the most out of what remains. The stocks these systems produce as trading candidates are what you will use to position your portfolio to experience lowered exposure to market risk as well as increased profit potential. To those systems we now turn.

beta:
FUNDAMENTALS-
BASED TRADING
SYSTEMS

THE PIOTROSKI F-SCORE SYSTEM

The evidence suggests that the market does not fully incorporate historical financial information into prices in a timely manner.

—Dr. Joseph Piotroski

If you landed here at the beginning of our systems chapters without reading the foregoing chapters, I'd like to kindly ask you to consider going back and reading at least Chapters 4 through 6. I can't fault you for jumping ahead; I do that myself with most books. But in this case, you may be setting yourself up for some confusion if you don't know about the tools described in Chapter 4 that are needed to trade these systems, and with which familiarity will be assumed in what follows. What's worse, without exposure to my cautionary notes in Chapter 5 and practical suggestions in Chapter 6, you may be positioning yourself for failure with these otherwise powerful trading systems. I have made good money with the following seven trading systems. I have also traded them and lost money (less than I've made, obviously; otherwise, I wouldn't be teaching them here!). What was the difference between the two? See Chapter 5!

With that warning aside, let me outline how each of the following seven system chapters will work. I will first describe the general thesis of the system by outlining the kinds of stocks the system is looking for. I will also suggest resources you may look to should you want to dig a bit deeper into the theory behind the thesis. Next, I will give you the parameters I use when I run the system for my own trading. Along with that, I will suggest what tools you may use to scan for stocks that fit the system. Since each of the seven systems is a hybrid of both fundamental and technical filters, the process of stock selection normally involves using more than one scanning and/or analysis tool. Then, in step-by-step fashion, you will see exactly how to work the scanning and analysis tools for best effect. Finally, we will examine a few price charts of some of the system's passing candidates.

INTRODUCING THE SYSTEM

Professor Joseph Piotroski was introduced to readers in Chapter 3. I described there how his 2000 paper published in the finance journal of the University of Chicago's Graduate School of Business helped to save my trading career. Entitled "Value Investing: The Use of Historical Financial Statement Information to Separate Winners from Losers," the paper outlines Piotroski's statistical analysis of what happens when you buy and short stocks based on criteria that are especially important to—get this!—*accountants*.

Most fundamentals-based trading systems are developed by finance guys with MBAs. While Piotroski holds an MBA from Indiana University (1994), his University of Michigan PhD (1999) and his academic position at Stanford are in accounting. This gives him a unique perspective. As it turns out, it is that uniqueness that makes this system so powerful.

What's also notable about Piotroski, at least judging by the year he received his BS degree, is that he is still a pretty young guy. In fact, he is younger than me, which makes him practically pubescent! Kidding aside, it's refreshing to know we are trading current theory. This is not a system excavated from a dog-eared copy of Ben Graham's *The Intelligent Investor* (HarperBusiness, 2005)—an awesome book, by the way—nor is it warmed-over Buffetology with a few modern tweaks. This is fresh stuff.

The Piotroski F-score system is considered a "value" system. This means that the dominant characteristic of the companies screened for is that they are undervalued as measured by a ratio of stock price to one or more bottom-line metrics, such as earnings, sales, cash flow, book value, etc. It also means that this system should, like all value systems, enjoy the greatest amount of success in volatile markets. Our version of it, however, turns that success quotient up a notch or two by harnessing it to one of my most powerful technical setups, one that can be traded in all market types.

At the heart of the F-score system is Piotroski's preferred measure of a stock's valuation: the ratio of stock price (SP) to book value (okay, this was Ben Graham's favorite too; some things never go out of style!). Book value (BV) is measured by subtracting total liabilities from total assets and then dividing that by the number of shares outstanding (SO). Thus, as companies expand operations, pay down debt, or buy back shares, their BV tends to move up, and thus, the ratio of SP to BV will move down. A low SP to BV metric, then, can indicate a company doing some nifty things to its bottom line, and that it is all happening under the radar, so to speak, because price is still low. On the other hand, a low SP to BV ratio can also indicate that its SP is falling off a cliff for reasons unrelated to BV. Thus, Piotroski learned that low SP to BV companies can generally be divided into two camps: ones showing true value and thus likely to rise in price, and ones that are merely cheap for good reason and thus likely to stay at a low share price.

There are, as of this writing, more than 1,200 publicly traded companies located in the bottom 20 percent of all price to book value scores. Piotroski's F-score was developed to determine which of those are worth buying and which are best avoided if not sold short. The score is the result of nine tests that assess the state of a company's finances. For every test the company passes, it scores one point on that item; any failed test receives a zero. A score of eight or nine is considered to be a high F-score, an indicator of financial strength and thus underlying value. The nine tests are as follows:[1]

- Is the return on assets for the last fiscal year positive?
- Is cash flow from operations for the last fiscal year positive?
- Is the return on assets ratio (i.e., net income/total assets) for the last fiscal year greater than the return on assets ratio for the fiscal year two years ago?
- Is cash flow from operations for the last fiscal year greater than income after taxes for the last fiscal year?
- Is the long-term debt to assets ratio for the last fiscal year less than the long-term debt to assets ratio for the fiscal year two years ago?
- Is the current ratio (i.e., assets/liabilities) for the last fiscal year greater than the current ratio for the fiscal year two years ago?
- Is the average shares outstanding for the last fiscal year less than or equal to the average number of shares outstanding for the fiscal year two years ago?
- Is the gross margin for the last fiscal year greater than the gross margin for the fiscal year two years ago?
- Is the asset turnover for the last fiscal year greater than the asset turnover (i.e., revenue generated by assets) for the fiscal year two years ago?

Reading this list is like reading an "Accounting 101" textbook, isn't it? These are just the kinds of concerns any good accountant brings to the table when going over a company's books. In fact, Piotroski discovered that companies that fail on seven or more of these tests are likely destined to languish in mediocrity, if not fall headlong into bankruptcy. He observed that nearly every company in Chapter 11 passed through the low end of the F-score range on its way there. On the other hand, companies that live near the top of the range are virtually free of accounting "red flags." The F-score is, in other words, tradable information of very high quality.

The following chart (Figure 7.1) demonstrates just how much of an edge is contained in these nine simple questions. Since 1998, the American Academy of Independent Investors has been tracking stocks that rise to the high

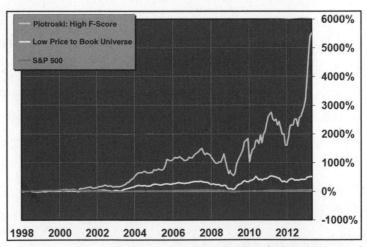

Courtesy of American Association of Independent Investors

Figure 7.1   Piotroski F-score system—performance over 15 years.

end (scores of 8 or 9) of the F-score. Look at how much outperformance these stocks attained (top line) compared to the universe of low SP to BV stocks (middle line) and the S&P 500 (bottom line).

Here is how we will play the Piotroski F-score system. In running this system, we are going to harness Piotroski's F-score scan to one my most powerful technical setups: the "Blue Sky Breakout" (longs) and "Blue Sea Breakdown" (shorts). This technical setup is a true inverse system in that the long and short versions each use the same parameters, only the short version (Blue Sea) reverses each parameter from bullish uptrend to bearish downtrend. The Blue Sky Breakout setup looks for stocks making new near-term highs when confirmed by the on-balance volume (OBV) indicator, which is also making new highs. The Blue Sea Breakdown setup looks for stocks making new near-term lows when confirmed by the OBV, which is also making new lows.

When we thus take the results of the fundamentals-based Piotroski F-score scan and require that those stocks further pass the technical test of price strength with a volume level that supports the move, we truly have our bases covered. We are buying stocks that are financially healthy but undervalued that have also drawn the attention of investors enough to push shares to new near-term highs. We are then also selling stocks short that are in trouble financially and that are also showing signs of strong selling pressure. That is how to neutralize the market!

FOR FURTHER RESEARCH ON THE SYSTEM

To my knowledge, Professor Piotroski has not yet published his system in book-length form. There are, however, a number of books that reference his research and the nine-point financial strength test. The best primary source is Piotroski's 2000 paper, which is surprisingly easy reading given the journal it was published in. Unlike most articles in financial journals, the mathematics involved in the paper requires no more skill than the ability to count to nine. If you would like to learn more about Joseph Piotroski's F-score system, you can check out the following resources:

- Joseph Piotroski, "Value Investing: The Use of Historical Financial Statement Information to Separate Winners from Losers." This is the title of Dr. Piotroski's original paper as it was published in the *Journal of Accounting Research* in 2000. I suggest accessing the more recent reprint, which is available through the University of Chicago Graduate School of Business at www .chicagobooth.edu. I assume that it is the same text as the original.
- John Reese and Jack Forehand, *The Guru Investor* (John Wiley, 2009): see Chapter 12, which discusses Dr. Piotroski's system at length.

- Dr. Piotroski's F-score is also described in Wesley Gray and Tobias Carlisle, *Quantitative Value* (John Wiley, 2012): Chapter 8.

To read more about the Blue Sky Breakout and Blue Sea Breakdown setups, see my *Trend Trading for a Living* (McGraw-Hill, 2007), pp. 176–180 and 208–213, respectively. I also have a couple of videos available to the public on www.Youtube.com that describe the longs version (Blue Sky). If you search YouTube for "Dr. Stoxx," you should see them. In these hour-long videos you will find a description of the Blue Sky Breakout setup as it is traded using the Dr. Stoxx Trend Trading Toolkit (TTTK) from MetaStock. For a more detailed study, you may be interested in two webinars I offer through our site, www.DrStoxx.com. They are entitled "How to Buy Breakouts" and "How to Short Breakdowns." They contain everything you need to know about this particular setup in both its long and short applications.

TRADING THE PIOTROSKI F-SCORE SYSTEM

Before you begin trading this system, please read and give some thought to the following disclaimer. I'm putting it at the head of every system:

What follows here for this system, as for each trading system in the book, is a step-by-step process you may replicate in order to find trading candidates that meet the system's requirements. No guarantee is being made that the tools used to find such stocks will not allow some stocks to pass through the filters that should not have passed for one reason or another. No screening tool is completely free of technical glitches. This is one reason why one should always apply to any short list of trading candidates further discretionary analysis of the sort we discussed in Chapter 5. Please note also that no claim is being made here that following the step-by-step procedure as stated will lead to profitable trading. It has in my case. But it may not in your case—or in mine going forward.

With that disclaimer out of the way, let's get down to work. Here are the tools needed to trade this system:

- (essential) Stock Investor Pro
- (option 1) MetaStock with the Dr. Stoxx Trend Trading Toolkit add-on
- (option 2) Stockcharts.com subscription with Blue Sky Breakout and Blue Sea Breakdown setups programmed

RUNNING THE LONGS VERSION

Step 1: Open Stock Investor Pro. The updater will run automatically if you are not loaded with the latest market data (weekly downloads). Once that is done, go to the Tools menu and pull down the Screen Editor tool.

Step 2: In the Name menu, pull down Piotroski: High F-Score. This opens four lines of screening filters for this system. In the fourth line, change the Compare To number from 8 to 7. Click Apply to run the scan. You should get at least 30 passing companies. If you get fewer than 30, change the 7 to 6 and run the scan again. Do not go under 6 (see Figure 7.2).

Step 3: Under the File menu, pull down Export Data. In the dialog box, save as an Excel spreadsheet. Save to your desktop or folder reserved for this system.

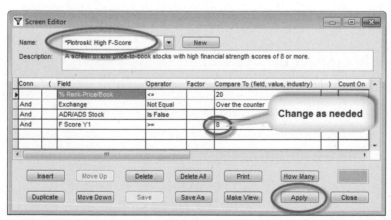

Courtesy of American Association of Independent Investors

Figure 7.2 Stock Investor Pro Screen Editor—Piotroski F-score system.

Step 4 (MetaStock option): Import the symbols from your Excel spreadsheet into MetaStock (MS) as a new chart list. Run the TTTK: Long Blue Sky Breakout Explorer from the Trend Trading Toolkit on the chart list. If the exploration returns no results, repeat steps 1 through 4 each day. As you build a larger watch list of high F-score stocks, you increase the chances of finding a good number of Blue Sky Breakout setups. If the Explorer shows that there are no Blue Sky Breakouts currently trading on the watch list of Piotroski high F-score stocks, you may apply the TTTK: Long Blue Sky Breakout Expert Advisor to each chart in the list. This will show all Blue Sky Breakout signals going back several years. Consider any signal valid that occurred within the past 20 trading days as long as the current price is *under* the closing price on the day of the signal.

Step 4 (StockCharts option): If you are not using MetaStock to run the technical part of this system, you may import the symbols from your Excel spreadsheet into another technical scanning service like Stockcharts.com. Run the Blue Sky Breakout scan on the watch list (see *Trend Trading for a Living,* pp. 176–180 for details on the parameters of this scan). You can create your own Blue Sky

Breakout scan by writing into StockCharts's Advanced scanning tool the following criteria:

- A new 40-day price high

- A new 40-day OBV high

- A new 40-day high in a momentum indicator (e.g., MACD or CCI)

Step 5: Do further discretionary analysis on any results from steps 1 through 4 and trade accordingly. Please note that the Piotroski scan as it is configured in Stock Investor Pro will turn up a number of "penny" stocks and/or stocks with very light volume. You can either add a volume filter to the SIP scan or to the StockCharts Blue Sky scan, or simply delete those symbols as you do your discretionary work on the charts.

*Step 6 (**position management**):* The Piotroski F-score system, like most of the systems in this book, does not require the use of stop-losses. Instead, you will let the system take you out of the trade. At each new rebalancing period, simply repeat steps 1 and 2. If any of your current open positions fails to pass the Piotroski screen, even when down at a 6 F-score, they need to be closed and replaced with a new position that passes the screen.

CHART EXAMPLES

The following are examples of stocks that passed at least eight of the nine Piotroski F-score tests and also showed a "Blue Sky Breakout" setup on their price charts. The first chart is of Aegean Marine (ANW), a company that supplies fuel and other materials to the shipping industry. ANW shows a nice entry signal in early January 2013 and promptly rallied from a 5.73 entry price to a high of 7.88, for a gain of over 37 percent in six weeks. In fact, ANW continued to rally, triggering a number of subsequent Blue Sky Breakouts. As of this writing, ANW is trading over $10 per share, for a gain of nearly 75 percent in only five months (see Figure 7.3).

Our next chart shows an even more robust move (Figure 7.4). SkyWest Airlines (SKYW) is a small airline company that services routes supplied by a number of larger carriers. Its business model is set up to benefit from the enormous traffic of the big hub carriers without any of the advertising and hub maintenance costs. Unlike the larger airlines, therefore, its fundamentals are consistently strong.

In mid-August of 2012, SKYW gapped up sharply on better-than-expected earnings, triggering a Blue Sky Breakout buy signal at a time when its Piotroski score was a robust 7 out of 9. From there, shares rallied upward over six months, nearly doubling in price.

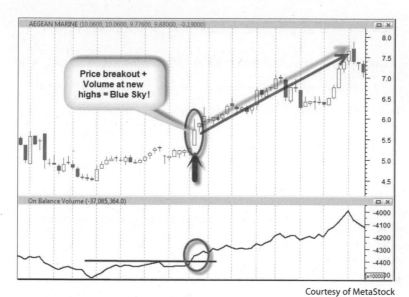

Figure 7.3   ANW long showing gains from the Piotroski F-score system.

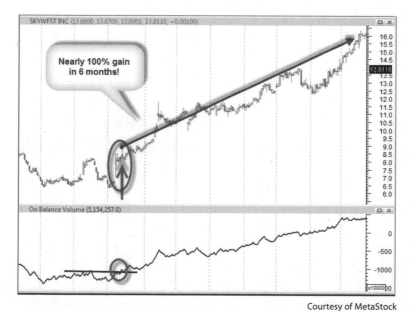

Figure 7.4   SKYW long showing gains from the Piotroski F-score system.

RUNNING THE SHORTS VERSION

Step 1: Run Stock Investor Pro. The updater will run automatically if you are not loaded with the latest market data (weekly downloads). Once that is done, go to the Tools menu and pull down the Screen Editor tool.

Step 2: In the Name menu, pull down Piotroski: High F-Score. This opens four lines of screening filters for this system. In the fourth line, change the operator from >= (greater than or equal to) to <= (less than or equal to) and change the Compare To number from 8 to 2. Click Apply to run the scan. You should get at least 30 passing companies. If you get fewer than 30, change the 2 to 3 and run the scan again. Do not go over 3.

Step 3: Under the File menu, pull down Export Data. In the dialog box, save as an Excel spreadsheet. Save to your desktop or folder reserved for this system.

Step 4 (MetaStock option): Import the symbols from your Excel spreadsheet into MetaStock as a new chart list. Run the TTTK: Short Blue Sea Breakdown Explorer from the Trend Trading Toolkit on the chart list. If the Explorer returns no results, repeat steps 1 through 4 each day without deleting any prior stocks already shortlisted. As you

build a larger watch list of low F-score stocks, you
increase the chances of finding a good number of
breakdown setups. If the Explorer shows that there
are no Blue Sea Breakdowns currently trading on
the watch list of Piotroski high F-score stocks, you
may apply the TTTK: Long Blue Sea Breakdown
Expert Advisor to each chart in the list. This
will show all Blue Sea Breakdown signals going
back several years. Consider any signal valid that
occurred within the past 20 trading days as long as
the current price is *above* the closing price on the
day of the signal.

Step 4 (StockCharts option): If you are not using
   MetaStock to run the technical part of this system,
   you may import the symbols from your Excel
   spreadsheet into another technical scanning service
   like Stockcharts.com. Run the Blue Sea Breakdown
   scan on the watch list (see *Trend Trading for a
   Living* for details on this scan). You can create
   your own Blue Sea Breakdown scan by writing
   into StockCharts's Advanced scanning tool the
   following criteria:

- A new 40-day price low

- A new 40-day OBV low

- A new 40-day low in a momentum indicator (e.g.,
  MACD or CCI)

Step 5: Do further discretionary analysis on any results from steps 1 through 4 and trade accordingly. Please see the additional note in step 5 for the longs side of this system.

Step 6 (position management): The Piotroski F-score system, like most of the systems in this book, does not require the use of stop-losses. Instead, you will let the system take you out of the trade. At each new rebalancing period, simply repeat steps 1 and 2. If any of your current open positions fails to pass the Piotroski screen, even when up at a 3 F-score, they need to be closed and replaced with a new position that passes the screen.

CHART EXAMPLES

The following are examples of stocks with low Piotroski F-scores that also showed a Blue Sea Breakdown setup on their price charts. The first chart is of AVEO Pharmaceuticals, an oncology drug research firm with several drugs in the Food and Drug Administration (FDA) approval pipeline. I normally do not like to short developmental pharma companies since even a hint of good news on anything in their pipeline can send shares soaring. I'll make an exception to that rule, however, when the Piotroski scale tells us that the company is just one FDA rejection away from bankruptcy. Like most experimental drug

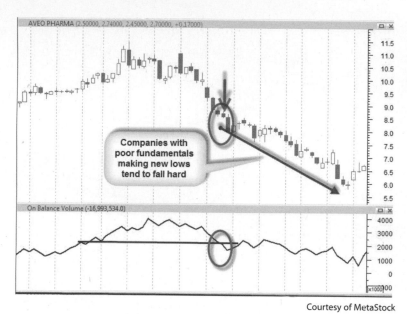

Courtesy of MetaStock

Figure 7.5   AVEO short showing gains from the Piotroski F-score system.

makers, AVEO's financials are not in great shape. Back in October 2012, the company's share price was also hitting new near-term lows on strong volume. It promptly lost over 40 percent of its value in five weeks (see Figure 7.5). As of this writing, nine months later, AVEO is resting on a base at $2.00 per share, for a total gain of nearly 300 percent!

Our second example is Molycorp (MCP), an exceptionally volatile stock that is a favorite with short-term swing and day traders. Molycorp is a mining and manufacturing company that turns rare earth minerals into industrial-grade product. MCP's financials are so bad it routinely carries an F-score of 1. In April 2012, MCP showed a Blue Sea Breakdown setup and promptly fell from around $27 per

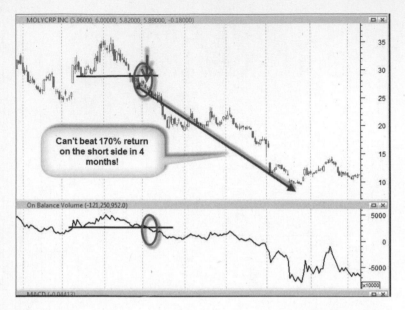

Courtesy of MetaStock

Figure 7.6   MCP short showing gains from the Piotroski F-score system.

share to under $10 in less than four months (see Figure 7.6). As of this writing, MCP is trading around $7 per share, having bottomed out with a low of $4.70, for a potential gain of over 450 percent!

CHAPTER 8

THE EARNINGS
ESTIMATE REVISION
SYSTEM

*There's a delay between when the analysts changed their
estimates or their recommendations and when the stock prices
respond, and you can use that delay to create and
trade portfolios.*

—Dr. Len Zacks

You met the founding father of the Earnings Estimate
Revision trading system, Dr. Len Zacks, back in Chapter 3.
I described there how his paper on stock price prediction, along with that of Professor Piotroski's, helped pull
my trading motivation out from the mire of the "random
walk" malaise and into the light of real-world statistics.
Stock price movement going forward can be reliably fore-
casted, so these two men claim—with hard evidence backing them up—as long as certain key data is known. For
Piotroski, as we saw in the last chapter, that data includes
the book value (BV) to stock price (SP) ratio and the
answers to nine accounting-like questions. For Dr. Zacks,
the essential data that impels future stock price movement

includes the changes made by companies and their analysts to the estimates of their future earnings per share.
Simply put, when companies and their analysts raise earnings guidance, the stock's share price normally responds
by rising over the near term as a new set of expectations
gets priced in. For the same reason, when guidance is lowered, the stock's share price normally falls over the near
term.

INTRODUCING THE SYSTEM

Dr. Len Zacks devoted his PhD research at MIT to dis-
covering ways quantitative research could be used to formulate successfully predictive models for stock prices.
After several years working for a major brokerage firm as
head of the quantitative research department, Dr. Zacks
published a paper that was to revolutionize the investing world. Dr. Zacks's paper, "EPS Forecast—Accuracy Is
Not Enough," first appeared in *Financial Analysts Journal*
in 1979. Until that time, EPS, or earnings per share, was
considered the most important piece of information about
a company. A company either had an EPS—i.e., they were
profitable—or they didn't; if they had an EPS, it was either
growing or it wasn't; and its ratio to share price was considered to be either under- or overvalued. That was largely
how the fundamentals of a company were measured prior
to the publication of Dr. Zacks's research. Zacks showed

that it is not earnings per se, but the forward-looking pro-
jection of how earnings are expected to change over time
that is all-important. A company may be losing money,
but if it can convince analysts that next year they will be
profitable, or at least less unprofitable than they are now,
their share price can and often will rise over the near term.

Where do these forward-looking projections come
from? First, from the companies themselves, and then
from the brokerage analysts who follow those companies
and regularly comment on their future earnings prospects. It normally works like this: Let's say company ABC
Widget, Inc., brings to market a new product it had been
developing. Similar products are made by Widget's com-
petitors, but this new version has a few novelties the company is sure will make it a strong seller. After a thorough
advertising campaign, preliminary sales figures show that
ABC Widget will likely grab 3 percent of the market out of
the hands of its rivals. This boost to Widget's bottom line
means that the earnings guidance it gave at its last conference call now needs to be revised. There are seven analysts
at major brokerage houses who follow ABC Widget. They
each receive a call from the head of the company's investor
relations with the news. The next morning, ABC Widget
receives two upgrades, three estimate revisions, and a new
significantly higher consensus price target. You know the
rest of the story: Shares of ABC Widget gap up at the open,
chop around for a few days as the sell-side guys work the

phones, and then run up to new highs as momentum builds heading into the next earnings announcement.

What Len Zacks has done with his research is find a way to step into the middle of that process in order to get on board stocks like ABC Widget before they make the big announcement. As the success of Zacks's ranking system for grading stocks (see Chapter 3 for details) demonstrates, this strategic method carries a very significant edge. Zacks developed a system, based on rigorous testing, that inputs the following four points of data: agreement among the analysts, the magnitude of their revised estimates, the accuracy of their past estimates, and the magnitude of past earnings surprises.[1] When these numbers are collected from the over 150 brokerage analysts tracked by Zacks Investment Research, the result is a ranking system that only gives a 1, or "strong buy," rank to the top 5 percent of all publicly traded stocks, and a 5, or "strong sell," to the bottom 5 percent of stocks. The "strong buy" designation is so prescient that it has resulted in an average of 2,000 basis points of alpha per year, every year, since 1988!

The American Association of Independent Investors (AAII) has been tracking the Zacks ranking system since 1998. While not identical to the proprietary algorithm used by the Zacks Rank, the system tested by the AAII uses three of its four key ingredients: agreement, magnitude, and surprise. The following chart shows how those results have fared over a 15-year look-back period (Figure 8.1). The top line represents all stocks that, among other things, have had

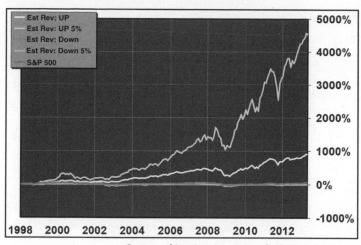

Courtesy of American Association of Independent Investors

Figure 8.1   The Earnings Estimate Revision system—performance over 15 years.

upward revisions of 5 percent or more from a consensus of at least five major analysts, the middle line is the whole universe of stocks that have had upward revisions of any magnitude, and the three intertwined lines at the bottom include the S&P 500 and stocks that have been revised downward.

Like the Piotroski F-score system, the Earnings Estimate Revision system has an identical inverse version. We will use a tweaked version of it to find quality short candidates. The inverse system scans for stocks that are showing downward earnings estimate revisions from a consensus of major analysts. As the following statistics from www.AAII.com show (Figure 8.2), this one factor alone is enough to cause a high degree of underperformance relative to the S&P 500. Figure 8.2 represents returns from stocks that have received downward earnings estimates

Performance	Passing Companies	Screening Criteria	Chart

	Est Rev: Down 5%	S&P 500
YTD Return:	9.3%	12.0%
Five Year Return:	0.4%	2.9%
Ten Year Return:	4.9%	5.7%
Inception:	0.2%	10.8%

Data as of 4/30/2013

The Est Rev: Down 5% Screen represents AAII's interpretation of the investment approach and is not determined by the original strategist. The list of **passing companies** represents a hypothetical portfolio, which is used to track the screen's performance on a chart.

Courtesy of American Association of Independent Investors

Figure 8.2   The Earnings Estimate Revision system (shorts)—performance.

revisions of –5 percent or more from at least five major analysts.

Here is how we will play the Earnings Estimate Revision system. There are two ways to filter out stocks on the front end (the fundamentals side) of the system. We can either use the screen that is preprogrammed into Stock Investor Pro (SIP), which mimics the Zacks Rank, or we can create a scan in Research Wizard (RW) using the Zacks Rank itself. I cannot divulge here the specific parameters used in SIP since that is available only to paying subscribers. What I can show you here is the RW scan, since the proprietary formula of what comprises the Zacks Rank, which is at the heart of the scan, is not disclosed.

Typically, stocks that pass through either of these filters are already showing some degree of momentum. Rather than chase stocks up and down, I prefer to time my entry. For this reason, on the technical side of the system, we are adding my most-used and all-time favorite setup: the "Pullback" (for longs) and its inverse setup, the "Relief Rally" (for shorts). The "Pullback/Relief Rally" setups identify trending price momentum—up for longs and down for shorts—that has also made a significant pullback to support (longs), or has rallied into resistance (shorts), without violating the dominant trend. It is at that point that we have our perfectly timed, technical entry point, one that reduces risk by taking some of the momentum off the table and increases profit potential by giving shares greater room to run before hitting resistance or support.

FOR FURTHER RESEARCH ON THE SYSTEM

Several resources are publicly available on the power of earnings estimates in general, and on the Zacks Rank system in particular. Dr. Zacks's 1979 paper is not easily found, but you can obtain an online copy by going to http://www.CFApubs.org, clicking Browse Publications, and then clicking *Financial Analysts Journal*. From there you will see a search bar on the right side of the page. Type in **Leonard Zacks**. This will bring up his paper entitled "EPS Forecast—Accuracy Is Not Enough." It will cost you $15.00 for the reprint unless you happen to be a CFA Institute member.

Dr. Zacks has a book out entitled *The Handbook of Equity Market Anomalies* (Wiley Finance, 2011). Chapter 3 describes the basis of his work on earnings estimate revisions. You might also want to visit the website associated with the book (www.hema.zacks.com). *Ahead of the Market* (Harper Collins, 2003) by Mitch Zacks, son of the founder, is the best book-length treatment of how analyst estimates and their revisions influence stock price. It is an excellent read and I strongly recommend it. I can also recommend Kevin Matras's *Finding #1 Stocks* (Wiley, 2011). Matras is vice president of Zacks Investment Research and a former commodities broker. While his book is mostly a primer for users of the Research Wizard, Matras's descriptions of various value and momentum stock screens using the Zacks Rank is an invaluable tool for those who wish to build their own stock scans, or who simply want to understand more fully the theory behind the Earnings Estimates Revision system used in this book.

The website www.Zacks.com is the hub of the investment research firm built upon the central insight of Dr. Len Zacks. The education page on the site (www.zacks.com/education) contains a wealth of information about the Zacks Rank. You will also find a video of Dr. Zacks describing his research.

For a description of the "Pullback" and "Relief Rally" setups, please see my *Trend Trading for a Living* (McGraw-Hill, 2007), pp. 158–165 and 194–198, respectively. You will also find a treatment of them as day trading systems in my *Micro-Trend Trading for Daily Income* (McGraw-Hill, 2010), Chapter 5. There I call the pair my "bread and butter system" because that is what these two powerful timing tools are. For a more detailed study, you may be interested in two webinars I offer through our site, www.DrStoxx.com. They are entitled "How to Buy Pullbacks" and "How to Short Rallies." They contain everything I know about this paired setup in both its long and short applications.

TRADING THE EARNINGS ESTIMATE REVISION SYSTEM

Let's get down to work. Here are the tools needed to trade this system:

- You will need either (option 1) Stock Investor Pro or (option 2) Research Wizard.
- You will also need (option 1) MetaStock with the Dr. Stoxx Trend Trading Toolkit or (option 2) a Stockcharts.com subscription with Pullback and Relief Rally setups programmed.

RUNNING THE LONGS VERSION

*Step 1 (**Stock Investor Pro option**):* Open Stock Investor Pro. The updater will run automatically if you are not loaded with the latest market data (weekly downloads).

Step 2: You will not need to edit this screen, so your next step is to go to the Portfolio window. Pull down

*EPS Est Rev Up 5%. Note that SIP also has a screen labeled ESP Est Revisions Up, but you do *not* want that one. Selecting the screen will open a Notebook with a list of all the stocks that have passed the filter. Each run of this screen should yield between 20 and 40 stocks.

Step 3: Under the File menu of SIP, pull down Export Data. In the dialog box, save as an Excel spreadsheet. Save the spreadsheet to your desktop or folder reserved for this system.

Step 1 (Research Wizard option): Open Research Wizard. The updater will run automatically if you are not loaded with the latest market data (nightly downloads). Click the Screens button. Open the SoW (Screen of the Week) folder. Click the Filtered Zacks Rank screen.

Step 2: The Filtered Zacks Rank is a very simple screen centered on a Zacks Rank of 1, but we will need to alter it to suit our purposes. I suggest the following changes:

- Add: Volume (20 days average) >100000

- Add: Current Price >5

- Delete the last line (line 3)

- Change the next line up (line 2) from >0 to Top #40

From that base, I suggest you do some back-testing and tweaking to formulate a robust formula for the fundamentals side of this screen. The screen as altered here, without any further additions, has performed well from 2003 to 2013, but as you can see from the chart in Figure 8.3, using a two-week rebalance period, it carries significant downside risk. Some of that risk will be mitigated with the addition of the short side of the system and the timing of entries using the Pullback setup. It is possible to flatten the curve even more by adding certain fundamental filters. A valuation filter of some kind—e.g., a price-to-sales ratio, or a P/E-to-growth ratio—with a threshold set at an undervalued level is often helpful for minimizing drawdowns. Kevin Matras's book mentioned earlier offers several excellent ideas for what works best when building scans in the RW.

Step 3: Under the Data menu of RW, pull down Export To Excel. In the dialog box, save as an Excel spreadsheet. Save to your desktop or folder reserved for this system.

Step 4 (MetaStock option): Import the symbols from your Excel spreadsheet into MetaStock (MS) as a new chart list. Run the TTTK: Long Pullback Explorer from the Trend Trading Toolkit on the chart list. If the exploration returns no results,

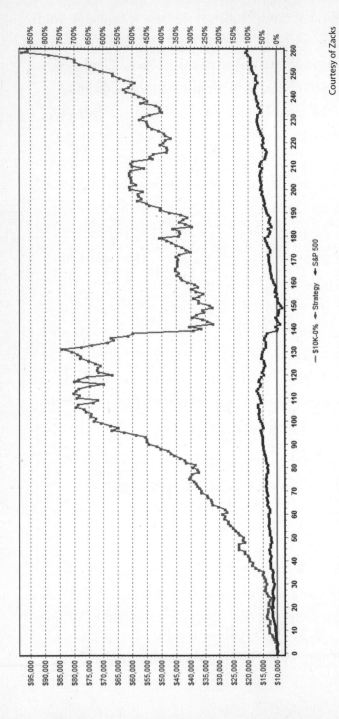

Figure 8.3 The Earnings Estimate Revision base screen (longs)—performance.

Courtesy of Zacks

— $10K-0% — Strategy — S&P 500

apply the Long Pullback Expert Advisor to each of the stocks in your charts list. This will show all Pullback setup signals over the past several years. Consider as valid any Pullback setup within the past 20 trading days, as long as current price is trading *under* the close of the signal day.

Step 4 (StockCharts option): If you are not using MetaStock to run the technical part of this system, you may import the symbols from your Excel spreadsheet into another technical scanning service like StockCharts. Run the Pullback scan on the watch list (see *Trend Trading for a Living*, pp. 158–165 for details on the parameters of this scan). The basic parameters for the Pullback setup are as follows:

- The stock is in an uptrend with a rising 50sma.

- The stock is trading above the 50sma.

- Stochastics (5) are <25.

Step 5: Do further discretionary analysis on any results from steps 1 through 4 and trade accordingly.

Step 6 (position management): The Earnings Estimate Revision system, like most of the systems in this book, does not require the use of stop-losses. Instead, you will let the system take you out of the trade. At each new rebalancing period, simply repeat steps 1 and 2. If any of your current open positions fail to pass the Earnings Estimate Revision screen, they need to be closed and replaced with a new position that passes the screen and satisfies the requirements of the Pullback setup.

CHART EXAMPLES

The chart in Figure 8.4 featuring Mohawk Industries shows just how powerful a profit generator a stock can be when upward earnings estimates are combined with the timed entries of the Pullback setup. Mohawk (MHK) is the largest flooring company in the world; as long as people keep

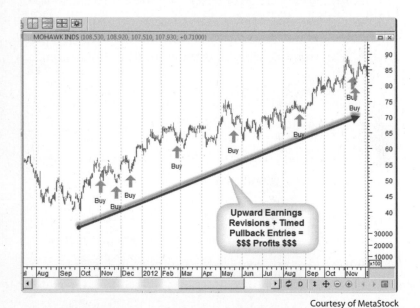

Courtesy of MetaStock

Figure 8.4   MHK—Earnings Estimate Revision system longs with the Pullback Expert Advisor applied.

building homes, Mohawk should continue to grow. In MHK's chart, we see a modest uptrend over a 12-month period, with price rising close to 100 percent. The TTTK: Long Pullback Expert Advisor from the Trend Trading Toolkit has been applied to this chart; it shows eight strategic entry points, each one profitable over the near term. In fact, the price of MHK's shares continued to rise to the $120 per share level (May 2013), for a full 167 percent return over 20 months!

In Figure 8.5 we see a chart of Ubiquiti Networks (UBNT) showing two nifty entries using this system. UBNT is a relatively "under the radar" wireless communications company with some very cool products in their pipeline. They are profitable and have been growing earnings at a triple-digit rate in recent quarters. With the Long Pullback Expert Advisor applied, we see two awesome entries just prior to earnings announcements that surprised to the upside. Quick-turn swing traders could have taken

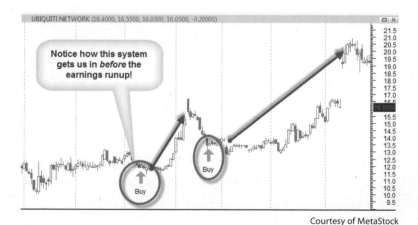

Courtesy of MetaStock

Figure 8.5   UBNT—Earnings Estimate Revision system longs with the Pullback Expert Advisor applied.

profits of close to 40 percent and 45 percent, respectively. Longer-term position traders would have seen a 78 percent return potential for the four-month holding period.

RUNNING THE SHORTS VERSION

Step 1 (Stock Investor Pro option): Open Stock Investor Pro. The updater will run automatically if you are not loaded with the latest market data (weekly downloads).

Step 2: You will not need to edit this screen, so your next step is to go to the Portfolio window. Pull down *EPS Est Rev Down 5%. Note that SIP also has a screen labeled ESP Est Revisions Down, but you do *not* want that one. Selecting the screen will open a Notebook with a list of all the stocks that have passed the filter. Each run of this screen should yield between 20 and 40 stocks.

Step 3: Under the File menu of SIP, pull down Export Data. In the dialog box, save as an Excel spreadsheet. Save the spreadsheet to your desktop or folder reserved for this system.

Step 1 (Research Wizard option): Open Research Wizard. The updater will run automatically if you are not loaded with the latest market data (nightly downloads). Click the Screens button. Open the SoW (Screen of the Week) folder. Click the Filtered Zacks Rank screen.

Step 2: The Filtered Zacks Rank screen is a very simple screen centered on a Zacks Rank of 1, but since we need the inverse screen here, you will need to change that to a Zacks Rank of 5. I suggest making the following additional changes to the base screen:

- Add: Volume (20 days average) >100000

- Add: Current Price >5

- Delete the last line (line 3)

- Change the next line up (line 2) from >0 to Bot #40

From that base, I suggest you do some back-testing and tweaking to formulate a robust formula for the fundamentals side of this screen. This particular screen has performed reasonably well from 2007 to 2013, particularly volatile years when a scan like this can be traded to advantage. The Zacks Rank 5 scan, without any further tweaking, returned 79 percent as a shorts-only scan, while the S&P 500 returned 32 percent return over the same period. This represents over 850 basis points of alpha per year!

Like the longs-only version of the scan, this part of the Earnings Estimate Revision system can go through rather lengthy losing periods. Much of that can be mitigated, however, with the addition of the longs side of the system and with the timing of entries using the Relief Rally setup. It is possible to flatten the curve even more by adding certain fundamental filters. On this side of the system, we would want to add valuation filters, as earlier, but with overvalued threshold values. Again, the Matras book mentioned earlier is helpful on this point; see especially the chapter entitled "Short Selling Strategies for Bear Markets" (Chapter 16).

Step 3: Under the Data menu of RW, pull down Export To Excel. In the dialog box, save as an Excel spreadsheet. Save the spreadsheet to your desktop or folder reserved for this system.

Step 4 (MetaStock option): Import the symbols from your Excel spreadsheet into MetaStock (MS) as a new chart list. Run the TTTK: Short Relief Rally Explorer from the Trend Trading Toolkit on the chart list. If the Explorer returns no results, apply the Short Relief Rally Expert Advisor to each of the stocks in your charts list. This will show all Relief Rally setup signals over the past several years. Consider as valid any Relief Rally setup within the past 20 trading days, as long as current price is trading *above* the close of the signal day.

Step 4 (StockCharts option): If you are not using MetaStock to run the technical part of this system, you may import the symbols from your Excel spreadsheet into another technical scanning service like StockCharts. Run the Relief Rally scan on the watch list (see *Trend Trading for a Living*, pp. 194–198 for details on the parameters of this scan). The basics of this setup scan are as follows:

- The stock is in a downtrend with a falling 50sma.

- The stock is trading below the 50sma.

- Stochastics (5) are >75.

Step 5: Do further discretionary analysis on any results from steps 1 through 4 and trade accordingly.

Step 6 (position management): The Earnings Estimate Revision system, like most of the systems in this book, does not require the use of stop-losses. Instead, you will let the system take you out of the trade. At each new rebalancing period, simply repeat steps 1 and 2. If any of your current open positions fail to pass the Earnings Estimate Revision screen, they should be closed and replaced with a new position that passes the screen.

CHART EXAMPLES

Almost Family (AFAM) supplies home health care services, including nursing and rehabilitation treatments. While its shares are undervalued, AFAM's earnings have been in contraction mode for a number of quarters. A Zacks Rank 1 stock two years ago, it is now languishing down in Rank 5

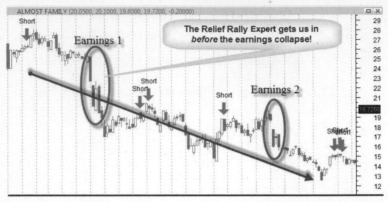

Courtesy of MetaStock

Figure 8.6 AFAM—Earnings Estimate Revision short with the Relief Rally Expert Advisor applied.

territory. In our chart example with the TTTK: Relief Rally Expert Advisor applied (Figure 8.6), we see several nice short entries highlighted, two of which came in advance of negative earnings announcements. The first signal returned 56 percent from peak to trough in less than eight weeks. The second trade, if taken at the earlier signal, would see a potential return of 45 percent in less than three months.

Rubicon Technology (RBCN) manufactures sapphire crystals—second only to diamonds for their hardness[2]—which are used in the light-emitting diode (LED) and optical industries. The stock is a favorite among quick-turn traders because of its volatility. In 2012, the company's earnings fell from a healthy $1.75 per share at the beginning of the year to negative numbers by the end of the year. This contraction of earning power was reflected in the share price, which took a massive hit. Note in Figure 8.7 shows how the Earnings Estimate Revision system with the Relief Rally

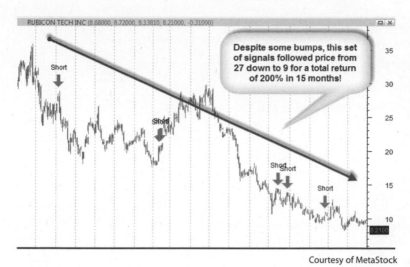

Courtesy of MetaStock

Figure 8.7   RBCN—Earnings Estimate Revision short with the Relief Rally Expert Advisor applied.

Expert Advisor from the TTTK applied got us in prior to the big move. In fact, RBCN's stock price went on to hit a low of $5 per share in February 2013, giving patient holders of the short a return of 440 percent in 21 months!

CHAPTER 9

THE O'NEIL CAN-SLIM SYSTEM

It doesn't pay to argue with the market. Experience teaches that fighting with the market can be a very expensive proposition.

—William O'Neil

This next system is an oldie but a goodie. First developed back in the mid-1980s—a full 10 years before I began trading—it has evolved into a spectrum of modified iterations, spawning a significant subculture of fans, detractors, users, and tweakers. One of the first true techno-fundamental hybrid systems ever developed, the CAN-SLIM system, as it is known, was one of the first systems I studied when I made the turn toward systems trading back in 1998 (after two years of losses). I'm sure that exposure planted the seeds that are now being harvested with this book.

The man who developed the CAN-SLIM system, William O'Neil, was introduced to you back in Chapters 2 and 3. He likely needs no further introduction. His best-selling book, *How to Make Money in Stocks* (McGraw-Hill, 1995), has appeared in at least four editions and has sold over

2 million copies. The book is so successful, it has inspired a cottage industry of "How to Make Money in…" books from some of O'Neil's protégés. I personally love O'Neil's book! Every time I pick it up, I get this little caffeine-like buzz in my stomach, which reminds me just how exciting it is to try and unravel the mysteries of the markets. There are two books everyone who wants to make money in the markets needs to read: first and foremost is Ben Graham's *The Intelligent Investor* (get the 2006 edition with Jason Zweig's comments attached); but when you are done with that, your next read should be *How to Make Money in Stocks*.

O'Neil first developed the CAN-SLIM method in 1960 as a student at Harvard's Business School. Three years later, at the age of 30, this method enabled O'Neil to become the top-performing broker at his firm, buy a seat on the New York Stock Exchange (the youngest ever to do so at that time), and establish the first computerized securities research firm, William O'Neil and Company, Inc., which in turn sponsored a print edition of O'Neil's research. In 1984, that paper became *Investor's Business Daily* (IBD), which is kind of like the *Wall Street Journal* on steroids. It held "must read" status for many traders and active investors. Today, the paper is in decline, suffering along with other print media from online competition, but at its peak, IBD claimed to have a readership of "nearly 1,000,000."[1] Fortunately for us, the print version of IBD has not disappeared; it has simply evolved with the times by going online. The paper edition has largely been replaced by Investors.com. All the important company research is there, along with great charts, commentary, stock tables ranked according to CAN-SLIM criteria (which we will be using in this system), and a wide variety of educational and investment research tools. Investors.com also has an evaluation tool that we will be using to trade two other systems in this book.

INTRODUCING THE SYSTEM

O'Neil's famous book introduced the investment world to what may have been the very first trading system to synthesize both technical and fundamental parameters. Known widely by its seven-letter mnemonic, CAN-SLIM, the strategy centers on three key dynamics: strong earnings growth, institutional sponsorship, and relative strength. Interestingly, O'Neil claims to have discovered CAN-SLIM in the same way I tried to discover a new momentum strategy. Remember my "500 stock experiment" from Chapter 2? Maybe I had his book in the back of my mind when I came up with that idea. Like my attempts to develop a "super system," O'Neil discovered the basics of CAN-SLIM by taking 500 of the most successful stocks from the past and asking the question, What did they have in common? He reasoned, like I did, that whatever they had in common must be the cause of their success. Thus, those stocks possessing the same traits may well be the next decade's winners.

Of course, O'Neil's reasoning suffers from the same fatal flaws that mine did. Just because successful stocks share certain characteristics does not mean that those characteristics were the cause of their success. Good thing for us, O'Neil did not stop with a mere 500 companies. Harnessing the power of one of the first computers available, O'Neil eventually analyzed over 1,000 stocks from the past 100 years. Using a more robust, data-driven methodology, O'Neil hammered together a system that not only made him a fortune—it has continued to do so for others. The list of all-star traders, investors, and portfolio managers who use CAN-SLIM as the basis for their research is long and growing longer. The popularity of books by O'Neil's disciples may serve to soften the edge of the system over time. But like all lasting truths, it will continue to have its seasons of fruitfulness.

The CAN-SLIM method is built around seven fundamental and technical conditions, which, according to O'Neil's research, are the common ground of all super-performing stocks. CAN-SLIM stands for[2]

- **C** stands for **Current earnings**. The company does not need to have positive net earnings from continuing operations, but it does have to show consistent growth (at least 25 percent) on a quarter-to-quarter basis. In addition, an acceleration in earnings growth in recent quarters is desired.

- **A** stands for **Annual earnings**, which should be up 25 percent or more in each of the last three years. In addition, annual returns on equity should be 17 percent or more.

- **N** stands for **New product or service**, which refers to the idea that a company needs to have a new offering of some kind that fuels the earnings growth seen in the first two parts of the mnemonic. This product or service should help the company achieve a new pricing power and better brand recognition. Think Apple's iPad or Starbucks adding breakfast sandwiches to their menu.

- **S** stands for **Supply and demand**. An index of a stock's demand can be seen in the rise and fall of trading volume of the stock, particularly during price increases and pullbacks. Volume levels should rise whenever share price rises, and volume levels should fall on pullbacks.

- **L** stands for **Leader or laggard?** O'Neil recommends buying "the leading stock in a leading industry." There is no real objective way to measure this, but O'Neil suggests using the *relative price strength rating* (RPSR) of the stock, a proprietary value that measures the stock's price performance over the past 12 months by reference to the rest of the market.

- **I** stands for **Institutional ownership**, which refers to the ownership of the stock by mutual funds and professional money managers. A marked increase in the percentage of ownership in recent quarters is desired as mutual funds, hedge funds, and investment banks begin to stockpile shares.

- **M** stands for **Market direction**, which is measured by the major averages: the S&P 500, the Dow Jones Industrial Average, the NASDAQ, and the NYSE Composite. O'Neil prefers investing during times of confirmed uptrends of these indices, as three out of four stocks tend to follow the general market pattern. When markets are in a downtrend, O'Neil recommends staying in cash or, for the more experienced, shorting stocks.

Since the CAN-SLIM strategy is essentially a growth stock filter, it can go through long stretches of dismal returns. The screen filters out strong growth companies at the top of their game. Sometimes, however, those at the top have nowhere to go but down. Competitor companies chasing the money can chip away at market share, or the debt the company took on to fuel its growth puts the squeeze on profit margins. Sometimes there is nothing

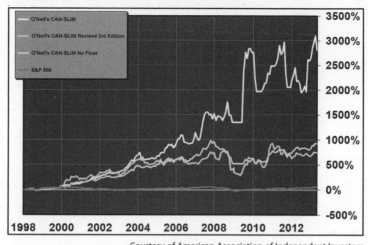

Courtesy of American Association of Independent Investors

Figure 9.1   CAN-SLIM system—performance over 15 years.

wrong with the company, but, whenever a season of "risk-off" concerns hammer the economy, big market players tend to prefer value stocks. The following chart of returns for the CAN-SLIM method (Figure 9.1) shows this phenomenon very clearly. First, we see that CAN-SLIM is a powerfully profitable system; but we also see that it can undergo very severe drawdowns (the standard version of CAN-SLIM is represented by the top line of the chart).

O'Neil advocated only buying CAN-SLIM stocks once they trade up to new price highs. We are going to break that rule. To help us cancel out a fair bit of the risk involved with this system, we will be adding two key technical filters—a simple, easily recognized price pattern setup (the "Bullish Base Breakout") and a volume indicator—to the long side of the fundamental base. The first of these additions takes some of the risk out of the trade by ensuring that we are only buying these growth companies when they are breaking out of price consolidation near support lows, and not when they are breaking out to new price highs after an extended run-up. The second addition virtually guarantees we are getting on board only when big money is also getting on board, for they are the ones with the financial power to sustain the breakout.

There is another problem with CAN-SLIM that we have had to address in our version of the system: To form the shorts scan by simply reversing the CAN-SLIM parameters—e.g., from 25 percent earnings per share (EPS) growth to 25 percent EPS decline, etc.—produces a system that yields poor shorting candidates. Stocks at the bottom end of the growth, institutional support, and relative strength spectrums tend to be stocks that have already bottomed out. They have little downside potential, and the risks of a short squeeze are high. For the short side of the system, therefore, we are going to abandon our usual "reverse the parameters" procedure and do something much more contrarian. The result is the one of the most exciting short-selling systems in this book!

FOR FURTHER RESEARCH ON THE SYSTEM

If you want to study the intricacies of CAN-SLIM, the best place to start is William O'Neil's bestselling book mentioned earlier. There are several editions out there. The one I prefer is McGraw-Hill's 2010 edition, which is subtitled,

Complete Investing System. It comes with a free month's subscription to Investors.com, which we will be using to trade this system, along with a free month to the online version of *Investor's Business Daily.* The book also comes with a helpful DVD that introduces you to all the tools available on the Investors.com website.

In addition to O'Neil's magnum opus, I can recommend a book written by two of O'Neil's disciples with a very provocative title: Gil Morales and Chris Kacher's *Trade Like an O'Neil Disciple: How We Made 18,000% in the Stock Market* (John Wiley & Sons, 2010). Chapter 1 offers a brief explanation of CAN-SLIM; Chapter 6 explains how the system can be used to short stocks (I have taken a few cues from this chapter); Chapter 8 gives us O'Neil's "10 commandments" for investing; and Chapter 9 offers some very cool recollections of what it was like to work with the founder during the 1990s Internet bubble and its aftermath. Fair warning: Chapter 10 contains a number of references to, for lack of a better term, "new age" teachings that I cannot endorse. While I am all for trading "in the zone," it should never be at the expense of one's spiritual health. With no disrespect intended toward the authors, I personally consider some of the teachings they reference in this chapter to be spiritually dangerous.[3] Fortunately, the authors reserved this short chapter for the end, and it does not interfere with the otherwise informative and interesting stuff that precedes it.

To the longs side of the system we will be adding a technical setup I call the "Bullish Base Breakout." This setup consists of a basic chart pattern coupled with a technical indicator, on-balance volume (OBV). The setup looks for stocks in a longer-term uptrend that have pulled back to a key support level and are showing price consolidation at that point. Price consolidation normally means that the trading range (highs to lows) of the stock's share price over a number of trading days is getting narrower. This consolidation normally forms a recognizable pattern, which I call here a "bullish base." The most common bullish base patterns are a rectangle, any of the triangles (ascending, descending, symmetrical), a falling wedge, an inverted head and shoulders, and a double/triple bottom. For further information about price patterns, along with rankings by track record, see the classic text by Thomas Bulkowski *Encyclopedia of Chart Patterns* (Wiley, 2005).[4] Consulting the Finviz.com "advanced chart" feature mentioned in Chapter 4 is also helpful here because it will draw in computer-generated price patterns. Remember, we want to see this consolidation pattern at or near an area of price support. This support can come in the form of a major moving average (50ma, 100ma, 200ma), a previous pivot low or lows, a lower Bollinger Band, or a trendline drawn under recent price lows.

The Bullish Base Breakout setup signals entry once we see the OBV indicator rise above a trendline placed above its most recent pivot highs. If you prefer something more objective (isolating the pivot highs can be more art than science), you can smooth the OBV with a three-period simple moving average (SMA) and then overlay that with a longer-term SMA like the 21-period. A new signal is triggered on the first bullish crossover of the two moving averages. Note that it is not enough for price to break out of its base; there must also be a confirming breakout in the OBV. The ideal is to see OBV break out above its pivot highs while price is still in consolidation. This indicates that although price is not moving much, shares are being accumulated in anticipation of a breakout. Thus, the setup is more aptly named "Bullish Base *Anticipated* Breakout." Our aim is to get on board a set of great growth stocks *before* they break out and then enjoy the full ride, not just the tail end of it. For a detailed description of the Bullish Base Breakout setup, along with more chart examples, please consult my *Trend Trading for a Living* (McGraw-Hill, 2007), pp. 181–189.

TRADING O'NEIL'S CAN-SLIM SYSTEM

Let's get down to work. Here are the tools you need to trade this system:

- (required): A subscription to Investors.com (about $15/month). Note that Stock Investor Pro (SIP) has the CAN-SLIM strategy preprogrammed into it, but its filters are so strict that it only returns a handful of stocks each week, and in some weeks none. It is, therefore, not suitable for our purposes.

- (option 1): MetaStock with the "Dr. Stoxx Trend Trading Toolkit" add-on.
- (option 2): A StockCharts subscription with the "Bullish Base Breakout" setup programmed.

RUNNING THE LONGS VERSION

Step 1 (Investors.com): Log in to Investors.com. On the right side of the home page you will see a menu with your name on it that looks like this (Figure 9.2). Click Screen Center.

Courtesy of Investors.com

Figure 9.2   Screen Center on Investors.com.

Step 2: At the Screen Center, find the header labeled Screen of the Day. To the right of that, find and click CAN-SLIM Select (as in Figure 9.3). This brings up a list of 60 to 100 stocks, sorted alphabetically, that pass most of the CAN-SLIM parameters (see Figure 9.3).

Step 3: Click the Export tab (upper right of the list) to export the list to an Excel spreadsheet. In that spreadsheet, sort the list of stocks by ascending

CAN SLIM® Select

Powered by
NorthCoast
Asset Management

The CAN SLIM® Select stock list tracks market-leading stocks that in general show strong earnings growth, positive institutional sponsorship, excellent industry strength, and solid sales growth, profit margins and return on equity. Stocks must also meet minimum price and volume levels. More

View by: Fundamentals ▾   ⊞Export | ⊞Print

Symbol ▲	Company Name	EPS % Chg (Last Qtr)	EPS % Chg (Prior Qtr)	Sales % Chg (Last Qtr)	EPS Est % Chg (Current Qtr)	EPS Est % Chg (Current Yr)	Tools
AAN	Aaron's Inc	5	12	2	6	7	✔️✉️Ⓜ️➕
ABT	Abbott Laboratories	5	4	2	-64	-55	✔️✉️Ⓜ️➕
ACAS	American Capital Ltd	0	8	-11	-57	-17	✔️✉️Ⓜ️➕
AEIS	Advanced Energy Inds	81	1500	6	6	47	✔️✉️Ⓜ️➕
AFCE	A F C Enterprises Inc	14	42	14	15	12	✔️✉️Ⓜ️➕
AMCX	Amc Networks Inc	42	-48	17	39	73	✔️✉️Ⓜ️➕
AOL	A O L Inc	95	28	2	39	14	✔️✉️Ⓜ️➕
ARRS	Arris Group Inc	32	33	17	4	45	✔️✉️Ⓜ️➕
AZZ	A Z Z Incorporated	39	54	14	24	32	✔️✉️Ⓜ️➕
BBRY	BlackBerry	-73	N/A	-36	111	N/A	✔️✉️Ⓜ️➕
BGFV	Big 5 Sporting Corp	3300	280	13	67	75	✔️✉️Ⓜ️➕
C	Citigroup Inc	32	63	-18	23	34	✔️✉️Ⓜ️➕
CACC	Credit Acceptance Corp	30	17	16	20	21	✔️✉️Ⓜ️➕
CINF	Cincinnati Financial	63	29	12	159	-5	✔️✉️Ⓜ️➕
CIT	C I T Group Inc	N/A	472	-22	360	N/A	✔️✉️Ⓜ️➕

Courtesy of Investors.com

Figure 9.3   CAN-SLIM select stocks on Investors.com.

(click Data tab and then click Sort) for each of the two EPS Est % Chg columns (Current Qtr and Current Yr). Note that in some versions of Excel you will need to unmerge all merged cells before sorting the columns. Once sorted, delete any stock at the top of the list that shows a negative number or N/A. In the example in Figure 9.3, you would delete ABT, ACAS, BBRY, CINF, and CIT. In this way we eliminate stocks that likely carry a low Zacks Rank as per the previous system.

Step 4 (MetaStock option): Import the list of remaining stocks into a watch list folder in MetaStock. From the Dr. Stoxx Trend Trading Toolkit, select the watch list of CAN-SLIM stocks and run the Long—Bullish Base Breakout Explorer. If the Explorer returns no results, apply the Bullish Base Breakout Expert Advisor to each of the stocks in your charts list. This will show all Bullish Base Breakout setup signals over the past several years. Consider as valid any Bullish Base Breakout setup within the past 40 trading days (note that this is a longer look-back period than the other systems), as long as the current price is trading *below* the close of the signal day.

Step 4 (StockCharts option): If you are not using MetaStock to run the technical part of this system, you may import the symbols from your Excel spreadsheet into another technical scanning service like StockCharts. Run the Bullish Base Breakout scan on the watch list (see *Trend Trading for a Living* for details on the parameters of this scan). The basic parameters for this scan are difficult to code into most scanning services, but they are as follows:

- Stocks in a long-term uptrend

- Current price in a consolidation pattern of some kind

- Consolidation pattern (rectangle, triangle, double bottom, etc.) is near an area of support

- OBV volume indicator is above a trendline placed over recent pivot highs

Step 5: Do further discretionary analysis on any results from the Bullish Base Breakout Explorer or scan and trade accordingly.

Step 6 (position management): The O'Neil CAN-SLIM system, like most of the systems in this book, does not require the use of stop-losses. Instead, you will let the system take you out of the trade. At each new rebalancing period, simply repeat steps 1, 2, and 3. If any of your current open positions fail to show up on the CAN-SLIM Select list, once filtered for negative estimate changes, they need to be closed and replaced with a new position that is on the list.

CHART EXAMPLES

Big 5 Sporting Goods (BGFV) is a chain of retail sporting goods stores with over 400 outlets, mostly in the Western part of the United States. The stock has been one of our most successful longs over the past year. It was this trading system that first brought it to my attention. It came up on the CAN-SLIM Select screen on Investors.com back in July 2012, sporting not only huge growth numbers, but also some pretty impressive value metrics (like a price to

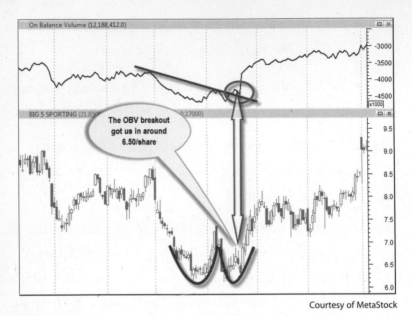

Courtesy of MetaStock

Figure 9.4   BGFV—CAN-SLIM system long showing entry signal.

sales ratio under 1.0 and a Piotroski F-score of 8). In the chart in Figure 9.4, you can see our original entry point. I had been stalking BGFV on our watch list after it printed a nice double bottom pattern at an area of previous price support. That pattern gave us the "bullish base" consolidation we needed. The entry signal then came once OBV crossed above its resistance trendline, as seen in the chart.

In the chart, BGFV appears to be fizzling out at around the $9 per share level. But in reality, it was just getting started. It is presently trading up near $22 for a 240 percent gain from our original entry! Note that there were four additional Bullish Base Breakout entries on the

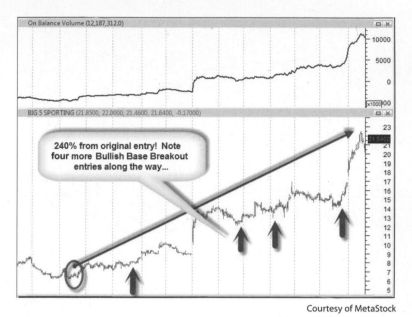

Courtesy of MetaStock

Figure 9.5   BGFV—CAN-SLIM system long showing four more entry signals.

way up (Figure 9.5). Each came as price consolidated right around the 50ma with rising volume balance.

The next company is for those who, like famed fund manager, Peter "Buy What You Know" Lynch, prefer to trade more familiar names. Whirlpool is the world's largest home appliance maker. It owns several well-known brands, including Maytag, Jenn-Air, and Amana. The company sports P/E-to-growth and price-to-sales ratios under 1.0, as well as a five-year projected growth rate of near 30 percent. And it happens to be a pretty nifty trading stock, with a beta of over 2.0 as of this writing, which

Courtesy of MetaStock

Figure 9.6   WHR—CAN-SLIM system long showing entry signal.

makes it at least twice as volatile as the S&P 500. The company had a rough couple of years following the 2007–2009 market crash, but once consumer credit stabilized, it has made regular appearances on the CAN-SLIM Select list. The stock gave its first and only Bullish Base Breakout in late June 2012 at a price that was just above the low established in 2011, which acted as support (see Figure 9.6). It has only gone up from there, trading as high as $134 per share for a potential return of 133 percent in 11 months!

As an aside, stocks that make it to the CAN-SLIM Select list tend to be very stable fundamentally. They can remain on the list for years. This may well be the case with WHR. One way I like to play stocks like this, especially when the Bullish Base Breakout signal comes after a significant selloff, is to sell naked puts (at the money, one month out) early in the run when implied volatility is still high. You run the risk of being assigned shares, of course, but at a substantial discount to the price at entry. Since you know the fundamentals of the company are sound, those are usually shares you want to own. As the position matures and premium on puts begins to dry up, I'll switch to writing covered calls. Together, this is a nice way to gain income from an uptrending stock without having to tie up so much cash.

RUNNING THE SHORTS VERSION

First, a preliminary note: As said earlier, we cannot simply reverse the parameters of the longs version of the CAN-SLIM screen to achieve a nice set of candidates for short sale. In fact, for the contrarians among us, that particular screen (the "anti-CAN-SLIM") is not a bad place to go looking for turnaround candidates to buy. So here is how we operate the shorts side of this system: We are going to use a different screening service in the Investors.com research toolkit to find stocks that have rallied hard for all the right reasons but are showing signs of topping out. We are looking for stocks to short that are at the top of all of Investors.com's fundamental tables but one. These are companies with some serious fundamental weaknesses but, for whatever reason, are trading at the top of the heap. What we are looking for is that moment of equilibrium in their ascent, when all the good news that propelled them higher is priced in and big money

Courtesy of Investors.com

Figure 9.7   Screen Center on Investors.com.

players start showing signs of profit taking. Our aim is to ride the selling wave down to a level more fitting to their earning potential.

Here is how we will play the shorts side of the "O'Neil CAN-SLIM" system:

Step 1 (Investors.com): Log in to Investors.com. On the right side of the home page you will see a menu with your name at the top that looks like Figure 9.7. Click eTables.

Step 2: At the eTables page, click the header labeled Main Tables. This will bring up a list of the top 300 stocks as screened by whatever criteria are selected in the header. The default ranking, which you will see when you first land on the page, is Smart Select Comp Rating. This is Investors.com's proprietary ranking tool. The table will show you the top 300 stocks as ranked by this composite indicator. Below the header you will find two sorting options:

primary and secondary. Set the primary sort to RS Ranking and toggle on the Descending option. The RS (Relative Strength) Rating measures the price performance of the stock as compared to all other stocks. An RS ranking of 99 means that the stock is outperforming 99 percent of all other stocks. Then set the secondary sort to SMR Rating and toggle on the Ascending option. SMR stands for "sales growth, profit margins, and return on equity." Investors.com uses a proprietary algorithm for ranking all stocks for their relative strength in these three areas. A stock given an "A" is in the top 20 percent of all stocks on the basis of these three areas of financial strength, while those given an "E" are in the bottom 20 percent. We are looking here for stocks that rank at "C" or below. Since all three metrics are foundational to the CAN-SLIM method, this is our way of reversing the longs version of this system.

Once you have the primary and secondary sorts set, click the Sort button. You should then see a table of stocks that looks something like Figure 9.8. We are going to use the stocks at the top of this sort to form a watch list of charts that we will monitor for short entry. To form this watch list, we need to look at a third indicator: the Acc/Dis Rating. You will see this rating in column 6. This is a ranking that was originally developed exclusively for the *Investor's Business Daily* paper. The rating

Primary Sort:	Secondary Sort (optional):
RS Rating ▾ ○ Ascending ◉ Descending	SMR Rating ▾ ◉ Ascending ○ Des

SmartSelect Comp Rating	EPS Rating	RS Rating (1ST)	Ind Group Relative Strength	SMR Rating (2ND)	Acc/Dis Rating	52-Week High	Closing Price	Price $ Change	Volume % Change	Vol. (1000)
Accelerate Diagnostics (AXDX) Develops culture-free analysis and medical diagnostic products for rapid bacteria										
46	3	99	B	E	B	9.20	9.22	0.38	81	114
CANADIAN SOLAR INC (CSIQ) Chinese manufacturer of ingot, wafer, solar cell, solar modules and other solar a										
85	49	99	A+	E	A+	10.65	9.40	0.05	-32	1454
CARDIONET INC (BEAT) Provides continuous, real-time ambulatory management systems and services fo										
69	21	99		E	A+	5.95	5.77	0.12	248	1472
CELLDEX THERAPEUTICS INC (CLDX) Develops vaccines for cancer and infectious and inflammatory diseases using a p										
82	34	99	A+	E	A	16.48	16.05	-0.04	-3	1438
China Information Tech (CNIT) Chinese provider of public security communication applications and geographic										
46	7	99	D	E	A+	3.23	2.80	-0.01	-90	23
CHRISTOPHER & BANKS CORP (CBK) Operates 686 christopher and banks and c.j. banks stores in 44 states with plans t										
84	70	99	B	E	B	7.92	6.60	-0.30	-18	206
CLEARWIRE CORP CL A (CLWR) Provides wireless broadband networks for delivery of residential and mobile inter										
61	43	99	D	E	A	4.56	4.63	0.16	-7	13218
Comstock Holding Cl A (CHCI) Builds single-family homes, townhouses and condominiums for first-time, early/se buyers										
38	17	99	C	E	D	3.65	2.87	0.16	-3	441
HASTINGS ENTERTAINMENT (HAST) Operates 138 entertainment superstores in 19 states offering music, software, per										
75	42	99	B+	E	A	3.70	4.16	0.52	706	67
HUTCHINSON TECHNOLOGY (HTCH) Manufactures suspension assemblies for hard disk drives, and medical equipmen										
88	54	99	A	E	A+	6.69	6.10	-0.39	-10	524
INSMED INC (INSM) Develops proprietary, advanced liposomal technology designed specifically for i										
69	2	99	A+	E	A+	14.30	12.61	-0.08	10	423
KERYX BIOPHARMACEUTICALS (KERX) Develops novel pharmaceutical products to treat cancer, renal disease and other										
67	48	99	A+	E	D-	9.98	7.30	0.33	-15	2119
M G I C INVT CORP (MTG) Offers private mortgage insurance enabling people to purchase homes in the u.s										
53	16	99	B-	E	A	6.60	6.07	-0.06	-66	4360
OLD SECOND BANCORP INC (OSBC) Holding co for old second national bank operating via 27 offices in cook, kane a										
86	80	99	B	E	A-	6.07	5.69	0.00	-94	3
RADIAN GROUP INC (RDN) Offers mortgage insurance and financial guaranty to mortgage and other lending										
41	6	99	B-	E	B+	14.34	12.73	-0.13	-41	4678

Courtesy of Investors.com

Figure 9.8   eTables sorted by EPS and SMR ratings.

is based on the degree of institutional buying (accumulation) and selling (distribution) a stock is seeing over the past 13 weeks. A stock rated A for Acc/Dis is experiencing heavy institutional buying; a stock rated E is seeing heavy selling. A stock rated C is showing a balance of buying and selling. Any increase in institutional selling usually leads to downward pressure on price. That is the signal to short we are looking for. Our goal is to find stocks that were at the top of the Acc/Dis but have since slipped a notch or two, signaling large block selling.

Step 3: From the stocks that rise to the top of the eTables sort, make a watch list in Investors.com of only those stocks that meet the following criteria:

- They have an RS Rating of 99 (column 3)

- They have an SMR Rating of C, D, or E (column 5)

- They have an Acc/Dis Rating of A or A+ (column 6)

- They are priced >$5 per share (column 8)

- They trade more than 100,000 shares per day (column 11)

You should find 10 to 20 stocks, maybe more, that satisfy these criteria each time you run the eTables sort. Save these stocks into a watch list by clicking the + button to the right of each stock in eTables. Simply select your watch list, and the stock is immediately placed into it. To view your watch list, click My eTables in the header bar, just to the right of Main Tables. This is the list of stocks we will monitor daily for our entry signal. I suggest running the eTables scan a couple times per week. Save into your watch list any new candidates that appear. The more stocks you have in the list, the less time you will need to wait for new short signals.

Step 4: Monitor your watch list each day for changes. We have a valid signal to short any stock in the watch list when we see the following two conditions met:

- An RS Rating that falls from 99 to 98 or lower, AND

- An Acc/Dis Rating that falls from A or A+ to A– or lower

Step 5: Do further discretionary analysis on any valid short signal and trade accordingly.

Step 6 (position management): The O'Neil CAN-SLIM system, like most of the systems in this book, does not require the use of stop-losses. Instead, you will let the system take you out of the trade. Open positions need to be monitored for their current RS, Acc/Dis, and SMR Ratings. This can be done daily or weekly, as preferred. Monitoring any less frequently than weekly is not recommended. For any open short position, cover at the next trading day's open when *any one of the following is true*:

- RS Rating rises to 99, OR

- RS Rating or rises 10 or more points from its lowest value since entry, OR

- Acc/Dis Rating rises to A or A+, OR

- Acc/Dis Rating rises six or more steps from its lowest value since entry (e.g., from D+ to B), OR

- SMR Rating rises to B

A cautionary note needs to be expressed concerning the short side of the CAN-SLIM system. The eTables sort we are using here highlights stocks with less-than-stellar fundamentals that are in strong rally mode. We enter them once they begin to top out, as indicated by a decline in relative strength *and* the presence of share distribution. This doesn't necessarily mean that we have entered at the top. Sometimes, what looks like a top turns out to be a shallow pullback before shares move sharply higher. Our exit strategy will normally get us out before too much damage is done, but it does mean that this side of the system can experience a number of false starts before we hit a big winner. The big winners are the bread and butter of this strategy. Not infrequently, we will be positioned short in a stock just before a major collapse, or even bankruptcy. If you are patient, you should eventually see a number of double-digit share prices fall to penny-stock status within several weeks of entry.

CHART EXAMPLES

This shorting strategy will frequently put companies that develop new pharmaceuticals on the short list of stocks to watch. I said previously that I'm not a fan of shorting developmental drug makers. However, this system frequently identifies such companies *after* the good news is out and shares have run up to unsustainable levels. Many times, that is a prime time to short the stock. With a few notable exceptions, developmental biotech firms have no earnings, negative profit margins, and repeatedly self-finance through shelf offerings, which dilute share value.

Such companies are no strangers to the SMR Rating of E. This financial ugliness in a post-good-news trading environment can make for a very unstable share price. This is where our anti-CAN-SLIM short strategy can really shine.

Such was the case with INFI. Late in 2012 through mid-March 2013, the company released results on a number of research trials that looked promising. Shares rallied from around $17 to a high of $50.51 on March 15, 2013, putting the stock on our watch list. Several weeks of choppy action later, we got our entry signal, as it became increasingly clear that the experimental evidence was not strong enough to warrant FDA approval anytime soon. The selloff was then increased by a number of share offerings.

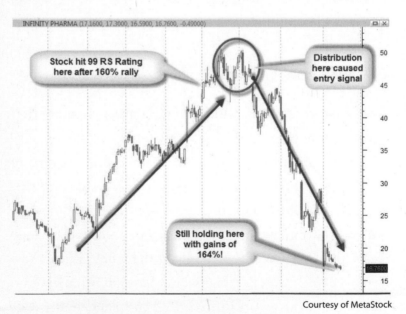

Courtesy of MetaStock

Figure 9.9   INFI—CAN-SLIM system short.

The INFI short is still open as of this writing, with a full 164 percent of profit from entry (see Figure 9.9). Note the nice double top formation.

Another prime CAN-SLIM short presented itself in Atossa Genetics, a health care company that specializes in manufacturing diagnostic products for breast cancer. Named after the first woman in history to be diagnosed with breast cancer—the wife of Darius the Great of Persia, circa 520 BCE—the company's two primary cancer detection tests received a lot of media attention when it snagged a key distribution contract, causing the ramp in shares into the March highs. Investors added $56 million to Atossa's market cap before they discovered that no reimbursement details were disclosed in the contract. For

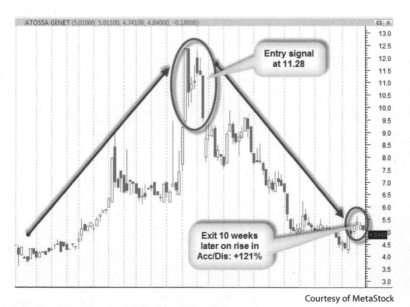

Courtesy of MetaStock

Figure 9.10   ATOS—CAN-SLIM system short.

a company with only around a quarter million in annual sales, this was hype ripe for shorting. CAN-SLIM shorts profited 121 percent in only 10 weeks with this setup (see Figure 9.10).

CHAPTER 10

THE CARR HYBRID SYSTEM

Sow your seed in the morning, and at evening let your hands not be idle, for you do not know which will succeed, whether this or that, or whether both will do equally well.

—Ecclesiastes 11:6

Every system described thus far contains at least one piece of information—a strategic idea, a technical indicator, a financial metric—that has been borrowed from someone else. I have neither the education nor the programming skills to be wholly original in the field of trading systems development; hence, the unashamed reliance on the brilliance of others. Dr. Piotroski gave us the F-score test, Dr. Zacks gave us the Zacks Rank, William O'Neil gave us CAN-SLIM; even the technicals-based systems in the next section of the book—and, for that matter, in my previous two books—can ultimately trace their roots back to pioneer strategists like John Magee, John Murphy, John Bollinger, Thomas Bulkowski, Nicolas Darvas, and George Lane, as well as a number of my peers in the trader training and advisory space.

If there is any system in *Market-Neutral Trading* I could truly call "original," you would think it would be the one described here, the one with my name attached to it. Truth be told, the only thing *truly* original in this system is the mix of ingredients; the ingredients themselves, for the most part, come from others far more capable. And even the mix itself is something I can't take full credit for. I believe that when I was putting this system together, I had some help "from above."

Let me explain. For several years I had been working on an original, long-short, techno-fundamental system that I could legitimately call my own. I was after my own CAN-SLIM, a pioneering system that would serve to build a fortune, launch a dozen hedge funds, and propel me into spheres of influence where I could make a difference in the world (I've since learned that influence built on wealth is vastly overrated). During these years of experimentation, there were plenty of false starts, some of which cost me money. There was one system in particular, however, that showed some promise. It back-tested well, though it was hardly the stuff of legend.

Toward the end of that experimental period, there was a night that changed everything. A guest pastor visiting our church spoke at our Tuesday night service. Afterward, he had a word of prophesy for me. He laid his hands on my shoulders and said, "You are a businessman." This was in itself startling because at that time I was still a tenured professor of religious studies.

Resigning from that position to trade and train traders full time—my current "business"—was still only a future hope at that point. He went on: "You are in a stuck place right now. You have been working on a formula [his exact words!] and there is a piece missing. The Lord says He will give it to you!"

The next day, I was out on a run. During the run, I recalled the experience from the previous night, wondering what it might mean. In the next moment, a phrase leaped into my head whose meaning I did not understand. The phrase was "free cash flow yield." I knew about "free cash flow"—income from operations after expenses are factored out—and I knew that "yield" is income produced by an asset, but I did not know what "free cash flow yield" (FCFY) referred to. I looked it up and discovered that there are at least three ways to configure FCFY: You can take free cash flow (FCF) and divide it by share price; you can take FCF and divide it by market capitalization; or you can take FCF and divide it by net income.[1] I plugged each one into my system and ranked stocks on that basis: longs with the best FCFY and shorts with the worst. No luck. There was a little improvement in returns, as one might expect, but nothing worthy of a divine revelation.

That evening I received an e-mail from a financial blog. I get this dispatch weekly and normally consign it to the recycle bin. This time, a title caught my eye. The article was about "free cash flow yield." I immediately clicked the link and read with great interest. The author claimed to be using a nonstandard way of calculating free cash flow yield that measures a company's earning power more accurately than the standard models. I took his formula, created a calculation expression for it, and added it to the system. When I ran the back-tester for the longs screen, I could not believe my eyes. It was like my original formula had taken steroids. The annual return on investment (ROI) over a 10-year look-back period—a stretch that saw an 8.1 percent annual ROI for the S&P 500—increased over 77 percent, from 13.2 percent annual ROI to 23.6 percent! For statistical and charted performance of the longs version of the Carr system, see Figures 10.1 and 10.2.

Developing the short side of the system took a bit more work. Simply reversing the parameters of the longs side proved profitable, but there was room for improvement. After some searching and experimentation,

from 04/11/2003 to 04/12/2013 1 week holding period		
STATISTICS ex.: $10,000 start	Strategy	S&P 500
Total Compounded Return %	741.8%	118.5%
Total Compounded Return $	$84,184	$21,851
Compounded Annual Growth Rate %	23.6%	8.1%
Win Ratio %	54%	58%
Winning Periods/Total Periods	282 of 523	302 of 523
Avg. # of Stocks Held	3.0	
Avg. Periodic Turnover %	72.1%	
Avg. Return per Period %	0.6%	0.2%
Avg. Winning Period %	4.5%	1.7%
Largest Winning Period %	26.5%	12.1%
Avg. Losing Period %	-4.0%	-1.9%
Largest Losing Period %	-21.4%	-18.1%
Max. Drawdown %	-77.1%	-54.7%
Avg. Winning Stretch (# of Periods)	2.2	2.2
Best Stretch (# of Periods)	9	9
Avg. Losing Stretch (# of Periods)	1.9	1.6
Worst Stretch (# of Periods)	9	6

Courtesy of Research Wizard

Figure 10.1   Carr Hybrid system statistics—longs.

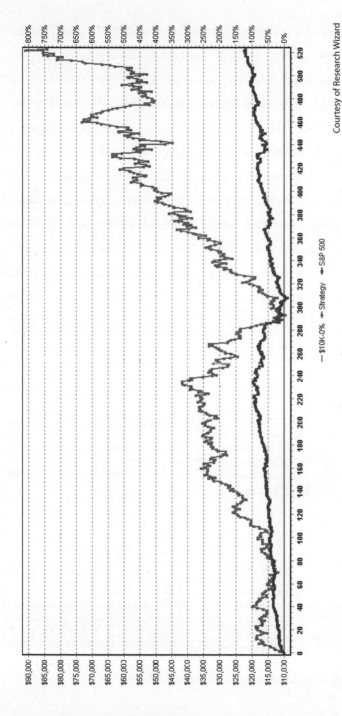

Figure 10.2 Carr Hybrid system ROI chart—longs.

Courtesy of Research Wizard

— $10K–0% ◆ Strategy ◆ S&P 500

I discovered a complementary short scan that added another 17 percent annual ROI to the returns (see Figures 10.3 and 10.4). This gives us a total return of the system, assuming full margin used for the shorts, of over 40 percent ROI per year! Try plugging your account balance into a spreadsheet and multiplying it by 1.4 ten times. You'll see just what a money maker this system is.

Keep in mind that the Carr Hybrid scans, long and short, were built and tested in Research Wizard (RW). As discussed in Chapter 4, the RW consistently shows a lag between back-tested and real-money returns, at least in my use of it. Still, with such a robust showing, and with discretionary stock selection at work, this is a system worth working with. I make no claim to the system being heaven-sent,

from 04/11/2003 to 04/12/2013 1 week holding period (SHORT)		
STATISTICS ex.: $10,000 start	Strategy	S&P 500
Total Compounded Return %	379.0%	118.5%
Total Compounded Return $	$47,902	$21,851
Compounded Annual Growth Rate %	16.9%	8.1%
Win Ratio %	50%	58%
Winning Periods/Total Periods	264 of 523	302 of 523
Avg. # of Stocks Held	3.0	
Avg. Periodic Turnover %	62.3%	
Avg. Return per Period %	0.4%	0.2%
Avg. Winning Period %	3.5%	1.7%
Largest Winning Period %	18.7%	12.1%
Avg. Losing Period %	-2.8%	-1.9%
Largest Losing Period %	-11.1%	-18.1%
Max. Drawdown %	-44.1%	-54.7%
Avg. Winning Stretch (# of Periods)	2.0	2.2
Best Stretch (# of Periods)	12	9
Avg. Losing Stretch (# of Periods)	2.0	1.6
Worst Stretch (# of Periods)	7	6

Courtesy of Research Wizard

Figure 10.3   Carr Hybrid system statistics—shorts.

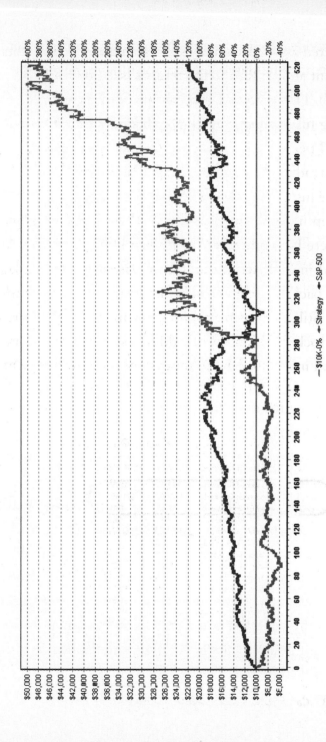

Figure 10.4 Carr Hybrid system ROI chart—shorts.

Courtesy of Research Wizard

— $10K-0% — Strategy — S&P 500

by the way. It falls far short of that standard of perfection. But I sincerely stand in awe of the way it all came together!

INTRODUCING THE SYSTEM

The longs version of the Carr Hybrid system is built on four key parameters: We are going to insist that the stocks show a high beta (i.e., they are more volatile than the S&P 500), that have recent net-positive changes to fiscal year estimates for earnings as stated by a significant number of analysts (something we borrowed from the Earnings Estimate Revision system in Chapter 8), that have strong free cash flow yields as defined in the next section, and whose price in recent trading is showing low relative strength (we don't want anything overbought) when compared to other stocks passing the same filters. Running this scan will give us a short list of tradable candidates on the long side. There is no further technical filter beyond the relative strength requirement.

The longs scan can be scaled to meet your particular needs. I've run back-tests on everything from 3 stocks weekly to 10 stocks monthly, and they are all profitable, just less so as you add more stocks and longer rebalance periods. Each time the scan is run, unless you see good reason to the contrary, you would close out any position that did not come through the filter and replace it with one that did (turnover is near 70 percent on both sides of the system).

The shorts side of the system, as mentioned earlier, is not exactly the inverse of the longs side. To improve performance, we needed to alter a couple of the filters. The shorts scan is built around four key parameters: We will be scanning for companies that are reducing earnings estimates, that show sluggish earnings growth relative to peers in the industry, that are overvalued relative to peers, and that are overbought. We have also found the best returns from this scan when we restrict our focus to small- and mid-cap sized companies. Small-cap companies are perceived as speculative investments and thus tend to fall fastest during market pullbacks, unlike their large-cap counterparts, which are thought to be "safe haven" investments during market volatility.

The version of this scan I use in my own trading was built in the Research Wizard. I took several cues for it from a longs-only system that is preprogrammed into the software and that was developed by Kevin Matras, vice president of Zacks Investment Research.[2] Kevin's "small-cap growth" screen is described in his book *Finding #1 Stocks* (Wiley & Sons, 2011). I found that when the parameters of the small-cap growth system were reversed and back-tested as a shorts-only system, the returns were strong. When I tweaked those parameters a bit, they became stronger still.

Trading the Carr Hybrid system requires no further step beyond running the long and short scans and buying and selling what the scans turn up. However, as explained in

Chapter 5, it is always best to do further discretionary work on the scan results to ensure you have the best candidates and the best entries. The Dr. Stoxx Trend Trading Toolkit add-on from MetaStock can help with that task by highlighting bullish and bearish technical setups on the charts. This information may aid the timing of your entries.

Alternatively, those with strong chart reading skills can simply analyze a good set of technical charts. This discretionary step is foundational; it adds a bit of "art" to the "science" of trading, which, as we said earlier, is the one essential thing required for consistent trading success.

FOR FURTHER RESEARCH ON THE SYSTEM

At the heart of the longs side of the Carr Hybrid system is the set of earnings estimate revision filters, discussed in Chapter 8, coupled with a rather unique valuation filter: a nonstandard version (at least as far as I can tell) of free cash flow yield. My source for this configuration of FCFY comes from an article authored by a financial blogger. The author's blog has not been updated since 2011, so he may no longer be active as a trader. Hopefully, he hasn't gone into hiding for some reason! In any case, he may not want the attention, so I will not reveal his name. You will see his formula for calculating free cash flow yield in step 1 later.

The best source for understanding the rationale behind the short side of the Carr Hybrid system is to read about the longs-only system, which is its basis. For that, you can read Kevin Matras's *Finding #1 Stocks: Screening, Backtesting, and Time-Proven Strategies* (Wiley & Sons, 2011), pp. 55–60. At the heart of Matras's system are two fundamental filters: a Zacks Rank of 1 or 2 coupled with a high rate of earnings growth. In our case, since we have developed this into a shorts system, we are looking for a Zacks Rank of 4 or 5 along with a low rate of earnings growth. For more information about the Zacks Rank, see the suggestions in Chapter 8. For a thoroughly modern discussion of earnings growth and why it tends to fuel stock price, I recommend Jason Zweig's "Commentary on Chapter 12" in Benjamin Graham's *The Intelligent Investor*. Zweig is a financial columnist and editor for publications like *Money* and *Time* magazines. His chapter commentaries in the 2006 version of the 1973 classic bring Graham's value-oriented theories up to date.[3]

TRADING THE CARR HYBRID SYSTEM

Let's get down to work. Here are the tools you need to trade this system:

- (option 1): Research Wizard. You will need to program in the filters for both sides of this system, but since both use the Zacks Rank, RW is the best choice for this system. Moreover, it has the small-caps growth system preprogrammed in, so changing that over to a shorts-only version is easily done (see later text).

- (option 2): Stock Investor Pro (SIP) from www.AAII.com. This has the earnings estimate revision filters we will use for both the longs and shorts systems preprogrammed in. You will then need to add the other filters to the scan.

RUNNING THE LONGS VERSION

Step 1 (Research Wizard option): Open RW and click Screens. In the Screening Criteria section, build a longs-only scan with the following parameters:

- Average volume >100,000 (adjust as needed)

- Average price >5 (adjust as needed)

- Beta (60 months) >1.5

- Zacks Rank <3

- # of Brokers in rating >4

- # Upward revisions in EPS for current Fiscal Year in past 4 weeks >0

- # Downward revisions in EPS for current Fiscal Year in past 4 weeks = 0

- Relative Strength 4 weeks = Bottom# 35

- % Change F(1) Est. − 12 weeks = Top# 21

- (Cash flow / Enterprise Value) $*$ 100 = Top# 14 (note that you will need to use the Calculation Expression Editor to create this filter)

- Relative % Change in Price in past 4 weeks = Bottom# 3 (adjust as needed)

Step 1 (Stock Investor Pro option): Open SIP and click Tools. Open the Screen Editor and pull down the EPS Est Rev Up 5% screen. Delete the last line of the scan (EPS Est Y1-% Rev-Last Month) and then save the scan, giving it a new name. You will now use this scan as a base. By itself, it should return at least 30 stocks. Most, if not all, of these stocks would qualify as a Zacks Rank 1 or 2. To this base add the following filters and then save the scan:

- Average volume >100,000 (adjust as needed)

- Average price >5 (adjust as needed)

- Beta (60 months) >1.5 (adjust as needed)

- % Rank (Cash flow / Enterprise Value) $*$ 100 $\geq$ 90 (note that you need to use the Custom Field Editor to create this filter; adjust as needed)

- % Rank Relative Strength 4 week $\leq$ 50 (adjust as needed to get desired number of stocks)

Note that with SIP, and unlike the RW, you cannot scan for the Top# or Bottom# of any category.

You can only filter out the stocks that rank in the top or bottom percentile in each category. Thus, you may need to adjust the percentile rank figures to attain the number of stocks you wish to trade.

Step 2: Run this scan at each rebalance period. Weekly is recommended, but this can profitably be done bimonthly or even monthly.

Step 3: Do further discretionary analysis on any results from steps 1 and 2, and trade accordingly.

Step 4 (position management): After running the scan at each new rebalance period, any stock you are currently in that fails to pass through the scan should be sold and replaced with a new position. Any stock you are currently in that passes through the scan should be rebalanced so that it matches the percentage of capital you are allotting to each position in this system.

CHART EXAMPLES

The long side of the Carr Hybrid system tends to focus its attention on a limited number of sectors. Industries like services, financials, and real estate companies tend to operate with greater cash flow; thus, they show up more frequently than other sectors. This is true of our first chart of Franklin Resources (BEN), a mutual fund company with $3 billion under management. BEN offers

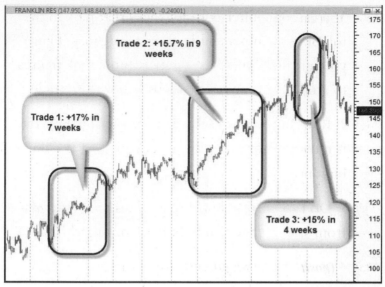

Courtesy of MetaStock

Figure 10.5   BEN—Carr Hybrid system long.

the Franklin Templeton line of funds and investments. The Carr Hybrid system marked three separate trades in BEN from June 2012 to June 2013. The exits were noted when the relative strength filter failed to pass the stock because it was showing too much price strength relative to other passing stocks. The two later entries came on pullbacks, which allowed the stock to pass the filter once again (Figure 10.5).

Stoneridge, Inc. (SRI) engineers and manufactures electronic components for commercial cars and vehicles. Even at its present price near $12 per share, it sports some very impressive valuation numbers, along with a projected growth rate of 35 percent. In 2013, SRI appeared on the Carr Hybrid scan twice. The first time came after an

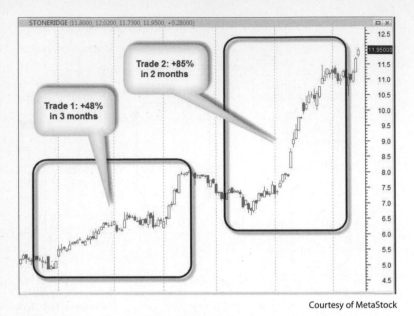

Courtesy of MetaStock

Figure 10.6   SRI—Carr Hybrid system long.

extended Bullish Base Breakout (see Chapter 9), and the
second time during a pullback. As you can see, both trades
led to quick, strong gains (Figure 10.6).

RUNNING THE SHORTS VERSION

*Step 1 (**Research Wizard option**):* Open RW and click
Screens. You have two choices here: You can either
open the Small Cap Growth screen and simply
reverse the operators (e.g., from > to <), or you
can build the scan that I use to pair the longs
version of this system by inputting the following
parameters:

- Average volume >100,000 (adjust as needed)

- Average price >5 (adjust as needed)

- Market value <$1 billion

- Zacks Rank >2

- Estimated 1 Year Growth Rate < (Industry Median $*$ 0.8)

- \# Upward revisions in EPS for current Fiscal Year in past 4 weeks = 0

- \# Downward revisions in EPS for current Fiscal Year in past 4 weeks >0

- Relative Strength 4 weeks = Top\# 35

- % Change F(1) Est. – 12 weeks = Bottom\# 21

- (Cash flow / Enterprise Value) $*$ 100 = Bottom\# 14 (note that you will need to use the Calculation Expression Editor to build this filter)

- Relative % Change in Price in past 4 weeks = Bottom\# 3 (adjust as needed)

Step 1 (Stock Investor Pro option): Open SIP and click Tools. Open the Screen Editor and pull down the EPS Est Rev Dn 5% screen. Delete the last line of the scan (EPS Est Y1-% Rev-Last Month) and then save the scan, giving it a new name. You will now use this scan as a base. By itself, it should return at least 30 stocks. To this base add the following filters and then save the scan:

- Average volume >100,000 (adjust as needed)

- Average price >5 (adjust as needed)

- Market value <$1 billion

- Estimated 1 Year Growth Rate < (Industry Median * 0.8)

- % Rank (Cash flow / Enterprise Value) * 100 ≤ 40 (note that you need to use the Custom Field Editor to create this filter; adjust as needed)

- % Rank Relative Strength 4 weeks <70 (adjust as needed)

Step 2: Run this scan at each rebalance period. Weekly is recommended, but this can be done bimonthly or even monthly.

Step 3: Do further discretionary analysis on any results from steps 1 and 2 and trade accordingly.

Step 4 (position management): After running the scan at each new rebalance period, any stock you are currently in that fails to pass through the screen should be sold. Any stock you are currently in that passes through the scan should be rebalanced so that it matches the percentage of capital you are allotting to each position in this system.

CHART EXAMPLES

Cirrus Logic, Inc. (CRUS) makes high-performance cir-
cuitry for use in a variety of household and industrial applications (think high-end dimmer switches). Unfortunately,
investors soured on the company late in 2012—even as the
sell-side guys were doing their best to prop up shares by
reiterating and raising targets—which caused the stock
price to take a hit. This sent shares tumbling over the next
six months, during which time CRUS appeared a number
of times on the Carr Hybrid shorts scan (Figure 10.7).

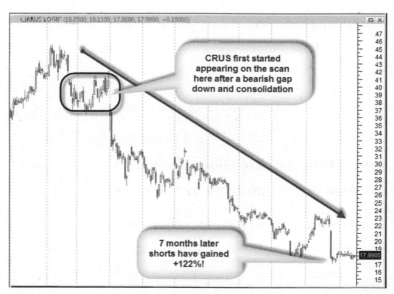

Courtesy of MetaStock

Figure 10.7 CRUS—Carr Hybrid system short.

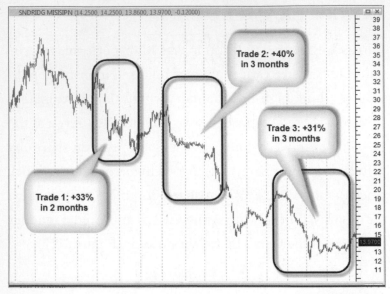

Courtesy of MetaStock

Figure 10.8   SDT—Carr Hybrid system short.

Our second short-sale example is of Sandridge Mississippian Trust (SDT), a fund that finances oil exploration. The stock was hit with a series of downgrades in mid-2012, which precipitated an 18-month selloff of shares. SDT pays a hefty dividend, so it was not one we shorted ourselves (the dividend is charged against profits), but the chart shows a picture-perfect set of short signals coming from the Carr Hybrid scan (Figure 10.8).

gamma:
TECHNICALS-
BASED TRADING
SYSTEMS

CHAPTER 11

THE BLUE SKY/BLUE SEA SYSTEM

*Sliding headfirst is the safest way to get to the next base . . .
and the fastest.*

—Pete Rose

After the years of study that I outlined in Chapters 2 and 3, I am at a place now where I can speak the dialect of "fundamental analysis" with at least a modest degree of ease. I have begun to teach webinars on how to determine a company's value and how best to tease out its potential for growth. I show my coaching clients how to use the nine-point stock grading tool I mentioned in Chapter 6, which is built around the most predictive of the fundamental metrics. My own trading is now so informed by fundamental analysis that I can no longer just "buy the price chart" as I used to do. That may still be a profitable venture, but why not increase the odds in your favor by covering all the bases? That is the thesis of this book, and the thesis informing these seven trading systems.

We come now to that part of the book that is truly my "comfort zone." In the three systems that are discussed in this and the following chapters, we are front-loading the technicals, with the fundamentals playing caboose. We will be using three time-tested, profit-proven scans that filter out stocks that we know are well positioned technically. Our next step will be to delete the stocks on those lists that are not also fundamentally sound. Once that is done, we will have a set of thoroughly vetted trading candidates. Of course, as earlier, the candidates who get our votes in the end will be those who also pass a final stage of discretionary analysis.

INTRODUCING THE SYSTEM

In this first of the three technical systems, we are starting with a technical setup that I have been using for over 10 years. The parameters have changed some over that time, becoming by turns more and then less complicated, but the foundational moves in price and volume have remained the same. In terms of winning percentage and moderation of drawdown, this is my most reliable technical setup. It is not my most profitable setup on a per diem basis (that is coming up in Chapter 13), but it does have the highest profit potential. If you are looking for a trading setup that is easy to run, with an awesome risk to reward ratio on a trade-by-trade basis, and one that lets you sleep at night, this is it. It reeks of technical soundness, fundamental safety, and good old common sense. It is an ideal system for newbie traders, and certainly should be added to any advanced trader's arsenal, if it is not already there.

We have already met both the Blue Sky Breakout and the Blue Sea Breakdown setups. These were the technical setups that we added to the Piotroski F-score system described in Chapter 7. The Blue Sky Breakout is a longs-only setup that screens out stocks making new price highs that are also showing strong volume accumulation at those new highs. In the trading system outlined here, we will also be making sure that those stocks carry the fundamental valuation and growth metrics needed to justify the new higher trading range, as well as reducing the possibility that they harbor anything that might cause a countertrend price implosion. The Blue Sea Breakdown is a shorts-only setup that screens out stocks making new price lows that are also showing strong volume distribution at those new lows. As we outline it here, we will also be putting these stocks through an additional filter that will help us avoid the possibility of a short squeeze, that is, a flurry of buying activity by short sellers as they scramble to cover their positions.

Following the technical setup just described, we will be putting our list of passing candidates through a simple but powerful two-step screening process that is designed to eliminate false breakouts. On the long side, we will define our best candidates as those that score reasonably high on either the Piotroski F-score test or William O'Neil's proprietary grading scale known as the Stock Checkup used on Investors.com. The F-score test is weighted more toward valuation (higher scores given to undervalued companies), while the Stock Checkup is weighted more toward earnings growth and relative price strength (higher scores given to companies with rising earnings and price). We are looking for both kinds of stocks; if a stock happens to pass both tests, so much the better. On the short side, we are looking for stocks that score below average on either the F-score test or the Stock Checkup grader. We will also favor candidates that are not too heavily shorted. If a stock can satisfy all three criteria, so much the better.

One potential drawback to this system is that during periods when the market is strongly trending, either up or down, you may find many more setups on the one side of this system than the other. If, for example, the market is in strong bull mode, you'll have plenty of great Blue Sky candidates to choose from, but a dearth of Blue Sea candidates and vice versa. For those who want to be 100 percent market-neutral, this presents a problem. This problem, however, has an upside. Stocks out of step with a bull market and making new lows are often great shorting candidates. This is equally true of stocks making new highs in a bear market. Fewer candidates to choose from doesn't necessarily reduce the system's profit potential; it may even enhance it.

FOR FURTHER RESEARCH ON THE SYSTEM

We discussed where to find information about the Blue Sky and Blue Sea setups in Chapter 7. They are both described in detail in my 2007 book *Trend Trading for a Living* published by McGraw-Hill. In addition, there are three videos on the web, free to the public, that describe the longs version (Blue Sky): two YouTube videos (search for "Dr. Stoxx") and an archived webinar at the Power Cycle Trading site (www.powercycletrading.com). E-mail Larry Gaines through the site if you cannot find it. Ask for the webinar by Dr. Carr on breakout stocks, and Larry will send you a link. As mentioned earlier, there are also two webinars on our site, www.DrStoxx.com, that give my fullest explanation of both the long and short applications of this setup.

As an aside, in the YouTube videos, you will hear me use the Blue Sky Breakout setup to make predictions about several stocks, including GRPN, HLX, NILE, and PCS. At the time the videos were made, those stocks had just landed on my short list for this system. As of this writing, less than three months later, all four stocks are nicely profitable. Two are trading 12 percent to 25 percent higher (HLX, NILE), one is up over 40 percent (GRPN), and a fourth was bought out at a 45 percent premium (PCS)! Fair warning: The two YouTube videos are, for the most part, promos for the Dr. Stoxx Trend Trading Toolkit. If you can get past the diversions that go with that task, you will find some nice visuals showing you what this setup looks like on the charts and how to go about selecting the best candidates among those that pass through the filter.

In addition to the technical setup, we will be using two of the fundamental grading tools on the longs side of the system. Both of these have been previously discussed:

Dr. Joseph Piotroski's F-score and the Stock Checkup grader on Investors.com, which is based in part on the CAN-SLIM strategy of William O'Neil. I refer you to Chapter 7 for further information about Dr. Piotroski's F-score ranking system and to Chapter 9 for the theory behind William O'Neil's Stock Checkup tool.

TRADING THE BLUE SKY/BLUE SEA SYSTEM

Let's get down to work. Here are the tools needed to trade this system:

- (option 1): Use MetaStock's Dr. Stoxx Trend Trading Toolkit (TTTK) if you do not want to program in your own scan. You will find both the long and short version of this system preprogrammed into the TTTK add-on. You also can program MetaStock's technical scanner (Explorer) yourself, but it does require familiarity with standard coding language.
- (option 2): Use StockCharts or another technical screening tool to search for stocks making the required Blue Sky or Blue Sea setup. You will need to write the parameters into the scanning software yourself, but the setup is a simple one. Stockcharts.com is especially user friendly.
- You will also need to bookmark the following websites. We will be using these to perform the

fundamental filters on whatever stocks pass our technical scan.

- ○ VectorGrader's Piotroski F-score grading tool (free) at www.vectorgrader.com/ stockrank
- ○ Investors.com Stock Checkup grading tool (requires subscription: $14/month)

RUNNING THE LONGS VERSION (BLUE SKY BREAKOUT)

Step 1 (MetaStock option): Open MetaStock and go to the Power Console. Click the Explorer. Select TTTK: Long Blue Sky Breakout and then click Next. From the Select List(s) To Explore table, highlight U.S. Optionable Stocks (see Figure 11.1) or any other list you wish to scan. Click Next and then click Start Exploration. Make a watch list of charts for all passing stocks.

Step 1 (StockCharts option): Create the Blue Sky Breakout scan in StockChart's advanced scanning tool. See step 2 for a general description of what you should be scanning for. For a more detailed description of the Blue Sky Breakout setup, see my *Trend Trading for a Living*, pp. 176–180. Run the scan and make a watch list of charts for all passing stocks.

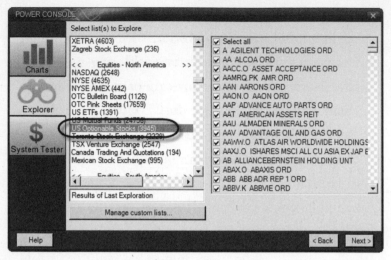

Figure 11.1   Starting Blue Sky Explorer in MetaStock.

Step 2: Sometimes, charts will pass through this scan that
are not valid "Blue Sky Breakout" setups. Moreover,
not all valid "Blue Sky" setups have the same upside
potential. Therefore, we want to strengthen our
short list of stocks by deleting any chart that fails to
show the following:

• A new 40-day (2-month) price high

• A new 40-day on-balance volume (OBV) high

• Plenty of "blue sky" between breakout price and
the nearest point of resistance, which could be a
trendline drawn over recent pivot highs, a horizontal
line drawn over price highs more than two months
ago, or the 200sma (simple moving average)

Step 3: Take any stocks that remain from step 2 and enter each symbol into VectorGrader's Piotroski rating tool (www.vectorgrader.com/stockRank). Keep on the list any stock that scores a 5 or higher. The higher the number, the better. For any stock that scores a 4 or less, go on to step 4.

Step 4: Take any stock that failed the Piotroski test from step 3 and enter the symbol into Investors.com's Stock Checkup feature (www.research.investors.com/stock-checkup). Keep on the list any stock that scores a 60 or higher out of 100. The higher the number, the better.

Step 5: Do further discretionary analysis on any results from steps 1 through 4 and trade accordingly.

Step 6 (position management): The "Blue Sky Breakout" system, like most of the systems in this book, does not require the use of stop-losses. Instead, you will let the system take you out of the trade. At each new rebalancing period, for any open position, check its Piotroski F-score, if that is what validated the setup, or the Investors.com Stock Checkup score, if that is what validated the setup. Any open position that falls below a Piotroski F-score of 5 or a Stock Checkup score of 60 should be closed and replaced with a new position that passes steps 1 through 5.

CHART EXAMPLES

Paychex, Inc. (PAYX) is an online resources company that helps businesses manage payroll, taxes, human resources, and a variety of accounting-related tasks. While only scoring a 4 on the Piotroski F-score rank, it regularly shows a Stock Checkup score in the 80s. After hitting a price low during the market crash of 2009, shares began to rebound before they consolidated around the $27 level late in 2011. The chart in Figure 11.2 shows a textbook "Blue Sky Breakout" as shares rally off their lows to print a new two-month high. OBV had already run to new highs, confirming that there was sufficient volume behind the move. Six months later, PAYX was trading near $34 for a 23 percent return (see Figure 11.2). Shares continued

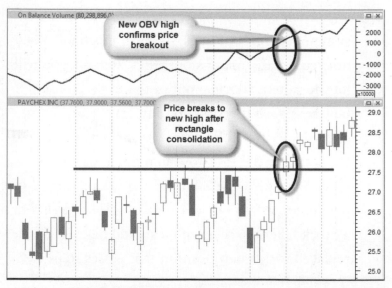

Courtesy of MetaStock

Figure 11.2   PAYX—Blue Sky Breakout long.

higher into 2013, hitting a high of $41.24, or over +50 percent, as of this writing.

Carriage Services, Inc. (CSV) is a "death care company"—or so Carriage styles itself—that shelters167 funeral homes and 33 cemeteries under its umbrella. Its growth model is all about convincing the mom-and-pop morticians to join the Carriage family. Carriage is to the funeral industry what Walmart is to the local five and dime. It has been a raging success if their stock price is any indication. Carriage is one of those rare companies that regularly scores well in both the Piotroski F-score (6+) and the Stock Checkup (90+). Though in recent times the company has had some trouble with debt financing issues, the stock was on fire in late 2012 through the first quarter

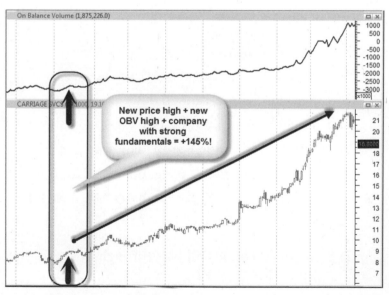

Courtesy of MetaStock

Figure 11.3   CSV—Blue Sky Breakout long.

of 2013. Shares hit their first "Blue Sky Breakout" signal in mid-August 2012, at a price of $8.85. Shares topped out on April 1, 2013, at $21.74, for a potential gain of +145 percent in about seven months (see Figure 11.3)!

RUNNING THE SHORTS VERSION (BLUE SEA BREAKDOWN)

Step 1 (MetaStock option): Open MetaStock and go to the Power Console. Click the Explorer. Select TTTK: Short Blue Sea Breakdown, then click Next. From the Select List(s) To Explore table, highlight U.S. Optionable Stocks (see Figure 11.1) or any other list you wish to scan. Click Next and then click Start Exploration. Make a watch list of charts for all passing stocks.

Step 1 (StockCharts option): Create the Blue Sea Breakdown scan in StockChart's advanced scanning tool. See step 2 for a general description of what you should be scanning for. For a more detailed description of the Blue Sea Breakdown setup, see my *Trend Trading for a Living*, pp. 208–213. Run the scan and make a watch list of charts for all passing stocks.

Step 2: Sometimes, charts will pass through this scan that are not valid Blue Sea Breakdown setups, Moreover, not all valid Blue Sea setups have the same downside potential. Therefore, we want to strengthen our short list of stocks by deleting any chart that fails to show the following:

- A new 40-day (2-month) price low

- A new 40-day OBV low

- Plenty of "blue sea" between breakout price and the nearest point of support, which could be a trendline drawn under recent pivot lows, a horizontal line drawn under price lows more than two months ago, or the 200sma

Step 3: Take any stocks that remain from step 2 and enter each symbol into VectorGrader's Piotroski rating tool (www.vectorgrader.com/stockRank). Keep on the list any stock that scores a 5 or lower. The lower the number, the better. For any stock that scores a 6 or more, go on to step 4.

Step 4: Take any stock that failed the Piotroski test from step 3 and enter the symbol into Investors.com's Stock Checkup feature (www.research.investors.com/stock-checkup). Keep on the list any stock that scores a 40 or lower out of 100. The lower the number, the better.

Step 5: For any stocks still on your watch list, go to www.Finviz.com (see Chapter 4) and input the symbols one by one. Check the short float figure. Short float is the percentage of the float—the number of shares available for trading—that are held in short positions. The higher the short float, the more shares have to be bought back by short sellers to cover their positions. If the stock starts to rise suddenly, short sellers will move quickly to cover their positions, causing a sudden drop in supply and a sharp rise in price. This is called a "short squeeze." A stock with a high short float is one that can "squeeze" higher much faster than one with a lower short float. We will, therefore, eliminate any stock that has a short float over 20 percent. The lower the number, the better.

Step 6: Do further discretionary analysis on any results from steps 1 through 5 and trade accordingly.

Step 7 *(position management):* The Blue Sea Breakdown system, like most of the systems in this book, does not require the use of stop-losses. Instead, you will let the system take you out of the trade. At each new rebalancing period, for any open positions, check their Piotroski F-score, if that is what validated the setup, or the Investors.com Stock Checkup score, if that is what validated the setup. Any stock whose Piotroski score rises above 5 or whose Stock Checkup number rises above 40 needs to be closed and replaced with a new position that passes steps 1 through 5.

CHART EXAMPLES

LG Display Company, Ltd. (LGL), a division of LG Electronics out of South Korea, is a maker of all things high-def. I used a 27"LG monitor for a while—paid close to $800 for it—and it worked just fine until rainbows started appearing on it. I like rainbows, just not on my monitor when I'm trading. No one would repair it. Today, the same monitor sells for under $300 at Sam's Club. We also own an LG fridge, their largest model. Five years later, it needed to be replaced. Am I a fan of the company? Hardly. So when LGL appeared on the Blue Sea Breakdown scan in May 2011, I was only too happy to short a few shares. The stock hit a low under $8 before bouncing back up (see Figure 11.4).

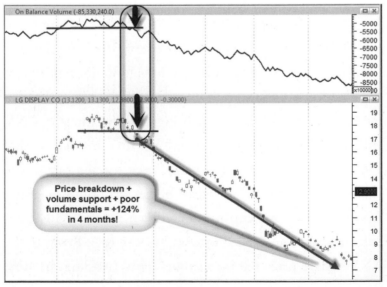

Courtesy of MetaStock

Figure 11.4   LGL—Blue Sea Breakdown short.

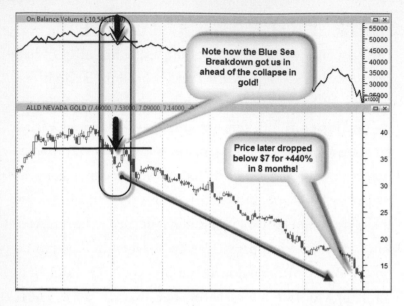

Courtesy of MetaStock

Figure 11.5   ANV—Blue Sea Breakdown short.

Allied Nevada Gold Corp. (ANV) is a mining and exploration company with some pretty lousy fundamentals. On paper, its growth projections look impressive and its valuation numbers are not horrible, but with gold prices falling off a cliff as they have been in recent months, ANV will likely fall short of expectations. Investors knew that back in October 2012, after the stock topped out in the low 40s. Sentiment for shares began dropping, pushing ANV's Stock Checkup number down into the 30s (it is currently at 9) and the Piotroski F-score to 4. From there, ANV's share price fell into single digits, handing the Blue Sea Breakdown shorts a nice gain of +440 percent on a buy-to-cover basis (see Figure 11.5).

CHAPTER 12

THE PULLBACK/RELIEF RALLY SYSTEM

The chance of bread falling with the buttered side down is directly proportional to the cost of the carpet.

—Anonymous

We come now to what I call my "bread and butter" system. It has been, over the span of my trading career, my most used system and, for that reason, the system that has most contributed to my family's income (hence, the nickname). It is the "old faithful" of trading systems. It can be traded on the monthly chart or the one-minute chart; on stocks, indexes, forex, and commodities. It works in bull markets, bear markets, and everything in between. It is so rooted in common sense, so reasonably constructed, that it cannot fail to produce profits no matter how many people latch on to it.

I cannot lay claim to the technical filter that lies at the basis of this system. That goes to a professional trader whose name I won't mention here. Shortly after he taught me this system, he was arrested. I'm not sure why, but I'd rather not draw any further attention to his plight. Regardless, his was the first technical system I learned, and from that time on, I've been hooked on technical analysis. While his ethics may have been questionable, the technical system he created is unquestionably both elegant and effective.

Like the Blue Sky/Blue Sea system we just looked at, the Pullback/Relief Rally system has the technical analysis part of it front-loaded, with the fundamental analysis part added on as a final set of filters. The technical setup is a simple one: Buy stocks in an uptrend that have pulled back enough to become technically oversold, and short stocks in a downtrend that have rallied enough to become technically overbought. To this simple setup we will add a set of fundamental filters that measure stocks for both valuation and growth. For our longs (the Pullback setup), we want stocks that are undervalued and showing signs of growing sales and earnings. For our shorts (the Relief Rally setup), we want stocks that are overvalued and showing signs of sluggish growth.

INTRODUCING THE SYSTEM

The Pullback/Relief Rally system is a long-short system that, in a nutshell, seeks to buy financially stable companies that are oversold and trading at support and to short financially unstable companies that are overbought and trading at resistance. The technical setup requires the use of three different indicators: simple moving averages, trendlines, and the stochastics oscillator. We use the moving averages to determine both the direction and the strength of the trend;

we use trendlines to make sure the pullback is still above support and the relief rally still below resistance; we use stochastics to detect both oversold and overbought levels; and we use candlesticks to signal our entry into each position (green or doji—a candlestick whose close is very near the open—for the pullback; red or doji for the relief rally).

The Pullback/Relief Rally system is the only system in the book that uses a stop-loss. On each new position entered, you will set a stop-loss as dictated by the individual chart, and at each new rebalance period, you will adjust the stop-loss accordingly if the position is trading at a new high-water mark. Target exit orders can also be used with this system if you desire greater turnover of positions. In the long run, however, they tend to reduce the profit potential of the system, so the recommended approach is to let the stop-loss take you out of the trade.

FOR FURTHER RESEARCH ON THE SYSTEM

The best resource for further research on the Pullback and Relief Rally technical setups is my book *Trend Trading for a Living* (McGraw-Hill, 2007), pp. 158–164 and 194–198, respectively, where the specific parameters and how to scan for them are discussed. I also offer two webinars through our site www.DrStoxx.com that give a more detailed study of both the long and short versions of the setup used in this system. In addition to my material, you will find a number of very good blog posts and You-Tube videos on the subject. Simply search for "trading pullbacks" and you will come up with plenty of resources.

You may also be interested in learning more about the stochastics oscillator. The word itself comes from the Greek *stochos*, which means "aim" or "target," and *stochastikos*, which means "aim at a target." The idea behind stochastics is that stock prices over time (think of them as arrows shot from a bow) tend to fall into a normative pattern (arrows embedded around the bull's-eye), but that now and then you get a few outliers. If those outliers are near the top of the pattern, the stochastics indicator will rise from a baseline of 50 toward the maximum value of 100. If the outliers are nearer the bottom of the pattern, the stochastics indicator falls from its baseline toward the minimum value of 0. The further the price is outside the pattern, either above or below, the sharper the rise or fall of stochastics will be. Once stochastics reaches a level considered extreme, the stock in question is considered to be either oversold or overbought.

The stochastic oscillator was one of the first technical indicators discovered. George Lane is largely credited as its inventor, but the real story involves others as well. The origins of the indicator date back to the 1950s, when the first technical analysts worked with pencils and rulers, hand-drawn charts, and lots of longhand mathematical formulas. For an interesting article on this piece of financial history, see George Lane, "Lane's Stochastics," in *Technical*

Analysis of Stocks and Commodities (May/June 1984): vol. 2, pp. 87–90. Also recommended is a nice summary article of the development of the indicator on a website called Knowledge Base (www.knowledgebase.mta.org) entitled "The Origins of the Stochastics Oscillator" by George Schade, CMT.

TRADING THE PULLBACK/RELIEF RALLY SYSTEM

Let's get down to work. Here are the tools needed to trade this system:

- (option 1): Use MetaStock's Dr. Stoxx Trend Trading Toolkit (TTTK) if you do not want to program in your own scan. You will find both the long and short version of this system preprogrammed into the TTTK add-on. You also can program MetaStock's technical scanner (Explorer) yourself, but it does require familiarity with standard coding language.
- (option 2): Use StockCharts or another technical screening tool to search for stocks making the required Pullback and Relief Rally setups. You will need to write the parameters into the scanning software yourself, but the setup is a simple one. StockCharts's scanning tool is especially user-friendly.

- You will also need to bookmark www.Finviz.com. We will use this site to run our fundamental filters on those stocks that pass through the technical setup scan.

RUNNING THE LONGS VERSION (PULLBACK)

Step 1 (MetaStock option): Open MetaStock and go to the Power Console. Click the Explorer. Select TTTK: Long Pullback and then click Next. From the Select List(s) To Explore table, highlight U.S. Optionable Stocks or any other list you wish to scan. Click Next and then click Start Exploration. Make a watch list of charts for all passing stocks. In a bullish market, you should be getting 10 to 20 stocks passing this screen, or more, depending on how many lists you are scanning. On a strong down-market day, or in a bear market, you may only get a handful of setups, if any.

Step 1 (StockCharts option): Create the Pullback scan in StockChart's advanced scanning tool. The general parameters of the Pullback scan are as follows:

- The 20sma >50sma

- The 50sma is generally in rising mode

- Stochastics <25 (adjust down as needed)

- Close >50sma

- Enter on first green candle or doji

Run the scan and make a watch list of charts for all passing stocks.

Step 2: It is rare for a chart to pass through this scan that is not a valid Pullback setup. Still, not all valid Pullback setups have the same upside potential. Therefore, we want to strengthen our short list of stocks by deleting any chart that fails to show the following:

- The 50sma is clearly rising over at least the past 10 trading days.

- The close is above the 50sma; a close above the 20sma is better.

- The close is above the support trendline drawn under the bottoms of recent pivot lows.

As an example of what is meant by this last requirement, consider the chart (Figure 12.1) of Educational Services, Inc. (ESI). ESI shows a nice recovery uptrend with one sideways consolidation (late April to early May) and one shallow pullback to the 20sma (late May). The selloff in mid-June is in every respect a valid Pullback setup according to our technical scan. The 20sma is above the 50sma, both moving averages are rising, price has closed on a green candle above the 50sma, and stochastics is

ESI ITT Educational Services Inc. NYSE   @ StockCharts.com
20-Jun-2013   Op 24.50 Hi 25.52 Lo 24.35 Cl 24.93 Vol 376.0K Chg +0.18 (+0.73%)

Support trendline with break of support

Courtesy of StockCharts

Figure 12.1   ESI—violation of a Pullback setup.

oversold. However, the price has broken below the support trendline drawn under the pivot lows of the trend. That support line will now act as resistance, thereby greatly reducing the profit potential of this setup. Therefore, we would pass on ESI and look at other charts on our list of passing candidates.

Step 3: Take any stocks that remain from step 2 and enter each symbol into www.Finviz.com. We will use Finviz to do our fundamental analysis as we whittle those stocks with valid Pullback setups down to only the very best candidates, technically and fundamentally. In this step, we are going to input each symbol and check two columns of data

in Finviz: the valuation column and the growth
column. We cannot expect perfect bullishness
in each of these categories. But our best long
candidates will, generally speaking, be those
showing strength in one without weakness in the
other, or (on the rare occasion) strength in both.

In the valuation column, we want to see as many
of the following as possible:

- Forward P/E < Current P/E

- P/S (price-to-sales) <2.0 (the lower the better)

- P/B (price to book) <2.5 (the lower the better)

- P/FCF (price to free cash flow) <30 (the lower the
  better)

- Debt/Eq (debt to equity) <0.3 (the lower the
  better)

In the growth column, we want to see as many
of the following as possible:

- EPS growth this year >20 percent (the higher the
  better)

- EPS growth next year = positive (the higher the
  better)
- EPS estimate for next quarter = positive (the
  higher the better)

- EPS growth next five years = positive (the higher
  the better)

- Sales growth Q/Q (this quarter vs. last quarter) > 10 percent (the higher the better)

- ESP growth Q/Q (this quarter vs. last quarter) > 10 percent (the higher the better)

The threshold values I have listed here are the ones I use; there is nothing magic about them. They are commonsense values collated from my research. You can adjust them as you see fit. I also support your overlooking what could otherwise be a problematic number because the company has what you consider to be a bullish catalyst and you think the risk is worth taking. That is the kind of discretionary trading we've been advocating in this book. But all things being equal, the guidelines listed here should help you sort out the best candidates from a list of valid Pullback setups.

As an example of how step 3 works in practice, see the following chart of Himax Technologies, Inc. (HIMX), a Taiwanese semiconductor maker with awesome fundamentals and strong price movement to match (Figure 12.2). During an uptrend in the first half of 2013, HIMX gave two clear Pullback entry signals: one in mid-March after HIMX printed a bullish engulfing candle, and one in late April on a doji candle. Both entries were profitable, showing potential one-month gains of 52 percent and 45 percent, respectively. But before we could enter HIMX, we had to check its fundamentals.

Figure 12.2   HIMX—chart with two Pullback setup signals.

As we moved to step 3 in our selection process and plugged HIMX into Finviz, we came up with the following fundamental analysis (see Figure 12.3). In every case, HIMX passed our requirements, with a very rare 5 out of 5 score for valuation and 6 out of 6 score for growth. This is highly unusual because companies that are undervalued are not often known for growing earnings at a triple-digit rate. The opposite is also true, that strong growth companies usually force investors to pay a premium for shares. The fact that HIMX is in the top rank for both value and growth made it a great candidate for the Pullback system. It is one of about 40 stocks that I

P/E	17.43	EPS (ttm)	0.30
Forward P/E	8.39	EPS next Y	0.62
PEG	0.70	EPS next Q	0.11
P/S	1.21	EPS this Y	400.00%
P/B	2.09	EPS next Y	47.28%
P/C	6.43	EPS next 5Y	25.00%
P/FCF	25.58	EPS past 5Y	-12.00%
Quick Ratio	1.90	Sales past 5Y	-4.30%
Current Ratio	2.30	Sales Q/Q	12.60%
Debt/Eq	0.17	EPS Q/Q	300.00%
LT Debt/Eq	0.00	Earnings	May 07 BMO
SMA20	-21.53%	SMA50	-20.05%

Courtesy of Finviz.com

Figure 12.3   HIMX—profile of a stock with solid fundamentals.

keep in a watch list of top performers and on which
I regularly apply the Pullback Expert Advisor from
the MetaStock Trend Trading Toolkit in order to be
alerted in real time whenever a new setup forms.

Step 4: Do further discretionary analysis on any results
from steps 1 through 3 and trade accordingly.

Step 5 (position management): As said, the Pullback/
Relief Rally system is the one system in this book
that requires the use of stop-losses. I suggest putting
a trailing stop-loss on all Pullback system positions.
For a detailed discussion of how to set stop-losses, I
refer you to Chapter 11 of *Trend Trading for a Living*.
I myself use three different types of stop-losses on
Pullback positions, depending on the trade:

• *Percentage stop-loss:* Subtract a percentage from
your entry price (normally 8 percent to 12 percent)

and set your stop-loss at that price. Note that more volatile stocks will require a wider percentage stop-loss. The greater risk taken on, however, is compensated for by the greater profit potential.

- *Chart support stop-loss* (my preferred method): From the chart I determine a likely area of support should the position move against me. This usually comes in the form of a recent pivot low, a major moving average, an unfilled gap, a support trendline, a lower Bollinger Band, or perhaps a place of former resistance. I set the stop-loss just under that price area.

- *Average true range stop-loss:* For those who prefer something more mechanical, you can check the average true range (ATR) value for the stock on the day of your entry. ATR refers to the average amount of price movement a stock makes from close to close over a certain number of days (14 is the default periodicity and works fine). Higher-priced stocks like AAPL (10) or GOOG (15) will have ATR values in the double digits. Lower-priced stocks like HIMX (0.40) will have smaller values. A stop-loss can be set at 3 (ATR) below your entry price. This gives you three typical days of selling before your stop gets hit. A larger multiple can be used, but then that also takes on greater risk.

Stop-losses on all Pullback positions should be moved up at each rebalance period if they have moved favorably since the last rebalance and are hitting a new high since entry. You can also put on a target exit order if you wish. Target exits can be set above your entry price using any of the stop-loss systems described earlier, only in reverse. Using both stop-losses and target exit orders will ensure a more active management of this system, and some traders prefer that. Others prefer to trade without setting a limit on profits, thus letting the stop-loss take them out of the trade. In the long run, trading without target exit orders will generate greater profit per position, but it can mean holding on to winning trades for long periods of time, thus diminishing the overall profit potential of the system. In short, using a target exit is a matter of balancing the costs of more active portfolio management against the costs of longer holding periods.

Note that users of MetaStock's Dr. Stoxx Trend Trading Toolkit can let the Expert Advisor select the stop-loss and target exit prices for them. For every new Pullback setup signal, an entry price and two values for stop-losses and target exit prices are automatically determined.

CHART EXAMPLE

The following is an excellent example of how the discretionary part of working a mechanical system like this can greatly increase your profits. Pharmacyclics, Inc. (PCYC) is a biopharmaceutical company that both develops and manufactures drugs that treat cancer, autoimmune diseases, and various conditions associated with aging. As a stock, PCYC has been on every active trader's "must watch" list due to its strong directional price momentum. In the second half of 2012 through the first quarter of 2013, PCYC triggered four Pullback buy signals (see Figure 12.4). Each signal proved profitable.

On the fundamentals side of the trade, PCYC has some good stuff going for it. As of this writing, the company

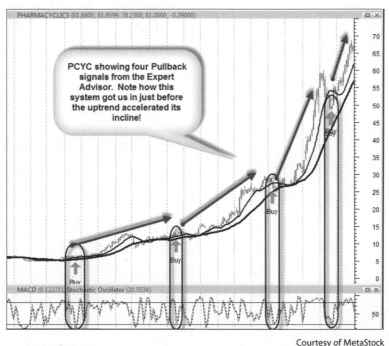

Courtesy of MetaStock

Figure 12.4   PCYC—four Pullback signals on MetaStock's Trend Trading Toolkit.

sports a triple-digit earnings per share (EPS) growth rate over the previous year and a 43 percent projected rate over the next five years. Sales are up 47 percent quarter on quarter. Those numbers in themselves are enough to push the stock from a "maybe" to a "likely" candidate. On the valuation side, however—like most companies in the biopharm industry—PCYC has issues. The company is all about growth. A Graham-Buffett stock this one is not! Discretionary traders, however, encouraged by the growth numbers, were able to drill down beyond the price multiples to see that the company had a number of important catalysts on the horizon. These included results from Phase II and Phase III trials and a new Food and Drug (FDA) designation for one of the drugs in its pipeline. In addition, the stock was being closely followed by large investment banks, and several mega-hedge funds were getting on board.

RUNNING THE SHORTS VERSION (RELIEF RALLY)

Step 1 (MetaStock option): Open MetaStock and go to the Power Console. Click the Explorer. Select TTTK: Short Relief Rally and then click Next. From the Select List(s) To Explore table, highlight U.S. Optionable Stocks or any other list you wish to scan. Click Next and then click Start Exploration. Make a watch list of charts for all passing stocks. In a bearish market, you should be getting 10 to

20 stocks passing this screen, or more, depending on how many lists you are scanning. On a strong up-market day, or in a bull market, you may only get a handful of setups, if any.

*Step 1 (**StockCharts option**):* Create the Relief Rally scan in StockChart's advanced scanning tool. The general parameters of the Relief Rally scan are as follows:

- The 20sma <50sma

- The 50sma is generally in falling mode

- Stochastics >75 (adjust up as needed)

- Close <50sma

- Enter on first red candle or doji

Run the scan and make a watch list of charts for all passing stocks.

Step 2: It is rare for a chart to pass through this scan that is not a valid Relief Rally setup. Still, not all valid Relief Rally setups have the same downside potential. Therefore, we want to strengthen our short list of stocks by deleting any chart that fails to show the following:

- The 50sma has been clearly trending down for at least the past 10 trading days.

- The close is below the 50sma; a close below the 20sma is better.

- The close is below the resistance trendline drawn over the tops of recent pivot highs.

As an example of what is meant by this last requirement, take a look at the following chart featuring LinkedIn Corporation (LNKD), the social media site for job seekers and business networkers. In June 2013, LNKD gave two Relief Rally signals (see Figure 12.5). Signal 1 should have been entered because it triggered entry under the resistance trendline set by the two previous pivot highs. Signal 2, however, should not have been taken

Courtesy of MetaStock

Figure 12.5   LNKD—two Relief Rally signals.

because it triggered above the resistance trendline. Moreover, though it is not clearly visible from this chart, the 50sma is falling on the date of Signal 1 relative to the previous week's trading, but is rising by the time we get to Signal 2, thus nullifying it as a valid signal. In fact, following the invalid Signal 2, LNKD has rallied as of this writing to a pivot high of 257. But over the long run, you will put the odds in your favor by keeping only to shorts below the resistance trendline.

Step 3: Take any stocks that remain from step 2 and enter each symbol into www.Finviz.com. We will use Finviz to do our fundamental analysis as we whittle those stocks with valid Relief Rally setups down to only the very best candidates, technically and fundamentally. We will be using the same data columns we used for the Pullback setup, only our threshold values have changed.

In the valuation column, we want to see as many of the following as possible:

- Forward P/E > Current P/E

- P/S (price-to-sales) >2.0 (the higher the better)

- P/B (price to book) >2.5 (the higher the better)

- P/FCF (price to free cash flow) >30 (the higher the better)

- Debt/Eq (debt to equity) >0.3

In the growth column, we want to see as many of the following as possible:

- EPS growth this year <20 percent (the lower the better)

- EPS growth next year = negative (the lower the better)

- EPS estimate for next quarter = negative (the lower the better)

- EPS growth next five years = negative (the lower the better)

- Sales growth Q/Q (this quarter vs. last quarter) <10 percent (the lower the better)

- ESP growth Q/Q (this quarter vs. last quarter) <10 percent (the lower the better)

Feel free to adjust my suggested threshold values as you see fit. I also support your overlooking what could otherwise be a very bullish number because the company has what you consider to be a bearish catalyst on the horizon and you think the risk is worth taking. That is the kind of discretionary trading we've been advocating in this book. But all things being equal, the guidelines listed here should help you sort out the best candidates from a list of valid Relief Rally setups.

Figure 12.6   WNR—chart with two Relief Rally signals.

As an example of how step 3 works in practice, see the chart featuring Western Refining, Inc. (WNR), an oil refiner and marketer (Figure 12.6). During an extended pullback in the first half of 2013, WNR gave two clear Relief Rally entry signals, both in mid-May. Both entries were profitable, showing potential one-month gains of 10 percent and 23 percent, respectively, with the second trade still open. But before we could enter WNR, however, we had to check its fundamentals.

As we moved to step 3 in our selection process and plugged WNR into Finviz, we took note of

the following fundamental data. WNR shows some
bullishness in terms of its valuation, sporting very low
P/S and P/FCF ratios, and its earnings growth this
fiscal year is exceptional. Four key negatives stand
out, however, which moved WNR to our shortlist
of viable candidates: a forward P/E greater than the
current figure, a projected contraction of growth next
year, a weak quarter-on-quarter sales figure, and high
debt-to-equity ratios (see Figure 12.7).

P/E	5.14	EPS (ttm)	5.40
Forward P/E	7.33	EPS next Y	3.79
PEG	0.67	EPS next Q	1.35
P/S	0.26	EPS this Y	176.90%
P/B	2.62	EPS next Y	-8.44%
P/C	9.69	EPS next 5Y	7.70%
P/FCF	6.98	EPS past 5Y	2.50%
Quick Ratio	1.20	Sales past 5Y	5.40%
Current Ratio	1.70	Sales Q/Q	-6.50%
Debt/Eq	0.79	EPS Q/Q	204.50%
LT Debt/Eq	0.61	Earnings	May 02 BMO
SMA20	-14.33%	SMA50	-14.33%

Courtesy of Finviz.com

Figure 12.7   WNR—profile of a stock with weak fundamentals.

Step 4: Do further discretionary analysis on any results
from steps 1 through 3 and trade accordingly.

Step 5 (position management): The Pullback/Relief
Rally system is the one system in this book that
requires the use of stop-losses. You will want to
put a trailing stop-loss on all Relief Rally system
positions. These can be determined using one

of the three methods mentioned in step 5 of the
Pullback setup, only the stop-loss would be placed
above your entry price instead of below it. Target
exit orders placed below the entry price may also
be used by traders desiring greater turnover in
positions. As noted earlier, users of MetaStock's
Dr. Stoxx Trend Trading Toolkit can have
their stop-losses and target exits automatically
determined for each new Relief Rally signal.

CHART EXAMPLE

Arcelor Mittal, SA (MT) was one of our few solid gainers
on the short side in the first half of 2013, an unusually bullish period. Along with GOL (a big winner) and MS (so far,
a loser), MT was one of our "three best companies to short
in 2013" bulletin, which went out on January 1, 2013. The
next day, MT opened at $17.64. As of this writing, MT has
traded as low as $10.83. During that period, the Expert
Advisor from the TTTK alerted us to two nice Relief Rally
setups. The first signal showed strong profit potential. The
second signal would not have been taken since it triggered
above what was then the resistance trendline. This saved us
from holding through three weeks of sideways price action
(see Figure 12.8).

On the fundamentals side, MT shows a number of
key weaknesses. It has a problematic debt-to-equity ratio, a

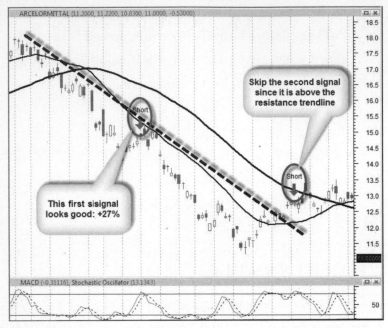

Courtesy of MetaStock

Figure 12.8 MT—chart with two Relief Rally signals.

fall in EPS this year of a whopping 368 percent, and nega-tive sales growth quarter on quarter. Having done previous due diligence on the company for our bulletin, it was easy to put this one on the list of candidates to short.

CHAPTER 13

THE MEAN REVERSION SYSTEM

Success is how high you bounce when you hit bottom.

—George S. Patton

We have now arrived at the final trading system in the book. You could say that I have saved the best for last: This is both my favorite trading system and my most profitable. It is also the riskiest (which I know will only endear it to some of you all the more!), and when not done properly, it can be the most frustrating, gray-hair-causing trading system man has ever invented.

With that said, the Mean Reversion system has impeccable credentials. Versions of it are used by some of the best-known and most successful technical traders and analysts. It has been tested and back-tested every way imaginable. It has proved itself profitable in all market conditions and on all security types and derivatives. When the Mean Reversion system is done properly, there is no more exciting, more profitable, and yet more (nearly) mechanical trading system out there.

The key thesis of the Mean Reversion system is that stocks that trade a statistically significant distance in price away from their mean (as measured in our case by a moving average) tend, once a point of equilibrium is reached, to revert to that mean in short order. What we are adding to this thesis is that when we limit stocks that have traveled far from their mean to only those showing strong growth potential (for longs) or the lack thereof (for shorts), we improve our odds significantly of a successful reversion. This reversion is what we trade.

INTRODUCING THE SYSTEM

Richard Donchian (1905–1993) is a name every trader should know. Among other things, Donchian is the founding father of the managed futures industry, inventor of the mutual fund, and pioneer of a trading style now called "trend following." He is more widely known among market technicians, however, for the development of a technical tool called the Donchian Price Channel. The Donchian Channel is deceptively simple: It draws horizontal lines over the highest high and under the lowest low of the last N periods. The idea is that as long as price trades within the channel created by the two lines, it is trading within a range. Once it breaks above or below the channel, the channel lines are raised or lowered accordingly. Rising lines mean a stock is making new highs and is in a bullish trend. Falling lines mean a bearish trend. Narrowing lines indicate a tightly coiled market ripe for breakout, either up or down. Widening lines suggest either increasing volatility or strong trending movement (see Figure 13.1).

Figure 13.1 SPY with Donchian Price Channel (20) overlay.

In his 1960 book *How to Make Money in Commodities* (published by Keltner Statistical Service), Charles Keltner took the Donchian Channel a step further. Instead of using highs and lows in price to determine channel values, he used a 20-period exponential moving average (EMA) to which was added twice the value of the 10-period ATR (average true range). Because EMAs and ATRs change every trading day, the Keltner Channel tool was more dynamic than the Donchian Channel and thus more responsive to small changes in price directionality. However, because ATR is less variable than price highs and lows, the bands tended to stay roughly the same distance from each other. Thus, the Keltner Channel renders a more recognizable trending pattern than Donchian's tool (see Figure 13.2).

The trading channel concept came into its maturity with John Bollinger (b. 1950), a market technician, financial analyst, and, pertinently, one of the pioneers in the

Figure 13.2   SPY with Keltner Channel (20, 2, 10) overlay.

synthesis of technical and fundamental analysis. Bollinger swapped out Keltner's ATR and exponential moving average for standard deviation (2.0) and the 20-period simple moving average. With this revision, Bollinger created trading bands that not only envelop most of the price action over time, but also are dynamic enough to show changes in both volatility and directionality (see Figure 13.3).

The Mean Reversion system we teach in this book uses Bollinger Bands as its primary technical tool. On the longs side of the system, we are looking for stocks that have traded outside of the lower Bollinger Band, but only after trading down to that level over several trading days (thus ruling out stocks that gap outside the lower band on bad news) and that are trading significantly under their "mean" (the 20sma). Our fundamental filter will be applied to these passing candidates; we will favor those stocks that show fundamental strength in terms of earnings growth (variously

Figure 13.3   SPY with Bollinger Bands (20, 2.0) overlay.

understood), a low debt to equity ratio, and institutional and/or insider buying.

On the shorts side of the system, we are looking for stocks that have traded outside of the upper Bollinger Band, but only after trading up to that level over several trading days (thus ruling out stocks that gap outside the upper band on good news) and that are trading significantly above their "mean." Our fundamental filter will then be used to select only those passing candidates that show fundamental weakness in terms of earnings deceleration and institutional and/or insider selling.

It would not be stretching the truth to say that for many years now I have been obsessed with Mean Reversion (MR) systems. The essence of the MR system is contrarian, which fits my trading profile perfectly. I'll throw in with the "buy high, sell higher" crowd when I need to; but as far as I'm concerned, the real fun happens when the "buy fear, sell greed" thesis is working. This can get you into trouble, of course, if you are not careful. You can go broke pretty quickly trying to catch the proverbial "falling knife" or short the runaway "freight train." There are ways to do it safely and profitably, however, and this system is one such way.

I have been working on an MR system for over 12 years. An early predecessor of the setup in this book was a very basic, longs-only Bollinger Band system I used to teach in my swing trading seminars called "Outside/Inside." It screened for S&P 500 stocks that had traded below the lower Bollinger Band (the "Outside" part) on strong volume and then had closed back within the lower band (the "Inside" part) on the next trading day. Money management involved using a percentage trailing stop and a percentage target exit with a 1.5 to 1 profit ratio. It proved profitable, but the system would suffer through some pretty nasty drawdowns during bear market periods.

Over the years I continued to work on the system. I studied John Bollinger's main book, *Bollinger on Bollinger Bands* (McGraw Hill, 2001), along with his webinar presentations. From Bollinger I learned a number of cool things one can do with the bands he invented—like establish certain price patterns—not the least of which was his "%B" metric: a measurement of how far price is from either of the two bands. I also purchased a number of different Bollinger Band systems from a technical analyst named Larry Conners, developer of the ConnersRSI indicator. Conners' statistical testing of a large number of different entry, position management, and exit strategies using the bands helped me tremendously as I worked toward finalizing the present system.

The Mean Reversion system detailed here is one that I recommend you *always* trade in market-neutral pairs no matter what the market is doing. This means that for every long position you take, you will need to find a short to mate it with and for every dollar you have in that long, you should put a dollar into the matching short. The long-short pairs are treated as a single position: They are entered at the same time and exited at the same time. If not done correctly, this can all go horribly wrong. Because we are fading the primary move, you can find yourself long a stock headed into bankruptcy, and at the same time, short a stock that is about to be bought out at a huge premium. There-fore, it is crucial for us to take steps to minimize those risks as much as possible.

Here is your incentive for persevering despite the risks: When done well, this system can hand you dou-ble-digit monthly returns and triple-digit annual returns regularly and reliably. I have been trading variants of this system for a dozen years now and know well what does and doesn't work. And even what does work well never does so all of the time. With that said, the system presented here is about as close as we can humanly get to Mean Reversion heaven. When it is working well, your trading log should look something like Figure 13.4. That spreadsheet is my trading log for an eight-week test of the MR system using a real-money account of $10,000. I put on between two and four pairs each week, always entering on Monday's open

Wk	$/side	$Account	Profit	ROI	Avg	LONG	Entry	Shares	Exit	Basis	P/L	ROI	SHORT	Entry	Shares	Exit	Basis	P/L	ROI
1	$2,500	$10,000	$329	13.2%		HOLX	17.19	145	17.57	$2,500	$54	1.1%	CALX	9.00	278	8.00	$2,500	$275	5.5%
	$2,500	$10,000	$510	20.4%	8.4%	AXIU	4.62	541	4.98	$2,500	$189	3.8%	KIOR	10.68	234	9.30	$2,500	$321	6.4%
	$2,500	$10,000	($66)	-2.6%		KIRK	10.35	242	10.33	$2,500	($7)	-0.1%	DGIT	8.54	293	8.73	$2,500	($59)	-1.2%
	$2,500	$10,000	$63	2.5%		STAA	8.90	281	8.31	$2,500	($169)	-3.4%	IDIX	9.73	257	8.82	$2,500	$231	4.6%
2	$2,709	$10,836	$284	10.5%		MXWL	6.75	401	6.81	$2,709	$20	0.4%	LCC	12.92	210	11.65	$2,709	$264	4.9%
	$2,709	$10,836	$121	4.5%	4.4%	VIP	7.19	377	7.69	$2,709	$185	3.4%	VHC	33.31	81	34.08	$2,709	($63)	-1.2%
	$2,709	$10,836	$64	2.4%		MWE	46.29	59	48.14	$2,709	$108	2.0%	AUY	15.58	174	15.82	$2,709	($43)	-0.8%
	$2,709	$10,836	$6	0.2%		LNG	11.81	229	12.18	$2,709	$63	1.7%	SMBL	7.09	382	7.28	$2,709	($76)	-1.5%
3	$3,771	$11,312	$48	1.3%		SWFT	9.24	408	9.77	$3,771	$212	3.9%	RGLD	76.44	49	79.75	$3,771	($164)	-3.0%
	$3,771	$11,312	$154	4.1%	-1.2%	ONE	11.21	336	10.90	$3,771	($108)	-1.9%	AUMN	5.63	670	5.23	$3,771	$261	4.6%
	$3,771	$11,312	($341)	-9.0%		MW	29.20	129	28.48	$3,771	($94)	-1.7%	WAC	21.28	177	22.66	$3,771	($246)	-4.4%
4	$3,724	$11,173	($261)	-7.0%		DV	18.05	206	18.71	$3,724	$134	2.4%	WPRT	29.14	128	32.22	$3,724	($395)	-7.0%
	$3,724	$11,173	$181	4.9%	3.3%	TWI	20.86	179	23.07	$3,724	$393	6.9%	OSUR	10.03	371	10.59	$3,724	($212)	-3.7%
	$3,724	$11,173	$454	12.2%		QLTY	10.46	356	12.04	$3,724	$559	9.9%	END	8.12	459	8.34	$3,724	($105)	-1.9%
5	$5,773	$11,547	$563	9.7%		LSCC	3.68	1,569	3.68	$5,773	($16)	-0.3%	DANG	6.79	850	6.1	$5,773	$578	10.3%
	$5,774	$11,547	$195	3.4%	6.6%	CROX	16.30	354	15.82	$5,774	($174)	-3.1%	BAC	8.15	708	7.62	$5,774	$368	6.6%
6	$4,101	$12,304	($224)	-5.5%		CROX	15.82	259	16.15	$4,101	$83	1.5%	BAC	7.62	538	8.18	$4,101	($307)	-5.5%
	$4,101	$12,304	($706)	-17.2%	-5.7%	AMBT	6.15	667	5.40	$4,101	($507)	-9.1%	FSS	5.55	739	5.81	$4,101	($200)	-3.6%
	$4,101	$12,304	$231	5.6%		LZB	11.41	359	12.38	$4,101	$345	6.0%	AVAV	25.62	160	26.32	$4,101	($114)	-2.0%
7	$3,868	$11,605	$1,207	31.2%		AMBT	5.40	716	7.00	$3,868	$1,139	19.7%	CX	6.78	571	6.65	$3,868	$68	1.2%
	$3,868	$11,605	($230)	-5.9%	10.7%	BCS	10.77	359	10.40	$3,868	($136)	-2.2%	LNG	14.5	267	14.84	$3,868	($93)	-1.5%
	$3,868	$11,605	$261	6.8%		LQDT	39.79	97	40.70	$3,868	$87	1.4%	STNG	6.68	579	6.37	$3,868	$174	2.8%
8	$3,211	$12,844	($219)	-6.8%		GRPN	8.93	360	8.33	$3,211	($219)	-3.6%	ETM	6.29	510	6.28	$3,211	($0)	0.0%
	$3,211	$12,844	$23	0.7%	0.0%	DEST	17.15	187	18.10	$3,211	$176	3.0%	NFLX	81.03	40	84.88	$3,211	($153)	-2.6%
	$3,211	$12,844	$183	5.7%		QLIK	18.28	176	18.35	$3,211	$11	0.2%	RBCN	11.16	288	10.55	$3,211	$173	3.0%
	$3,211	$12,844	$15	0.5%		SWFT	8.31	386	8.45	$3,211	$50	0.9%	KEYW	10.84	296	10.95	$3,211	($36)	-0.6%
			$2,846	85.5%	3.3%														3.3%

Figure 13.4 Carr's trading log—Mean Reversion system over eight weeks.

and closing on Friday's close. Only two of the eight weeks were not profitable. The average gain per week, including the losing weeks, was +3.3 percent. This is about in line with previous and subsequent tests of the system. The total return on investment (ROI) was over 28 percent, or roughly +170 percent annualized with the compounding of gains.

FOR FURTHER RESEARCH
ON THE SYSTEM

I strongly recommend doing some background work on this system, even if you did not do so for the previous six systems. The Mean Reversion system you will be learning in this chapter is potentially the most profitable system in the book. It is also the most volatile. There are periods when things can, and probably will, go horribly wrong. Thus, having a working knowledge of the theory behind the system can go a long way toward instilling the confidence you will need to keep at it through the inevitable drawdowns.

Your first stop in learning more about the components of this system is John Bollinger's aforementioned book *Bollinger on Bollinger Bands*. The whole book is worth the read, but for our purposes here, Chapter 20 contains the critical discussion. The book is supported by a separately sold DVD set that goes by the same name. This is the course I took several years ago. I recommend it as a supplement to the book, or an alternative to those who are reading averse (though since you have read my book this far, you couldn't be too averse!). Bollinger's two websites, www.Bollingerbands.com and www.Bollingeronbollingerbands.com, are also worth a browse. They contain a number of free articles, interviews, and helpful charts.

The aforementioned Larry Conners has a website, www.TradingMarkets.com, that contains a number of articles and videos on Bollinger Bands. The course I purchased is also sold there, as well as on Amazon, entitled "Trading with Bollinger Bands: A Quantified Guide." It is worth the price for its thorough research on a wide variety of entry and exit strategies using the Bollinger Bands. Conners will show you the differences in returns that occur when, for example, you hold an extra day, average into the position, use specific %B figures, etc. The systems themselves are similar to, and nicely complement, what we present here in this chapter.

On my site, www.Drstoxx.com, I offer a trading manual that gives detailed guidance on trading the Mean Reversion system, as described here. You will be shown how I weed out the best candidates, how I pair longs and shorts for the best market-neutral positioning, and various ways to manage the positions given different levels of risk tolerance.

For the fundamentals side of the system, you can do no better than to read Louis Navellier's *The Little Book That Makes You Rich: A Proven Market-Beating Formula for Growth Investing* (Wiley, 2007). Written for the layperson, Navellier's short primer on buying growth stocks offers a full, easily assimilated explanation of the various components that go into his proprietary Portfolio Grader we mentioned back in Chapter 4.

We will be using the Portfolio Grader in this system. Understanding the theory behind the Grader's evaluation can go a long way toward giving you the background knowledge that will help you trade this system with confidence.

TRADING THE MEAN REVERSION SYSTEM

Let's get down to work. Here are the tools needed to trade this system:

- (option 1): Use MetaStock's Dr. Stoxx Trend Trading Toolkit (TTTK) if you do not want to program in your own scan. You will find both the long and short versions of this system preprogrammed into the Long + Short Mean Reversion Scan in the TTTK add-on. With a single click of the mouse, you can scan the markets in real time for current MR setups. I have coded this system into two other scanning services—StockCharts and NinjaTrader—and neither one gives me as many viable candidates as the MetaStock tool.
- (option 2): Use StockCharts or another technical screening tool to search for stocks making the required MR long and short setups. You will need to write the parameters into the scanning software

yourself, but the setup is a fairly simple one. Stockcharts.com is especially user-friendly.

- You will also need to bookmark the following website. We will be using this free service to perform a basic but very effective fundamental analysis on whatever stocks pass our technical scan:

  ○ Navellier's Portfolio Grader navelliergrowth .investorplace.com/portfolio-grader/

RUNNING THE LONGS VERSION

Step 1 (MetaStock option): Open MetaStock and go to the Power Console. Click the Explorer. Select TTTK: Long + Short Mean Reversion Scan. From the Select List(s) To Explore table, highlight U.S. Optionable Stocks or any other list you wish to scan. Click Next and then click Start Exploration. Make a watch list of charts for all passing candidates.

You should get 6 to 10 passing candidates each day. Since this scan targets price extremes, you will normally have more long candidates than shorts in downtrending markets, more short candidates than longs in uptrending markets, and fewer candidates of both sorts in nonvolatile markets (e.g., with the VIX < 15). When the general market is itself outside the upper or lower Bollinger Band, you may see dozens of passing candidates come through the scan.

In this case, it is best to modify the moving average filter. When you open the Edit function for the TTTK: Long + Short Mean Reversion Scan, you will see the following code line:

$$C < Mov(C,20,S) * 0.9$$

Simply change the 0.9 multiplier to 0.87 and run the scan again. Keep lowering the multiplier if needed until you attain a list of only 10 to 15 passing candidates.

Step 1 (StockCharts option): Create the Mean Reversion longs scan in StockChart's advanced scanning tool or in another online technical scanning tool. The parameters of this scan are as follows:

- Stocks > $5/share and >100,000 per day trading volume

- Yesterday's close < Lower Bollinger Band

- Yesterday's close >10 percent below the 20sma

- Each of the previous three days before yesterday's close show a %B <0.25

- Today's close > Lower Bollinger Band

Run this scan and make a watch list of charts for all passing candidates. In certain market conditions, you may get more stocks than you can handle. In this case, you can raise the requirement from 10 percent below the 20sma to 12 percent or higher until a list of 10 to 15 candidates is attained. You may also alter the %B figure as needed (higher for more candidates, lower for fewer).

Step 2: Take your list of passing candidates and input them, one by one, into Navellier's Portfolio Grader. When you do so, you will see 11 categories, each with a grade ranging from A (best) to F (worst). There are three general categories: Fundamental, Quantitative, and Total. We are only interested in the Fundamental grade. The Quantitative grade is Navellier's proprietary formula, and since he is big on relative price strength, our long candidates trading below the lower Bollinger Band will not fare well there. The Total grade factors in both the Fundamental and Quantitative grades, so we can ignore that one too. We are interested here only in the company's fundamental strength.

Your best candidates for the long side of the MR system will show an A or B for its Fundamental grade. We can occasionally take a C stock if pickings are slim and we like the trade for other reasons. For best results with this system, pass on any stock showing a Fundamental grade of D or F. If you have a number of A and B candidates, give favor to those with the highest grades in the first four growth categories: Sales Growth, Operating Margin Growth, Earnings Growth, and Earnings Momentum. Two or more A's in those categories are a good indicator that we have a strong candidate for this system.

Step 3: Do further discretionary analysis on any passing candidates from steps 1 and 2. At the least, this should involve plugging each symbol into www.Finviz.com and checking the headlines for any possible "deal breaker" story about the company. Stocks usually hit extreme prices for good reason, but these setbacks can provide profitable trading opportunities as they bounce back to the mean. What we want to avoid in this important step is getting into any company that is experiencing systemic problems. These can include things like accounting scandals (remember WorldCom?), an unexpected Food and Drug Administration (FDA) rejection, wells that run dry, and so on. We want to avoid these things. We can buy the shakeout from things like disappointing earnings, subpar same-store sales numbers, or a major downgrade because these are usually taken in stride by good companies. But we want to avoid the more serious stuff that can hold even good companies underwater for months at a time.

This system works best when traded in market-neutral fashion with long-short pairs. Thus, once you have completed step 3, you will want to run steps 1, 2, and 3 for the shorts side of the system (described later) and trade accordingly.

Step 4 (position management): There are a number of ways to manage the paired positions in the MR system. I recommend reading the Conners material noted earlier to give you some great ideas to work with. My own real-money trading suggests that two strategies work best. The one that generates a higher win percentage as well as return per trade requires the ability to trade during the trading day. The other strategy works slightly less well but can easily be implemented in after-hours trading. The two options are as follows:

- For those who can trade during the day:
  - Exit any MR system long-short pair using a "market on close" order after three full trading days have passed since entry, if and only if
    - Either the long or the short position is trading at or beyond the 20sma (above the 20sma for the long; below for the short), or
    - Ten trading days have passed since entry, whichever comes first.
  - Repeat steps 1 through 3 and replace the closed pair with a new long-short pair at the next market open.

- For those who cannot trade during the day:
  - Exit any MR system long-short pair using a "market on open" order on the next market day after:

□ At least five trading days have passed since entry and the pair is profitable, or

□ Ten trading days have passed since entry, whichever comes first.

○ Replace any closed pair with a new long-short pair at the next market open by repeating steps 1 through 3.

CHART EXAMPLES

Strum, Ruger and Co. (RGR) is a firearm manufacturer of the Rambo and Dirty Harry sort. This puts the company right at the center of a long-standing and increasingly heated cultural debate. Politics aside, the company's shares are reliably volatile—probably because of the political tension—which makes it a perfect stock for the MR system. Moreover, its fundamentals are as solid as the recoil of a .44 Magnum. It has earned either a B or an A on Navellier's Portfolio Grader in 11 of the past 12 months. In the following chart, you will see three MR long signals, each of which was profitable within two weeks of trading (see Figure 13.5).

Hawaiian Airlines, Inc. (HA) began as a regional airline back in 1929 with two small planes serving residents of the islands. Today, it serves 8 million passengers a year who fly all over the Pacific Rim. Though hard hit in 2013, HA has been known as a strong growth stock with its acquisition of new planes, hubs, and destinations. It is also a prime

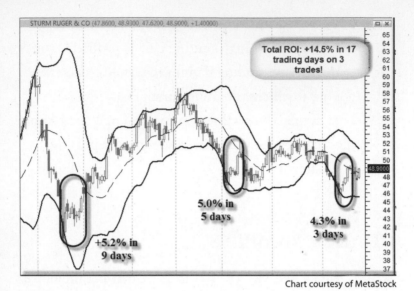

Figure 13.5   RGR—Mean Reversion system longs.

study in Mean Reversion: It has signaled 10 MR longs since January 2009, 8 of which were profitable. In the following chart (Figure 13.6), you will see two of those signals straddling either side of a downtrend.

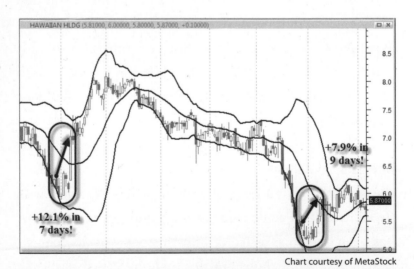

Figure 13.6   HA—Mean Reversion system longs.

RUNNING THE SHORTS VERSION

Step 1 (MetaStock option): If you ran the TTTK scan looking for longs, then you already have a list of short candidates, since the one scan highlights both sides of the system. If you have too many short candidates to deal with, open the Edit function for the TTTK: Long + Short Mean Reversion Scan. You will see the following code line:

$$C > Mov(C,20,S) * 1.1$$

Simply change the 1.1 multiplier to 1.13 or higher. Run the scan again. Keep raising the multiplier as needed until you attain a list of only 10 to 15 passing candidates.

Step 1 (StockCharts option): Create the Mean Reversion shorts scan in StockChart's advanced scanning tool or in another online technical scanning tool. The parameters of this scan are as follows:

- Stocks > $5/share and >100,000 per day trading volume

- Yesterday's close < Upper Bollinger Band

- Yesterday's close >10 percent above the 20sma

- The previous three days before yesterday's close show a %B >0.75

- Today's close < Upper Bollinger Band

Run this scan and make a watch list of charts for all passing candidates. You should get 3 to 10 candidates each day. As noted earlier, in certain market conditions, you may get more stocks than you can handle. In this case, you can raise the requirement from 10 percent above the 20sma to 12 percent or higher until a list of 10 to 15 candidates is attained. You may also alter the %B figure as needed (lower for more candidates, higher for fewer).

Step 2: Take your list of passing candidates and input them, one by one, into Navellier's Portfolio Grader (see step 2 in the previous procedure). Your best candidates for the short side of the MR system will show a D or F for its Fundamental grade. We can occasionally take a C stock if pickings are slim and we like the trade for other reasons. Pass on any stock showing a Fundamental grade of A or B. If you have a number of D and F candidates, give favor to those with the lowest grades in the first four growth categories: Sales Growth, Operating Margin Growth, Earnings Growth, and Earnings Momentum. Two or more F's in these categories signal a strong candidate for the short side of the MR system.

Step 3: Do further discretionary analysis on any results from steps 1 and 2. As for the longs, this should involve checking the headlines for any possible "deal breaker" story about the company. What we want to avoid in this important step is getting into any company that is undergoing structural change that can radically shift earnings momentum. These can include things like an unexpected FDA approval, a hot new product, an unexpected mining or drilling find, and so on. We want to avoid these things. We should be willing to fade news like better-than-expected earnings, sizzling same-store sales numbers, or a major upgrade in an otherwise financially unsound company because as soon as the euphoria has worn off, we know those shares are likely to fall hard. What we want to stay out of are the things that give troubled, beaten-down companies a new lease on life.

I wish to underline this last point. Having a strong sense of what stories propel stocks higher or lower is a critical facet of the kind of discretionary trading we spoke about in Chapter 5. This particular skill—interpreting the news cycle—is essential to making any trading system work well, but especially one like the MR system, where both the rewards and the risks are inherently high.

*Step 4 (**position management**):* The shorts side of the MR system is managed the same way the longs side is managed. Once either side of the pair hits the exit requirements (see step 4 in the previous procedure), the other side should be closed as well. Long-short pairs should always be entered on the same day and exited on the same day.

CHART EXAMPLES

Biolase, Inc. (BIOL) is a medical equipment maker that, among other things, makes dental lasers, pain treatment applications, and 3-D imaging machines. The shares of the company are favored among the momentum day-trading crowd and thus have a way of getting ahead of themselves. Its chart looks like a silhouette of the Grand Tetons. Once these peaks reach equilibrium, where supply and demand match up evenly, it is time to put on the short position. The MR system is designed to catch these reversals of momentum. In the following chart (Figure 13.7), you will see three such shorting opportunities.

Theravance, Inc. (THRX), according to its website, is "a biopharmaceutical company with a pipeline of internally discovered product candidates and strategic collaborations with pharmaceutical companies."[1] Like most drug developers, its fundamentals range from questionable to scary. It currently carries a Portfolio Grader grade of D, with F's in three of the four growth categories. On April 18, 2013, THRX gained FDA approval for a drug that treats chronic obstructive pulmonary disease (COPD). Of course, this caused the shares to gap up sharply on the news, triggering two successive MR short signals. FDA approvals,

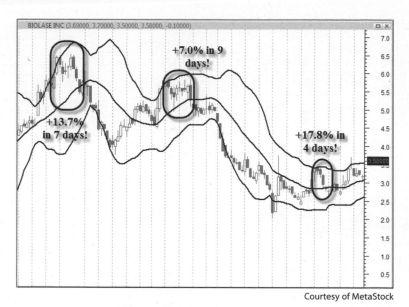

BIOLASE INC (3.69000, 3.70000, 3.50000, 3.58000, -0.10000)

+7.0% in 9 days!

+13.7% in 7 days!

+17.8% in 4 days!

Courtesy of MetaStock

Figure 13.7   BIOL—Mean Reversion system shorts.

however, fundamentally change the earning power of the company, so we decided against the trade (it would have been a narrow loss after the 10-day stop-out). On May 13, 2013, the company came out with more good news: A large biotech firm, Elan, was backing four drugs being developed by THRX in exchange for 21 percent of revenues once approved. While this is certainly good news for THRX—they now have the capital to ramp up their R&D programs and thus grease the pipeline—it will not materially affect earnings until the drugs are approved and come to market. That could be years away. Moreover, in digging deeper into the story, I learned that the safety profile of at least one of these drugs looks questionable.

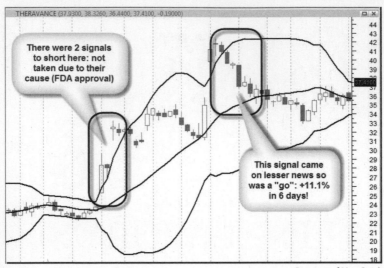

Courtesy of MetaStock

Figure 13.8   THRX—Mean Reversion system shorts.

Thus, the May signal was given a green light. See Figure 13.8 for the outcome.

PART FIVE

delta:
FINAL WORDS

CHAPTER 14

NEVER, EVER GIVE UP!

Success is not final; failure is not fatal:
It is the courage to continue that counts.

—Winston Churchill

I have come to construct a new paradigm for success in any endeavor in life, including trading: Success is not defined by winning, but by persevering through failure. Success is not about doing a thing flawlessly; it is about doing it passionately, however imperfect your doing of it is. If you are truly passionate about trading, if you can envision the benefits it can bring yourself and others, and if you are willing to slog through weeks, months, even years of what may look to others like failure, without ever giving up, then you are a successful trader in my book!

Success as a trader of the stock market is not about finding a winning system and obeying its rules. It's not about going all "Zen" and trading like a robot. It's simply this: not giving up! The process is simple: Learn as much as you can, find a good mentor, try different methods, stick to what works, and never, ever give up! You will suffer setbacks, I guarantee it. There will be times when you want to quit. Don't! There is no shame in failure, unless it causes you to quit. Don't let shame win. Resolve now to keep on trying, no matter what. As Winston Churchill said, "When you are going through hell, keep on going!"

Be patient with your trading. Like all fine crafts, it takes time to master. You can trade your way to wealth beyond your wildest dreams, but it will not happen overnight. In trading, it's okay to be slow. It took me 13 years of trading to build a sizeable, "trade for a living" portfolio (remember, I started with $2,000). Then we gave it all away and started over. With trading, it's not about the money. As soon as it becomes about the money, you have set yourself up to lose it.

Make your trading about *how* you trade, and prosperity will follow. Trade in such a way that you are a better person because of it—more patient, more forgiving, more generous, less anxious—and you will already have your success. Let trading humble you (and it will). Let it put the knife to your pride and self-sufficiency. Become someone whom God can entrust with riches, and whether or not riches come, your life will be blessed. "It is not about winning the prize," said the apostle Paul. "It is *how* you run that counts."[1]

Ultimately, successful trading is about trust. When King David was on his deathbed, having lived a life filled with ups and downs, great victories and costly defeats, he gave his son, Solomon, these parting words, "Be strong, my son, and trust God. Walk in the paths He lays out for you and you will always have success."[2] Trading success is not found by trusting in a system, or a book (even this one!), or a coach. It is found by trusting in the One who works through the system, the book, and the coach to bring you to where He wants you to go. I've learned, through many tough trials, that where He wants you to go is exactly where you want to be!

Notes

Chapter 1

1. For a full discussion of these new mutual fund types, see Armfeld and Somos, "Performance, Risks and Benefits of Active-Extension Strategies," a master's thesis in finance submitted to the Stockholm School of Economics, February 8, 2008. The thesis may be accessed at http://www.hhs.se.

2. At the end of the last century, less than 2 percent of all assets under management in alternative investments were in shorts-only funds. See Jansen, Chadha, Kodres, Mathieson, Sharma, and Eichengreen, *Hedge Funds and Financial Markets* (International Monetary Fund: June 1998), p. 30.

Chapter 2

1. This kind of research into "superperformance" stocks is nothing new, and may have been in the back of my mind as I built my test. William O'Neil, who is introduced later in this book, describes the same kind of research he conducted as he developed his famed CAN-SLIM system. For details, see later text and *How to Make Money in Stocks* (McGraw-Hill, various editions). Prior to O'Neil's book, back in 1977, Richard Love published a book, now out of print, on his work into what causes the best-performing stocks to move so strongly. See Richard Love, *Superperformance Stocks* (Prentice Hall, 1977). Love's work was referenced by two current traders, David Ryan, in his interview with Jack Schwager for *Market Wizards* (Wiley, 1989), and Mark Minervini for *Stock Market Wizards* (Wiley, 2012), both of which I read.

2. Thomas Bulkowski, *Encyclopedia of Chart Patterns* (Wiley, 2005).

3. For an insider's look at what goes on at these kinds of meetings at a large investment bank, see Greg Smith, *Why I Left Goldman Sachs: A Wall Street Story* (Grand Central Publishing, 2012).

4. Robert Edwards and John Magee, *Technical Analysis of Stock Trends*, 10th edition (CRC Press, 2012). The original was published in 1948.

Chapter 3

1. The founding father of EMT, and a proponent of RWT, was American economist Eugene Fama. Fama spent his teaching career at the University of Chicago and earned the Nobel Prize for Economics in 2013, largely for his influence on modern theories of the movements of stock prices. He coauthored a much-used textbook, *The Theory of Finance* (Holt Rinehart & Winston, 1972), with Nobel Prize winner Merton Miller. Somewhat ironically, Fama is currently investment research director at a firm that manages $214 billion.

2. The history of RMT can be traced to a French stock broker named Jules Regnault who in 1863 published a book on the subject. The mathematical justification of the theory was added in 1900 by French mathematician Louis Bachelier in his PhD dissertation entitled "The Theory of Speculation." Professor Eugene Fama of the University of Chicago's Booth School of Business was the first to translate the academic language of RMT into laymen's terms in his 1965 article, "Random Walks in Stock Market Prices," published in the *Financial Analysts Journal* (51 (1), September–October 1965).

3. Cf. Burton Malkiel, *A Random Walk Down Wall Street*, 10th ed. (New York: W. W. Norton & Co., 2012), Chapter 5.

4. In a memorable passage from *A Random Walk Down Wall Street*, Malkiel narrates an experiment he performed with his students. Each was given a hypothetical stock worth $50 and told to flip a coin each day to determine the stock's current price. If heads, they moved the price up $0.50 and if tails, they moved it down the same amount. After several weeks of this, they had a "price

chart" to which they then applied technical analysis. The charts were then taken to a certified market technician who, upon seeing the chart, told Malkiel that he should immediately buy the stock. Of course, the technician was dismayed to learn the truth. *Ibid.*, p. 143.

5. *Ibid*, p. 26.

6. Cf. Luke 19:13 where Luke's version makes this command to "trade" explicit. Luke's "parable of the 10 minas," when compared to Matthew's "parable of the talents," was likely a separate parable told by Jesus on a different occasion. But it teaches the same basic tenets about stewardship and the fear of investing what God has given to us. "Trade with these" likely meant, in Jesus's day, to buy products at a discount, set up a market stall or small storefront, and sell the items for a profit (not unlike eBay's virtual storefronts today).

7. Matt. 25:21.

8. The figures used in this table are based on information taken from AAII.com, the website for the American Association of Individual Investors. The 10-year average annual return from 2002–2012 listed on the site was applied to the 13-year period to arrive at a total return on investment (ROI) to match that of the S&P 500. As with all financial information posted on websites, even one as professional and as well respected as AAII, certain disclaimers apply. Here is the pertinent part of the disclaimer found on the site: "The opinions and analyses included herein are based on sources believed to be reliable and written in good faith, but no representation or warranty, expressed or implied, is made as to their accuracy, completeness, timeliness, or correctness. Neither we nor our information providers shall be liable for any errors or inaccuracies, regardless of cause, or the lack of timeliness of, or any delay or interruptions in the transmission thereof to the users. All investment information contained herein should be independently verified."

9. The citations and returns listed in this paragraph can be found in the original article (Selected Paper 84): Joseph Piotroski, "Value Investing: The Use of Historical Financial Statement Information to Separate Winners from Losers," Chicago Graduate School of Business, January 2002. They are also summarized on a variety of websites devoted to Piotroski's system.

Chapter 4

1. Thomas K. Carr, *Trend Trading for a Living* (McGraw-Hill, 2007), p. 29.

2. Nicholas Carson, "The Death of the PC: A Full Report from *Business Insider*," Jan. 9, 2013. Accessed April 8, 2013, on Businessinsider.com.

3. From "About AAII" on www.aaii.com.

Chapter 5

1. Cf. Proverbs 1:4, 2:11, 3:21, 5:2; Isaiah 28:26.

2. A thinker I find very helpful on this point is scientist and philosopher Michael Polanyi. In his most important book, *Personal Knowledge: Towards a Post-Critical Philosophy* (University of Chicago Press, 1974), Polanyi developed the theory that much of what we know, especially of things that we are passionate about or carry great meaning for us, is not taught or learned from books. It is transmitted to us by our culture and the various experiences we have within it.

3. At Kingdom Capital, we named our managed account "The 8:18 Fund" for this reason.

4. See Acts 18:3–5.

5. The Greek "tekton" used in Mark and Matthew to describe Jesus's learned profession more rightly refers to a "handyman" or someone who could do anything from building a bridge to fixing a leaky roof. In today's terms, He might be called an employee of the civil engineering department.

6. Cf. Luke 5:1–11.

Chapter 7

1. The following parameters of the Piotroski F-score have been adapted from the website of the American Association of Investors (www.AAII.com), which is described in Chapter 4. While the particular page this information is taken from is password-protected, the criteria are widely available online and

are described in detail in the paper Piotroski published, also available online.

Chapter 8

1. This information comes from a document entitled "The Zacks Rank: Harnessing the Power of Earnings Estimate Revisions," which is found on the www.Zacks.com website.

2. Information taken from the company website (www.rubicontechnology.com).

Chapter 9

1. Cited in "Investor's Business Daily" on *Wikipedia*. Article accessed June 2013.

2. Description is taken in part from the article "CAN-SLIM" on *Wikipedia* (accessed June 2013), as well as information taken from www.investors.com/ibd-university. I also edited and added text for the sake of clarification.

3. For one example, the teaching cited on pp. 340–341 that success should be measured by how much joy we feel when doing something, and that joy and "feeling good" bring into play a "law of attraction" whereby we "enable the universe to deliver our desires." To make emotions the master of our choices is, in my estimate, a prescription for disappointment, if not outright disaster.

4. The *Encyclopedia of Chart Patterns*, though well worth adding to your trading library, is rather expensive. It can sometimes be found in public libraries in major U.S. cities, however. For a shorter and more affordable treatment of the same topic, try: Thomas Bulkowski, *Getting Started in Chart Patterns* (Wiley, 2005).

Chapter 10

1. For more on free cash flow yield, see "Free Cash Flow Yield" in *Webster's New World Finance and Investment Dictionary* (Wiley, 2010). There are also articles on the topic in the online sources Investopedia.com and Ehow.com.

2. "Small-cap growth" is found in the Screen of the Week folder in Research Wizard. It is also described in Matras's book *Finding #1 Stocks: Screening, Backtesting, and Time-Proven Strategies* (Wiley & Sons, 2011), pp. 55–60.

3. Benjamin Graham, *The Intelligent Investor* (Collins Business Essentials, 2006).

Chapter 13

1. www.Theravance.com/About. Accessed June 25, 2013.

Chapter 14

1. 1 Cor. 9:24. My paraphrase of the original.

2. 1 Kings 2:2–3. My paraphrase of the original.

INDEX

Note: Page numbers followed by an italic *f* or *t* refer to the figure or table on that page.

ABOUT THE AUTHOR

Dr. Thomas K. Carr (aka "Dr. Stoxx") is the founder and CEO of DrStoxx.com (formerly Befriend the Trend Trading). He holds MPhil and DPhil degrees in philosophy and theology from the University of Oxford. He served for 16 years as a tenured professor. Dr. Carr currently is a full-time trader, market analyst, trading systems developer, and trainer of traders. His management company, Kingdom Capital (est. 2012), manages The 8:18 Fund.

Dr. Carr is the bestselling author of *Trend Trading for a Living* (McGraw-Hill, 2007) and *Micro-Trend Trading for Daily Income* (McGraw-Hill, 2010). Together they have sold over 40,000 copies and have been translated into Chinese, Japanese, and Korean. Dr. Carr's insights into the markets have been published in *The Wall Street Journal, US News & World Report, Investor's Business Daily*, and *Technical Analysis of Stocks and Commodities*.

In 2002, Dr. Carr launched his first advisory letter, "The Trend Trade Letter," followed by "The ETF-Reversal Letter" (2007) and "The Cheap Stocks Letter" (2010). In July 2013, Dr. Carr launched DrStoxx.com, a "one-stop shop" for stock traders. Its stated mission is to become the number-one online site for stock picks, market analysis, and trader training. Today, DrStoxx .com offers three premium advisory letters, trading systems manuals, trader training webinars, a one-on-one coaching service, and a managed account service.

Dr. Carr seeks to integrate his faith into everything he does. His business enterprises are expressions of his desire to honor God and steward His gifts wisely. He is helped in this work by his gorgeous wife, Ina, who holds a master's degree in leadership management, and by his three brilliant kids: Natasha, Nadia, and Nathan.

Put what you've read to the test

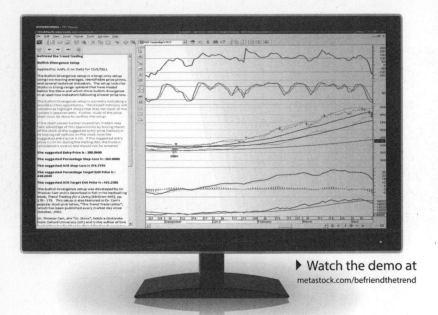

▶ **Watch the demo at**
metastock.com/befriendthetrend

You've read about neutralizing the market. Now go long AND short using Dr. Stoxx's Trend Trading Toolkit. The Trend Trading Toolkit combines some of the most popular trending technical analysis indicators into one powerful MetaStock add-on featuring explorations, expert advisors, and templates.

Dr. Stoxx's time-tested strategies will help you identify entry positions in trending instruments. In addition to identifying entry points, this toolkit also identifies proper stop losses and target levels for your trades. It includes two real-time strategies for use with MetaStock Professional, nine strategies designed for a daily time frame, 13 explorations, and six templates. Two pre-filter explorations are also included, helping you find high beta stocks ideal for trading.